# VASILY I. KELSIEV

## AN ENCOUNTER BETWEEN THE RUSSIAN REVOLUTIONARIES AND THE OLD BELIEVERS

# VASILY L. KELSIEV

## An Encounter Between the Russian Revolutionaries and the Old Believers

by
**PAUL CALL**

ANY

This book is for

TIM KANATISEW,
a Native of the land called America

Library of Congress Catalog Card Number 78-78270
ISNB 0-913-124-36-2

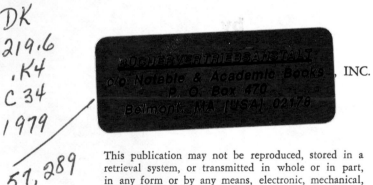

PRINTED IN THE UNITED STATES OF AMERICA
BY
ATHENS PRINTING COMPANY

# Acknowledgements

I am indebted to several people and foundations for this publication. Professors Byrnes, Thompson, and Soulis were the inspirers and the critics of the undertaking. Fred Johnson patiently read the early versions of the manuscript and offered many suggestions for its improvement. The Woodrow Wilson and Ford Foundations provided financial aid. Elizabeth Meyendorff rendered an invaluable service by her careful proofreading of the manuscript and Margaret Raymond indexed the volume. Finally, I am immeasurably indebted to my wife, who (not unlike Avvakum's faithful consort) urged me on with the task in spite of the discomforts it sometimes brought into our daily existence.

# About the Author

Born in Russia, Dr. Paul Call spent three years in a German prison camp during World War II. Following service with the United States Army in Europe, he returned to study at American universities. He earned a M. A. and a Ph. D. degree from Indiana University. He has written on Tolstoy and Pushkin in several scholarly journals and his major work pertaining to the Russian peasantry will be published in the summer of 1979. Dr. Call has been on the faculty of the History Department, University of Manitoba, Winnipeg, Canada, since 1963.

# CONTENTS

The Author Among the Old Believer Cossacks

Vasily Ivanovich Kelsiev

Alexander Ivanovich Herzen (right)
and Nikolai Platonovich Ogarev

Kondraty Selivanov
From Orel Gubernia
Founder of the Castrates

The Castrates
Prophetic Inebriation of a Woman

The Castrates
Prophetic Inebriation of a Man

Castration

The Castrates
A Mass Ritualistic Dance

Paul of Belokrynitsa
The Founder of the Old Believer Hierarchy

Ambrosius
A Greek Bishop who was converted to the Raskol and became
the first Metropolitan of the Old Believers

Osip Semenovich Goncharov
An Ataman of the Nekrasovtsy

[The sign translates as: "My life is bitter on earth."]

# ГДИ ІСЕ ХЕ СНЕ БЖІИ ПОМИЛОУИ НАСЪ ГРѢШНЫХЪ.

Слоучилаѧ пора приходитъ, положеніѧмъ сроки вышелъ, й народъ по разнымъ мѣстамъ стали пошевеливатьсѧ. Не сегоднѧ такъ завтра й христолюбивое воинство наше пойдетъ на Москвѣ выборныхъ ѿ Народа на Земскій Соборъ сзанкать со всей Земли, а лиходѣевъ за границу, къ нѣмцамъ прогонѧтъ. Принимайте же воинство съ честью, съ хлѣбомъ съ солью й съ колокольнымъ звономъ, каждый по своей вѣрѣ, потому что й вѣрами всѣмъ можно будетъ полною утвердить волю. За всѣхъ вышедшихъ ратовать за васъ молитесь Бгу й помогайте кто чѣмъ можетъ. Гдѣ нельзѧ будетъ тотчасъ поднѧться, вы, выбирайте тамъ себѣ тишкомъ военное начальство: десѧтниковъ, сотниковъ, полковниковъ, воеводъ, какъ в старину. Тоже, оружіе припасайте, какое кто можетъ. Й другъ съ другомъ совѣтуйтесь осторожно. Крови лишней не проливайте безъ нужды людей не избивайте, въ піѧнство й въ грабежъ никому вдаватьсѧ не позволѧйте. А вставайте честно, ѻтецъ съ сыномъ, тесть съ зѧтемъ, братъ съ братомъ, й стойте дружно за Землю Свѧторусскую за Міръ Народъ Бжій: не торопко, да й не мѣшкотно. Чтобы завести у насъ порѧдокъ по Бжьему, а не понѣмецкому, й не пофранцузскому, й не поанглійскому: чтобы Землѧ Свѧторусскаѧ немедленно вышла йзъ подъ рабства, й досталась своему законному йспоконному владѣтелю Народу Свѧторусскому, безъ ѻбрѣзки, й безъ выкупа. Чтобы управлѧласѧ, судиласѧ й расправлѧласѧ, й подати раскладывала народъ самъ собой, своими людьми: а не чиновниками грабителѧми й притѣснителѧми. Чтобы досталась народу й Землѧ й Волѧ. Чтобы войско впередъ набиралось только йзъ охотниковъ, а теперешнимъ бѣднымъ солдатамъ была бы волѧ домой йдтить, кто пожелаетъ. Чтобы царствовала у насъ своѧ правда, а не чужѧ кривда. До кого ѐто дойдетъ, й кто ѐто поймётъ, й Міръ за собой поведетъ, тотъ людѧмъ великое добро сдѣлаетъ, а себѣ заслужитъ ѿ Гда праведное воздаѧніе, ибо за ближнихъ своихъ дшу свою полагаѧ. Крестьѧне й мѣщане, дворовые й міргане, купцы й попы, казаки солдаты й. ѻфицеры, старовѣры й всѧкіе разновѣры: казенна мірское́дна власть проходитъ, мірскаѧ народнаѧ приходитъ, иностраннаѧ исчезаетъ, свѧторусскаѧ наступаетъ.

Имѣющіи оуши слышати да слышитъ. аї числѧ мца Февруаріѧ текущаго года. Аминь.

"Slushnaia pora prikhodit"
A Proclamation lithographed and distributed by Vasily Kelsiev

Archpriest Avvakum

Patriarch Nikon

Tsar Alexis

The Solovetskii Monastery

# PREFACE

In the 1860's the Russian radical intelligentsia emerged as an influential socio-political force. In spite of ideological and organizational fragmentation within its ranks, the intelligentsia remained united on one basic demand—the fundamental socio-political reorganization of Russia. In their search for ways to achieve this goal some members of the radical or revolutionary intelligentsia explored the possibility of creating the nucleus of a revolutionary force from an element within Russian society which had stood in defiance of the church and the state for two centuries. This element, numbering some ten million adherents, was the religious Dissent or the Raskol.

The members of the intelligentsia who were most active in trying to win the support of the Raskolniks for the revolutionary cause comprised the small group of revolutionaries associated with *Kolokol* or *The Bell*—an anti-tsarist Russian-language newspaper published in London and subsequently in Geneva. This segment of the intelligentsia, who will be referred to as the Kolokol Group, determined upon various schemes for enlisting the Raskolniks in the revolutionary movement. They attempted, for example, to obtain the Raskolniks' support for the summoning of the Zemsky Sobor or Assembly of the Land, and at least one member of the Group went among the Raskolniks for the purpose of moulding them into an active revolutionary force. That member was Vasily Ivanovich Kelsiev—a youthful and imaginative radical intellectual. It is Kelsiev's activities among the Raskolniks which will constitute the central subject of this study.

The very fact that extensive communications were established for a time between the revolutionaries and the Raskolniks stands out as a unique aspect in the history of the two elements, for the former were professed atheists and politically oriented toward Western radicalism and the latter were devoutly religious men with strong attachments to the traditions of the old pre-Petrine Russia. On what basis was it possible for the Raskolniks to seek the friendship of those whom they considered to be the servants of Antichrist? Why did some of the revolutionaries believe that the traditionally conservative Raskolniks constituted a latent revolutionary force? What common ground was there on which these seemingly antithetical elements could seek to cooperate with each other? These are some of the problems which will be explored here.

Although no attempt will be made to present a systematic history of the Raskol, aspects of its historical background relevant to its political character in the 1860's and vital for understanding Kelsiev's attraction to that religious movement will be treated in considerable detail. Since some of the members of the Kolokol Group, such as Alexander Herzen and Nicholas Ogarev, are well-known historical personalities, no detailed treatment of their general activities will be included. That is to say, their lives, their ideas, and their political work will be dealt with only insofar as they relate to the main theme of this monograph.

This study is based on primary source materials. The treatment of the early history of the Raskol draws heavily on Avvakum's writings, which are available in *Russkaia istoricheskaia biblioteka*, XXXIX, 1927; the collected documents on the life and work of Patriarch Nikon, in William Palmer's *The Patriarch and the Tsar*, 6 vols.; and Nikolai I. Subbotin's *Materialy dlia istorii raskola za pervoe vremia ego sushchestvovaniia*, 9 vols. The secret government reports on the Raskol edited by Vasily I. Kelsiev (*Sbornik pravitel'stvennykh svedenii o raskol'nikakh*, 4 vols.) were indispensable for the understanding of Kelsiev's attraction to the Raskol. The correspondence of members of the Kolokol Group and of some influential Raskolniks published in *Literaturnoe nasledstvo,* especially volumes XLI-XLII and LXII, contains information dealing directly with Kelsiev and his activities among the Raskolniks. Of the biographical and collected works, Herzen's have been very useful. Kelsiev's *Ispoved'* or *Confession*, published in *Literaturnoe nasledstvo*, XLI-XLII, has special significance for this study since it is the chief source on his revolutionary career and especially his work among the Raskolniks living in the Ottoman Empire, about which little has been recorded elsewhere.

Unless otherwise indicated, all dates in this text will be in accordance with the Gregorian calendar. Proper names which have an English equivalent or have been anglicized through usage, will be used in their English form. Thus, "Paul" rather than "Pavel," "Alexander" rather than "Aleksandr," "Herzen" rather than "Gertsen," and "Kelsiev" rather than "Kel'siev" will be used. This rule, however, does not apply to names appearing in an initial citation of Russian sources. The terms Zemsky Sobor and Raskol will not be italicized, and the plural Raskolniks rather than raskol'niki will be used.

A few years ago I had the opportunity of becoming acquainted with a group of descendants of the Old Believer cossacks whose activities constitute an important segment of this study. Living in isolation in Turkey for more than two centuries this community of cossacks seems to have instilled in its individual members a capacity for remaining confident and constant in the face of the ever-changing and often menacing uncertainty which tends to disturb and at times overpower many of their contemporaries. These unique people bolstered my belief that the fragment of the human story with which I am concerned here is worth telling. It is to the children of these Old Believer cossacks that I wish to dedicate this volume.

# CHAPTER I

# THE FORMATIVE PROCESS

As a political figure, Vasily Ivanovich Kelsiev (1835-72) was to a large extent a product, in part a maker, and most certainly a victim of the period known in Russian history as the 1860's.[1] The opening of that turbulent period could be likened to the burst of spring descending upon Russia after a long and severe winter. The stirrings of that anxiously-awaited thaw began to reverberate within the heavy layers of ice, which had grown thick during the long and frigid reign of Nicholas I (1825-55), with the sounds of the cannonade at Sebastopol. The Alexandrian spring that followed seems to have sent hundreds of rivulets hurrying across the vastness of Russia, spreading the message of liberty and awakening the hopes of the oppressed multitudes from the bustling boulevards of St. Petersburg to the muddy streets of Siberian outposts. The 1860's, according to a contemporary, must be characterized not so much by the events that were taking place as by the spirit of animation one sensed within Russian society. The unusual intellectual dynamism of the sixties emerged just as naturally and organically as the new growth appears on a meadow exposed to the sun. "As soon as the Crimean War ended [1856] and everyone had breathed the fresh air of the new age, all intelligent people in Russia—from the highest to the lowest classes—began to think as they had never thought before. Their thoughts were aimed in one direction: in the direction of freedom, in the direction of the development of better conditions for each and for all."[2] The sudden freshness in the air inspired confidence and hope. As

13

Russian children greet the arrival of spring, young Emperor Alexander II (1855-81) seemed to utter the joyful words "Spring is here!" when he addressed the nobility in March 1856 and called for the liberation of the serfs. "Spring is here!" echoed the restless university students of lower social origin as their ranks began to swell because of Alexander's liberal policies. "Spring is here!" peeled the uncensored Russian-language periodical, *The Bell*, from the misty British Isles. "Spring is here!" muttered a bearded peasant from the province of Kursk as he replaced his lice-infested underwear with the patched but clean pair which he had been saving for his funeral.

The 1860's were a period of many positive developments both in Russia and within the broader panorama of history. The liberation of the serfs by Alexander II may have been the most significant humanitarian reform the Romanovs or any other rulers of Russia ever carried out. By this reform more than forty million individuals acquired a legal human identity. This was the period of national unifications in Western Europe, of the emancipation of the slaves in America, and of the enactment of important political reforms within the British Empire. On the intellectual front, both in Russia and in the West, the 1860's were years of passionate debates over the theories advanced by Charles Darwin. Tolstoy, Turgenev, and Dostoevsky reached their creative maturity in the 1860's. The industrial revolution began to inundate Central and spill over into Eastern Europe. It was with considerable justification therefore that Lenin reduced the description of that complex period in Russian history to a concise, yet meaningfully descriptive, label: the beginning of capitalism in Russia.

The vigorous response of Russian society to the promising developments of the 1860's, however, was not consistently directed along a constructive path. Instead of rejoicing over the prospects of their emancipation, the peasants intensified their violence against the existing order.[3] Unlike their predecessors of the previous two decades, the circles of politically-minded intellectuals of the 1860's were no longer mere samovar-centred philosophical debating societies but active revolutionary cells favouring violent methods. The first centralized all-Russian revolutionary organization, *Zemlia i Volia* or Land and Liberty coalesced during this period. Proclamations and manifestoes were spread throughout the Empire calling for the outright destruction of the existing order. And the hunt for the Tsar, the Liberator, which in 1881 led to his assassination, was initiated in the 1860's.

Possibly even more significant than the change in the overt actions was the change that took place in the spirit of optimism which characterized Russian society at the beginning of the period. Although Tolstoy was already expounding his ideas on nonviolence, it was Chernyshevsky's call for a solution to Russia's problems with an axe that incited the imagination of the politically-minded radical intellectuals. An active negation was one of the principles the radical intelligentsia chose to follow.[4] In its extreme form, this negative approach meant a devotion to an ideology demanding the destruction of all principles, codes, and institutions embodied within human society. It meant that one must actively strive to villify and discard everything that society had sanctified and venerated. In the eyes of the negatively-oriented intellectuals the heroic deeds of yesterday became deeds of infamy. Law for them existed in order to be violated, and the usefulness of religion was now seen only in its accentuation of atheism. The greater the sanctity of a belief or an institution, the more destructive was to be the attack against it. Utility was to be the sole measure of value for boots as well as Shakespeare, and effectiveness in negating the existing reality was to be the determinative factor of unity. This urge toward homo-titanism, which descended on Russia in the 1860's, sapped the Russian political intelligentsia of its creative energies for many decades thereafter, much as a malignancy within the bloodstream drains a living organism of its vitality.

Vasily Kelsiev was a representative of the radical intelligentsia of the 1860's, and his thoughts and actions in many ways reflected the mood and the intensity of activism which characterized that element. Born in St. Petersburg, Kelsiev began his education in a private boarding school, spent ten

years in a commercial school, and for two years studied
Oriental languages at the University of St. Petersburg. From
the fragments of information available about his family, it
appears that his ancestors were of the gentry class, but at the
time of his birth they were so thoroughly impoverished that
their social origin had little real meaning in their lives.
Vasily's maternal grandfather was a clergyman. His father,
who served as a minor official in the St. Petersburg custom-
house, died in 1852, when Vasily was seventeen. Vasily's
widowed mother was left with three sons and three daughters.
In view of their material difficulties, the Kelsievs felt fortunate
that Vasily, because of his noticeable linguistic aptitude, received financial assistance from the Russian-American Company and, therefore, was able to complete his education in
a commercial school and to attend university.[5] In his study of
Oriental languages, Kelsiev concentrated on Chinese, in
preparation for a career in the field of commerce.

The engraving reproduced here is the only visual image
of Kelsiev that is available. At twenty-five he was apparently
fair-haired, had shifty penetrating eyes, an angular head, and
a smile with a touch of sadness begging sympathy.

He entered the commercial school at the age of ten, and
during the ten years he spent there (1845-55) he and his
world became transformed. According to his own assessment,
the genesis of his nihilism could be traced to his experience
at the commercial school. In contrast to the strict religious
life he led at home, conditions at school were such that he
soon forgot about such accepted practices as fasting two days
a week. He was bewildered to discover that in his school the
icons—an object of special veneration at home—were extremely small and were soiled by flies. The prayers before
and after classes were repeated apparently out of a desire for
formality, and the Divine Law was taught in such a way as
if intended to convince the children that the subject was "an
unavoidable superfluity." There were eight tutors at his
school, and of these only two were Russians, and later there
was actually only one. Neither the inspector nor the school
master was of the Orthodox faith, and since the students
looked at them as men of great learning, they, the students,

came to suspect that "mental development and Orthodoxy" were not necessarily complementary to each other.[6]

Another characteristic of the educational institutions which Kelsiev attended, especially the university, was the superficiality of intellectualism. That superficiality, he thought, had produced a lasting effect on his individual development and was an important cause of the spread of negative thinking among the Russian intellectuals in general. In these institutions, according to Kelsiev, everything was taught, but nothing was learned thoroughly. "The encyclopaedism of our education," he observed, "our attitude of knowing it all, and our inclination to judge everything without a thorough knowledge of anything gave us the confidence to advance solutions to any complex problem of science and life and skillfully put down the challenges advanced by our opponents, snowing them under with the trumpery of our pseudo-erudition . . . it is precisely because we were not sufficiently trained to distinguish between the facts and the hypotheses that we became materialists."[7] That pseudo-intellectualism bore a political connotation and led to the wide-spread practice of judging one's academic qualifications on the basis of his political "progressivism." Beginning with their religious adulation of the natural sciences the politically-minded intellectuals of the 1860's tended to view their academic subjects not as sources for learning about objective reality but as instruments for reinforcing their political commitments. This prostitution of scholarship was a far more serious barrier to learning in nineteenth-century Russia than were the ever-present hindrances of the tsarist government. The extent to which Kelsiev's own intellectual superficiality was a reflection of the educational conditions of his time is difficult to measure with any degree of precision. Nonetheless, in comparison to Herzen, Ogarev, and Bakunin, with whom he became affiliated later in life and who were educated before the Russian universities became so thoroughly politicized, it cannot be said that Kelsiev attained a broad liberal education.

Probably no other factor in Kelsiev's life had had as strong and lasting an influence on him as literature. He was born two years prior to Pushkin's untimely death, and the years of his childhood and his youth were in the history of Russian literature the years of Gogol, Lermontov, Tiutchev, Belinsky, Dostoevsky, Goncharov, Ostrovsky, Turgenev, and Nekrasov. His was the time of the Golden Age of Russian literature— an age when whole generations of literate Russians "ripened" in the world of literature long before they reached maturity in the real world. Denied the freedom of direct political expression, the Russian political intelligentsia concentrated its attention on literature as a medium for expressing political ideas. Thus, the publication of a new novel, a new poem, or a new issue of a journal was regarded by Kelsiev and many of his contemporaries as an extraordinary event—an event which usually evoked passionate debates. Under the spell of literature, Kelsiev became what Dostoevsky called *literaturnyi chelovek*—a man who psychologically lives in the world of literature even though he may lack the courage to contribute creatively to that world. The literary talent of such a man is usually in the state of a perpetual, and therefore sterile, potentiality. Kelsiev, as we shall see, was more fortunate than many others in that respect, for his writings did see the light in print—dim though that light was.

In addition to the inevitable Pushkin, Kelsiev found in his family library the works of the eighteenth-century Russian classicists, including those of Sumarokov, Kheraskov, Kniazhnin, Derzhavin, and Karamzin. At the commercial school he was exposed to the translated works of French classicists, and became especially enamoured by Dumas's *Three Musketeers*. He claimed that the sentimental writings of these authors played an important role in determining his outlook on life in his early youth. According to his own reflection on the subject, classical literature "had that strange characteristic which in a fascinating fashion separated the reader from his surroundings, led him into a new world— a world of splendour, heroism, and deep passions; a world without squabbles and the vanities of daily existence. The common problems of daily life simply did not exist for that literature . . . It called for heroic deeds, induced day dreaming, and engendered in one's soul the instincts for everything great and beautiful." [8] By the middle of the century, however, the popularity of sentimental classical literature had declined in Russia, and the literature that appealed to the radical intelligentsia had a quite different effect on young Kelsiev. Byronic disillusionment, he claimed, led to the analytical method of Dickens, then to the sarcasm of Gogol, and ultimately to the numerous less gifted but "mercilessly brave" analysts who taught Russian youth to penetrate into their own souls and the souls of others. These negatively-minded analysts tore off the laurel of sentimentalism from the male hero and robbed the female of her fairy-like and angelic qualities. This negation, which began as a reaction against the excessively sentimental ways of classical literature, encouraged a negative approach to life.

Kelsiev regarded this new literary trend, which was called the "Natural School," as having been an important medium for the development and expression of nihilistic attitudes among the radical intellectuals of his generation. This movement emerged in Russia in the 1840's, with Gogol (d. 1852) and Belinsky (d. 1848), and by the 1860's it had become thoroughly politicized by radical writers such as Chernyshevsky and Dobroliubov. In his last years at the commercial school the world of sentimental literature was gradually replaced in Kelsiev's life by the new, nihilistic, politically-oriented world of the Natural School. The Natural School, he later complained, crushed and dislocated everything. It proclaimed all the standards governing human society as artificial and superfluous. Kelsiev claimed that the adherents to that literary movement came to regard humans as simple mortals who needed no values other than those dictated by the necessities for their own survival. Without values and standards there could be neither heroes nor villains. "Subsequently, when the Natural School, with that unbelievable speed possible only in Russia, squeezed out everything associated with Romanticism, and we, the thirteen- and fourteen-year old boys behind school desks, began to negate everything important and heroic and to slander each other with vulgarities, we became what Lermontov foresaw that we would become . . . 'the emaciated fruit ripened before its time'. We hardly knew the life of youth with all its bright hopes." Un-

der the impact of Gogol's invective, according to Kelsiev, one
began to analyze and criticize his fellow men. As a result, "a
painful spleen would penetrate into one's soul, and one begins
to recognize one's own shortcomings . . . , begins to pluck one's
own entrails out . . . and begins to suspect that the world of
heroic deeds, of poetry, and adventure is not merely remote
but does not exist." [9]

Due to such a strong predilection for politics and literature among them, it was a short step for many a Russian radical
from being a *literaturnyi chelovek* to becoming a political
man or "politman." A politman is one who leads a religiously
political life. Just as a *literaturnyi chelovek* is a suffering
rather than a creative writer, so a politman is seldom a practicing politician. He is not a politician by profession—he is
possessed with politics. He suffers throughout his life with
political pains, views the surrounding reality in political
terms, and associates even the most mundane of his personal
activities with his political goals. Kelsiev saw himself to be
such a politman. He began as a *literaturnyi chelovek*, and
without ceasing being one he became a politman. As a politman he thought politically, worked politically, and politically
he dissipated his personal life as if it were a burdensome
superfluity. Having experienced extreme hardships and constant failures in his revolutionary activities, he asked himself
at one point why it was that he did not abandon his political
life and become a private citizen—"a salesman or a watch-
maker." The answer he gave was that such a reversal was
a virtual impossibility, for he felt himself to be a political
addict. Addiction to politics, he though, was just as real and
serious as the addiction to tobacco or alcohol.[10]

In addition to being influenced by nihilistic literature
Kelsiev's inclinations toward political radicalism were also
stimulated by the general mood prevailing in Russia at the
time. Born only a decade after the Decembrists' uprising, he
grew up in an atmosphere of mysterious whispers about the
political events of 1825. His was the time when children would
overhear the enticing whispers of their parents, would discover
the secret notebooks their parents had kept, and memorize the
forbidden verses these notebooks contained about the Decem-

brists. To the children this air of secrecy was a curtain hiding from them an exciting and mysterious world of adventures comparable to the adventures of their literary heroes. The revolutionary events of 1848, moreover—even though Kelsiev was still only thirteen years of age at the time—impressed upon his responsive mind the fact that the world of adventure was not confined to literature. The suppression of the Hungarian revolution by the Russian army the following year and the arrest of the Petrashevtsy—a Russian socialist group— filled the capital with a feeling of anticipation of important political changes. The words "republic, uprising, and disorder," Kelsiev later recalled, "were heard from all sides." Instead of liberalizing changes, however, a deeper secrecy fell upon Russia. In those days hardly any of her citizens knew much about Russia," for both her past and present were shrouded in bureaucratic secrecy," and one had to turn to foreign sources to learn about his own country. The fact that those sources were usually prohibited led many Russians to attribute undue importance to them, and the secrecy imposed by the government led the people to ask themselves what it was that the government was hiding from them. Under these circumstances the conclusion at which Kelsiev and many of his contemporaries arrived was that the government was conspiring against its own people."

Kelsiev entered the University of St. Petersburg in 1855, when Russia was fighting in the Crimean War (1853-56). The defeats Russia suffered in that war served to mirror the hitherto hidden abuses and corruption of the bureaucratic system Nicholas I had maintained and stimulated thereby a feeling of hostility toward the government. This hostility was especially strong among the university students, and Kelsiev thus became directly exposed to the ideas of political radicalism. Whereas at the outbreak of the war he seriously thought of volunteering for military service, now, studying at the University, his political negativism triumphed over his feeling of patriotism, and instead of defending his country he "spitefully rejoiced" in its defeat.

Kelsiev's university years coincided with years of alienation between fathers and sons, years when respect for one's

country began to be regarded by the young generation as a mark
of political degeneracy. Under such conditions, as Kelsiev
later admitted, the Russian way of life became "completely
alien" to the radical intellectuals.

> To suppose that the government, too, sincerely de-
> sired well-being for Russia . . . seemed insane in
> those days. The words "government" and "evil"
> were almost synonymous. Russia's hopes were placed
> on the young generation . . . and every impudent
> youth regarded himself to be more capable and more
> experienced than all the statesmen of Europe. Ex-
> perience, diligence, and a constructive preoccupation
> were no longer valued; caution and thoughtfulness
> appeared to be pretentious. It was a feverish period:
> everyone rushed about as if half awake—awakened
> by the cannonade of Sebastopol, with the eyes not
> yet accustomed to light, the mind to reason, and
> hands to labour.[12]

Initially this negativism was directed specifically against the
government, but soon everything associated with the existing
system became subjected to rejection and abuse. Writing some
years later, Kelsiev recalled that there was hardly anyone
among his acquaintances at the University who really knew
the difference in quality between Russian and English cloth.
"Yet, if I were to say that my coat was made of English cloth,
they would look at it with curiosity; but if I were to say that
my coat was made of cloth from the factory of some merchant
named Sinebriukhov, that would be the end; without inquiring
into the real quality of the cloth, nobody would honour it
with any special attention." [13] Such was the general mood he
became exposed to at the University; these were the conditions in which he matured.

Kelsiev, too, learned to idolize everything associated with
the West. He explained his adulation of the West by the fact
that the West was the forbidden fruit and that the Russian
political system offered no alternative which could merit a
sincere respect from its people. The forbidden foreign books

seemed to him almost an expression of supernatural wisdom, and his credulity was based not so much on their contents as on the strictness of their prohibition. Such a correlation between the intensity of the government's efforts in denying its people access to certain Western ideas and the strength of the radical intelligentsia's belief in the validity of these ideas led Kelsiev to regard the most radical ideas of the West as being the most profound. He blamed government censorship not only for his own alienation but also for contributing to the development of nihilism as such. As the religious intolerance and restrictions led to the emergence of "all kinds" of sects, he thought, so political censorship made unavoidable the emergence of extreme forms of opposition such as nihilism.

Undoubtedly, the most penetrating characterization of the Russian radical intelligentsia as a whole was made by its own members in the well-known collection of essays titled *Vekhi* or *The Signposts*, published in 1909. The extent to which the characteristics of the intelligentsia described in *Vekhi* coincide with the characteristics manifested and often recognized in himself by Vasily Kelsiev is worth noting. In these essays one reads, for example, that the intelligentsia was deeply religious, if by religiosity one understands "a fanaticism and a passionate devotion to a select idea—*idée fixe*—which on the one hand may lead to self-sacrifice and great heroic deeds and on the other to an abnormal exaggeration of the entire perspective of life and a feeling of destructive intolerance of everything that does not coincide with the demands of the given idea." The intelligentsia, according to the *Vekhi* writers, lived in an atmosphere of anticipation of a great social miracle, of a universal cataclysm in the eschatological sense. "To become a hero, and thus become a saviour of mankind, is possible only through a heroic deed far exceeding the limits of the ordinary call of duty. This is the dream that lives in the souls of the intellectuals, and even though it might be fulfilled only by a few individuals, this dream serves as the guiding principle of life for the entire intelligentsia." Because of the idealization of their own mission in life, the intelligentsia, one of the *Vekhi* writers suggested, lost sight of the real humans it aspired to save. The Russian people, in whose name the radical intellectuals sought to sacrifice themselves, were not the actual people of Russia but an abstraction formulated by and existing in the minds of these intellectuals. A member of the radical intelligentsia, according to another *Vekhi* contributor, was not an altruist. Although he aspired for the happiness of mankind, "his real interests are devoted not to the living people but only to his idea—namely, the idea of happiness for all mankind. In sacrificing himself for this idea, he does not hesitate to sacrifice others as well." His love for the oppressed is negated by his hate for the oppressors, and thus in effect he hates the very mankind he professes to love.[14] It would also seem reasonable to assume that such a passionate idealizer of mankind would be inclined to become antagonistic toward humanity because of the latter's unavoidable failure to live up to the standards he projects for it in his idealization.

In the course of his preoccupation with the attainment of salvation for this abstract humanity, many an individual member of the intelligentsia, according to one of the *Vekhi* intellectuals, allowed his own life to pass him by. "What was our intelligentsia doing in the past half-century?" that *Vekhi* contributor asked himself, and he provided an answer which strongly reflected the paradoxical predicament the individual intellectuals had imposed upon themselves.

A bunch of revolutionaries went from house to house, knocking at the door and summoning: "All, out into the street! It is shameful to sit at home!" and people of different convictions poured into the city square. Lame, blind, armless—none remained at home. For a half a century now they have been milling around in the square, lamenting and arguing. At home there is filth, poverty, disorder, but the master of the house has no time for that. He is among the people; he is bringing them salvation; and being there, of course, requires less effort and is more interesting than doing the unpleasant work at home. No one really lived—all were engaged (or at least made it appear as if they were engaged) in

public affairs. They did not live even from the pure
sense of egotism; they did not rejoice in life; did not
enjoy freely its amusements; but snatched pieces of
it and swallowed them whole, feeling lustful and
shameful at the same time, like a mischievous dog.
This was a peculiar kind of asceticism: not so much
an abstention from the personal physical existence
as an abstention from being in control of it. Personal
life went on somehow, on its own accord, sullenly
and with convulsions.[15]

In looking at Kelsiev, one finds it easy to recognize in
him many of the same characteristics the *Vekhi* writers
attributed to the radical intelligentsia collectively. As was
the case with Chernyshevsky, Dobroliubov, and Shchapov, for
example, Kelsiev was of clerical ancestry. While professing
to be an atheist, he, like so many others of his generation,
retained throughout his life an intense feeling of religiosity,
which manifested itself in his devotion to the idols he happened
to worship at any given time. He was inclined to commit
himself totally to a cause only to reject it and become devoted
just as deeply to an ideal or cause which might be its opposite.
He actively yearned for a cause that would lead to an ultimate
goal, and, although he was never quite certain of the essence
of that goal, he was willing to pay any price for its attainment.

Herzen placed Kelsiev among the residue of the socialistic Petrashevtsy and thought that he retained some of their
dignity and all of their shortcomings. He described Kelsiev
as a young man who seemed to have studied everything in
the world but learned nothing thoroughly. Because he was
constantly criticizing everything that was commonly accepted,
Kelsiev, according to Herzen, weakened all of his common
sense values and utterly failed to develop any of the habits
of a disciplined mind. In Kelsiev's skeptical gropings, Herzen
recognized an admixture of mystical fantasy and regarded
him as a nihilist with religious proclivities, "a nihilist in a
deacon's cassock." In Herzen's view, Kelsiev combined the
traits traditionally held to be peculiarly Russian with a nega-

tive approach to reality. "He worked spasmodically and spasmodically he idled. He easily grasped new problems but just
as easily lost interest in them, and he tried to squeeze every
issue to its last drop and more." Kelsiev rejected the basic
principles, precepts, and values in which he had been brought
up in his early childhood, but failed to replace them with an
integrated system of his own.

> He rejected the old; he lost his hold on all firm
> ground; he pushed away the shore; and, grasping his
> head with both hands, he set out upon the open sea.
> He was equally suspicious of belief and disbelief,
> toward the Russian ways and the ways of the West.
> Only one thing was rooted in his breast, and that
> was a deep and passionate awareness of the economic
> injustices which existed in contemporary societies.
> His acute awareness of these injustices led him to
> despise and hate the old order and to develop a
> mystical yearning for social theories which would
> remedy all of these social ills.[16]

Herzen's appraisal of Kelsiev was confirmed by another
member of the intelligentsia of the 1860's. Nicholas V. Shelgunov, a prominent radical publicist, regarded Kelsiev as a
typical representative of the intelligentsia of his generation.
According to Shelgunov, Kelsiev began his career by negating
and questioning, and he came to believe in the need for a
basic change of all moral assumptions.

> Having unreservedly committed ourselves to the left-
> ist trends of Europe we then went further, and none
> of us was willing to believe that such a beginning
> would be premature. The social point of our protest
> was our general indignation and hatred of the eco-
> nomic disorder of our society. Since solutions could
> be found only in the new socio-economic theories,
> we threw ourselves upon these theories. It was to
> this intellectual type that Kelsiev belonged. He was
> smitten by a new wave that washed him off the old

shore, and, head first, he threw himself into an unknown sea.

Some of the dominant characteristics Shelgunov attributed to the radical intellectuals of the 1860's, among whom he placed Kelsiev, befit the latter as an individual rather well. "A slight inclination toward exaggeration; a slight capacity for critical judgment; a slight trace of goodwill; a great deal of egotism, especially a desire to play a role and to be the centre of attraction; exaggeration of one's own powers; an imagination preoccupied with the luring imagery of important deeds; even some boastfulness—emanating from the same source of egotism and the satisfaction of seeing oneself wearing a halo; and, always, a great deal of cowardice." [17]

Kelsiev's own appraisal of himself as a member of the radical intelligentsia was expressed in even more vividly dramatic terms than those used by Herzen and Shelgunov in their comments about him. Instead of plunging into a metaphorical sea, Kelsiev saw himself as a knight challenging a malevolent supernatural power. He cites in his memoirs a tale from Russian folklore—a tale about a knight who, having defeated all his earthly enemies, called forth an enemy from another world, and was gratified to see that not one but two supernatural warriors were sent against him.

> The Knight fell upon the warriors and with all his
>     might cut them in half.
> There were now four of them, and they were all
>     alive.
> The fearless Knight fell upon them and with all
>     his might cut them in half.
> There were now eight of them, and they were all
>     alive.
> With all his might the Knight cut them in half.
> There were twice as many now, and they were all
>     alive . . .
> Not only was the Knight cutting them,
> But his stallion was trampling them down . . .
> But their number kept growing and growing,

And against the Knight they kept charging and
    charging.

He and his fellow-radicals, Kelsiev concluded, were also such
knights. "We challenged a power that was not of this world,"
he wrote. "We challenged it in spite of censorship and the
severe regulations of the time, disregarding everything in the
world in order to attain the latest secrets of knowledge . . .
We challenged this power and struggled against it, struggled
to the death. This was far from being a childish struggle, for
some of us ended up in Siberia and others became emigrants." [18]
    Kelsiev was one of those who emigrated. He left Russia
in 1858 as an employee of the Russian-American Company.
His destination was Alaska, where he was to be employed in
a clerical capacity and where he planned to do some ethnographic studies among the native people. By that time he was
married, and his wife, Varvara Timofeevna, with a new-born
daughter, accompanied him on his journey. Both he and his
wife were enthusiastic about their travel and about his prospective career. A few days following their departure, however,
Varvara, still infirm from the recent childbirth, began to experience severe hemorrhages. The ship physician advised them
to disembark at the nearest port, and, as disappointed as they
were over the failure of completing their intended journey,
the Kelsievs came ashore at Plymouth, England. That event
proved to be the beginning of a long Jobean decade in the
brief life of this defiant, nihilistic Russian "knight" of the
1860's.
    In spite of his preconceived admiration for everything
Western, when he first arrived in England, Kelsiev did not
plan to become an emigrant. In May of the following year,
however, he went to London and paid a visit to Alexander
Herzen. Herzen, who himself had migrated from Russia in
1847, was an idol of the Russian intelligentsia, and Kelsiev,
like many others, had revered the very sound of his name.
Herzen advised Kelsiev against emigration, but this served
only to reinforce the latter's sudden decision for doing so.
With romantic bravado Kelsiev swore to the editor of *The
Bell* and his associate, Nicholas Ogarev, that he would devote

his entire life to revolutionary work with them and promised to begin contributing articles to their periodical. Disregarding the warnings from the two experienced emigrants about the hardships a Russian political refugee might encounter abroad, Kelsiev moved his ailing wife and child to the British capital and in November of that year notified the Russian consulate of his decision to remain abroad permanently.

"I became an emigrant," he wrote some years later, "because it was impossible for me to do otherwise." He claimed that his decision was dictated by the general mood characterizing the Russian youth at that time. "One needs to work, one needs to propagandize—this is a sacred duty of every contemporary Russian," he kept telling himself. He was then twenty-four years of age. The only Russia he had seen was a fraction of the whole: from St. Petersburg to Novgorod, and even that he saw only at a glance. His life in St. Petersburg was bookish, and his political theories, therefore, were mainly derived from books and from conversations with youths similar to himself. Of the West he knew even less, yet he idealized that alien world and believed that everything associated with the West was superior to anything Russian. His idealization led him to the conviction that full "human development and the latest word in science and thought existed only in the West." He became an emigrant in part because he was convinced that in the West—"the world of mysterious forbidden books, the world of free speech"—he would be able to learn the real truth, which he would then communicate to his native Russia."

His confidence in the West, one must hasten to note, did not endure for long. In the same reminiscences in which he described his earlier enthusiasm for everything Western he also expressed agreement with Herzen about the hardships of a political emigrant's life there. When a Russian emigrant arrives in the West, Kelsiev observed, he expects every Westerner he meets to embrace him for being such an ardent believer in liberty and progress as to abandon his native country and come to the West. "He goes to the West because of his convictions, confident that he would live among people who are sympathetic to his cause, respectful of his ideals, and believing in the same thing he believes. But alas! Not only in

France or England, but in America itself they look at him as if he were a wild animal!" [20]

The suddenness of Kelsiev's decision to remain abroad—a step involving the sacrifice of a rather promising career with the Russian-American Company, the abandonment of his relatives and his native country, and the risk of retaliation from the Russian government—was consistent with both the prevailing mood of his time and his character. It was with some justification that in his later years, because of his political vacillations, Kelsiev's enemies compared him to a weathervane. At the university, for example, he was devoted to the study of Oriental languages, then at one point he suddenly abandoned this subject for the natural sciences, only to return once again to the former discipline. Dobroliubov, who was acquainted with him at the university, observed that although Kelsiev was a man "who thinks seriously" and who "has a powerful spirit and thirst for action," he revealed excessive touchiness in his personal life.[21] This touchiness often manifested itself in an abrupt change in his course of action, and his decision to become an emigrant, as we will see, was one of several such important decisions he made seemingly on the spur of the moment.

Alexander Herzen, a master in characterizing those he met, noted at the time of Kelsiev's arrival in London that the new Russian emigrant, a tall young man "with a square head covered with a mop of hair," was frantically seeking an all-absorbing cause. Herzen noticed in him much "that had not yet been brought to order and had not yet been reconciled," but little that appeared to be insincere or vulgar. The basic sincerity in Kelsiev's character, recognized by nearly all of those who have left accounts of him, indicates that his apparent instability was not the caprice of an indecisive mental weakling but a manifestation of his excessive concern with the general problems of his time. Herzen recognized that Kelsiev's decision to remain abroad was motivated not only by his desire to flee from the burdens he felt in his homeland and by his need to find a place of refuge, but also by his conviction that "he was going somewhere," although just where he did not know. "Like most of the other young Russians of his generation,

Kelsiev had not yet found any definite goal. He was searching for his goal, and in the meantime he was surveying the surroundings and bringing to order, and possibly disorder, the entire mass of ideas grasped at school, in books, and from life. There was turmoil inside of him . . . That turmoil was the essential problem by which he lived, waiting for this or that idea to which he could dedicate himself." [22] The rapid vacillation in Kelsiev's behaviour, then, including his sudden decision to become an emigrant, places him clearly within the ranks of his generation of the political intellectuals who were absorbed in an intense search for solutions to the predicament in which they found themselves due to their alienation from existing reality.

In London, Kelsiev settled down in Fulham, and it is on the masterful pen of Alexander Herzen that we must rely for our description of the life there of this political refugee who consciously sought to exchange his own and his family's happiness for the future happiness of mankind. Herzen observed that the district in which Kelsiev settled was populated by "mat, ash-coloured Irishmen and various other emaciated proletarians." In that section of London, according to Herzen, one did not hear the sounds which were representative of life in other parts of the city: one never heard there the cries of the food vendors or the barking of dogs or the rattling of horse carriages. Among the typical sights in Fulham would be "some lean cat, with its fur ruffled and covered with coal dust, which would come out and tread across the roof to a chimney, arching its back and thereby revealing that it had become chilled within the house." [23]

The level of Kelsiev's material well-being in London was fully consonant with the general material level of the district in which he lived. On one occasion he attended a meeting of Polish socialists and was asked to make a speech there. The meeting place was well-heated, yet, in spite of his embarrassment and discomfort, he spoke wearing an overcoat, for his jacket was too tattered to be exposed. It is interesting to note that he told the Poles on that occasion that many Russians, including himself, had no desire to see Poland dominated by Russia. Ever since the conquest of Poland "by Peter the Great," he informed them, Poland had been a serious economic burden to Russia. According to Kelsiev, his speech was greeted with enthusiastic applause, and the following day the *Morning Chronicle* carried an article which stated that a "famous" Russian poet-revolutionary spoke before a gathering of Polish socialists and called for the liberation of Poland. No mention was made of the error in Kelsiev's speech regarding the conquest of Poland by Peter the Great, and Kelsiev concluded that those who attended the meeting must have been even less knowledgeable in the field of Polish history than he.[24]

On his first visit to the Kelsievs in Fulham, Herzen witnessed a heart-breaking scene. Vasily Kelsiev was not at home, but "a very young, very unattractive woman [Kelsiev's wife]—lean, lymphatic, eyes filled with tears—sat by a matress on the floor, on which a year or a year and a half old child with a high fever was tossing, suffering, and dying." This child, the Kelsievs' first-born, did die soon after Herzen's visit, and another daughter was born shortly thereafter. The poverty in which the Kelsievs lived was extreme, but the sickly, twenty-year old woman faced it with dignified meekness.

> It was difficult to suspect from looking at her sickly, scrofulous and weak appearance, what power, what strength of dedication resided in her meek body ... She was, and she wanted to be, what has later been called a nihilist: she combed her hair in an unusual manner, she dressed slovenly, smoked heavily, feared neither advanced thoughts nor bold words; she did not act pretentiously before the patrons of her family, she did not speak about her sacred duty nor the sacrifices which she performed daily, and she did not speak of the lightness of the cross which rested upon her young shoulders. She did not dally with her struggle against poverty, instead she did everything: sewed and washed, fed the child, cooked the meat, and cleaned the house. She was a firm friend to her husband ...[25]

Herzen's is the only specific description of Kelsiev's consort that is available. Varvara Timofeevna, born Shcherbatova (1840-65), apparently possessed some literary abilities, for during her residence in London she translated one of George Sand's novels from French into Russian. After her marriage to Kelsiev she lived under the spell of romanticism, hero-worshiping her husband and consciously minimizing her own intellectual capacity in order to accentuate his. Varvara Timofeevna, as one of her acquaintances in London noted, "was meek, and she was enraptured by his intellect. She never dared to challenge any of his fantasies." [26] Whether it was because of her meekness or rapture over her husband's intellectual prowess is difficult to say, but Varvara Timofeevna did endure, and ungrudgingly, a tragic life of extreme hardships. She was, moreover, sincerely devoted to the nebulous goals for which the *Weltschmerz*-ridden soul of her husband so passionately yearned.

These, then, were the general circumstances in which Vasily Kelsiev—a tall, square-headed, long-haired man of twenty-five, with a sickly chain-smoking wife and a gravely ill infant, a refugee in a foreign land—set out to change the socio-political order of Russia. His was a Herculean task. Where does one begin with such an undertaking? How is it possible for an individual to find a way to tear asunder such a complex, powerful, and amorphous entity as the socio-political order of an empire extending from the Baltic Sea to the Pacific Ocean? Even Kelsiev, with his high aptitude for a total commitment in pursuit of a goal, lacked a clear plan as to the ways and means to initiate such an enormous task. In spite of his idealism, therefore, his actions in London were largely determined by the daily circumstances of his life, even though he usually succeeded in justifying these actions in terms of his imaginary political mission.

At the time of his initial meeting with the publishers of *The Bell*, Kelsiev offered to begin his crusade against the Russian political order by writing about the civil rights of Russian women. Herzen suggested that his articles for *The Bell* should deal with land distribution instead, for this was the time when preparations for the liberation of the serfs were being made in Russia. Kelsiev, however, insisted on his own proposal and wrote an article on women's civil rights. Herzen found the article to be of such an inferior literary quality that he refrained from publishing it. This in effect terminated Kelsiev's journalistic contribution to *The Bell*. Unable to find other means for supporting himself and his family, Kelsiev reluctantly accepted a semi-patronage from Herzen: he agreed to serve as a tutor to Herzen's daughter and as a substitute proofreader for *The Bell*. This unimpressive sinecure with *The Bell* could only be viewed by Kelsiev as a temporary engagement; nevertheless it proved to be the beginning of his active affiliation with that small yet influential centre of the Russian revolutionary movement of the 1860's which will be referred to in the present context as the Kolokol Group.

The nucleus of the Kolokol Group consisted of two men: Herzen and Ogarev. They were the founders and the publishers of the anti-tsarist Russian-language newspaper *Kolokol* or *The Bell*, which was published in 1857-65 in London and from May 1865 to its closure in July 1867 in Geneva. In 1859 Kelsiev and in 1861 Bakunin became actively affiliated with the two publicists, and many others both in Russia and abroad assisted them in their revolutionary work. In a few cases the assistance of the others was financial, but mostly these supporters served as clandestine correspondents for and distributors of the London publications. Unlike Kelsiev and Bakunin, however, none of the others made the London facilities of *The Bell* their permanent place of political work.[27]

Herzen was the dean of that informal association. One of the most colorful and influential personalities of the nineteenth-century revolutionary intelligentsia, Alexander Ivanovich Herzen (1812-70) was the son of a German woman whom his father, a Russian nobleman named Iakovlev, brought to Russia as his mistress. Born in the year of Napoleon's romantic, albeit tragic, dash across the Russian steppes, Herzen was thirteen when Nicholas I came to power in the midst of the Decembrists' revolt. The execution of the five Decembrist leaders on Nicholas's order made a deep impression on the sensitive youth; and according to an often repeated story, Herzen and his friend Ogarev swore an oath to avenge the death of the fallen leaders. Unlike the vows of most other youths this one was fulfilled: working together, Herzen and Ogarev spent their lives struggling against the tsarist political system.

Having experienced exile for political activities as a student, Herzen abandoned his native country in 1847 and was destined never to return. With the aid of James Rothschild, of the famous financial concern, he was able to induce the Russian government to transfer the wealth he had inherited from his father to Western Europe. Thus, unlike most political refugees of his or any other time, Herzen enjoyed the freedom of Western Europe in comfort. Under the spell of George Sand's romantic novels, Herzen's sentimentally tender wife Natalie (1817-52) applied some of the precepts of literary romanticism by becoming intimate with a German romantic poet George Herwegh. Upon learning of his wife's infidelity, Herzen betrayed his professed adherence to the codes of romantic literature and for months raged violently with common jealousy. Natalie Herzen began to wilt from sorrow and died in childbirth at the age of thirty-five, leaving her beloved husband struggling with a conscience perpetually kindled by a feeling of guilt for her death. Then, in 1856, his childhood friend Nicholas Platonovich Ogarev (1813-77), with his youthful wife, also named Natalie (1829-1913), joined Herzen in London as an emigrant, and another dramatic chapter opened in the latter's colorful life. Like Herzen, Ogarev was of the nobility, was opposed to the political system existing in Russia, and was a romantic by inclination. The Ogarevs settled in Herzen's residence, and Natalie—an imaginative romantic idealist, sixteen years younger than her perpetually-philosophizing and rather monkish husband—fell in love with the older but more handsomely masculine widowed Alexander Herzen. While continuing to live in the same house with Ogarev and remaining legally his wife, Natalie bore Herzen three children. Remaining loyal to his lifelong friend, who was now the father of his wife's children, Ogarev spent the rest of his life withering away from a deep ever-smoldering pain. The love of an English prostitute named Mary Sutherland failed to save Ogarev from burning himself out with alcohol.

Michael Alexandrovich Bakunin (1814-76) lived a life far more dangerous than and nearly as intricate as Herzen's. Born of a noble and well cultivated family in the province of Tver, Bakunin spent three years as a cadet in an artillery school in St. Petersburg. In 1833 he was commissioned as an ensign in artillery, but some two years later resigned his commission and moved to Moscow. In Moscow he became a devout Hegelian. Herzen and Ogarev, who at the time belonged to a more politically oriented circle, were among his close acquaintances there. By the time of his departure for Berlin in 1840, Bakunin was already noted for his extreme political radicalism, for the spontaneity of his behaviour, and for his propensity to incur debts on a permanent basis. Studying at the University of Berlin, Bakunin became disenchanted with Hegelianism and with philosophy in general; and at the time of the revolutionary unrest of 1848 he decided that the making of revolutions was the profession for which he had been yearning. Living to him now meant struggling, and there was hardly an upheaval in Europe in his lifetime in which he did not participate. In 1849 he was arrested in Saxony for his revolutionary activities and was condemned to die, but the following year was handed over to the Austrian government. In Austria he was in turn sentenced to death but was handed over to the Russian authorities. In Russia he spent six years confined in the Peter-and-Paul and Schluesselburg fortresses and then was permanently banished to Siberia. In 1861, however, he escaped from Siberia and, travelling by way of Japan, San Francisco, and New York, came to London to join associates of his Moscow days, Herzen and Ogarev. The decade he spent in prisons and exile did little to dull his enthusiasm for the destruction of the existing European political order. Upon his arrival in London he resumed his revolutionary activities and continued to be as generous with promises as before.

These three members of the Kolokol Group—Herzen, Ogarev, and Bakunin—were among the most prominent of Russia's political theorizers. Bakunin was the most original of the three, Herzen the most versatile and influential, and Ogarev the most concise and thoughtful. Herzen is best known for his theory of peasant socialism, in which he advocated a fusion of Western socialist concepts with the Russian peasant communal organization. Possibly the strongest testimony to Herzen's eminence as a political thinker lies in the fact that nearly all of the diverse socialistic groups emerging in Russia after the 1860's claimed him as their political progenitor. Bakunin is well known for his ideas on anarchism, and his theories of violent negation are truly original in the annals of Russian political thought. He believed that the masses were inherently inclined toward violence. This passion for destruction, he thought, would spontaneously manifest itself in a perpetual wave of violence leading to the annihilation of all existing institutions and to the ultimate liberation of the individual. The general mood of Bakunin's teaching was probably most clearly revealed in his oft-quoted pronouncement that the passion of destruction is a creative passion.

Ogarev's Boswellean figure has been almost hidden in the shadow of his Dr. Johnson. This is unjust to the meek poet and sufferer. For his moral precepts, his vital idealism, his subtly daring existence, and for his political theories, Ogarev deserves to be recognized on his own merits. In the light of recent documentary publications on the revolutionary movement of the 1860's it is becoming increasingly evident that Ogarev's political thought was far from being a mere footnote to Herzen's political theorizing. Ogarev reveals in his writings a much more penetrating understanding than Herzen of the need for economic reorganization in achieving any basic political changes in the Russia of their time. He may even be credited with having originated the concept of "going to the people," which was applied in the 1870's. Many of the ideas that are to be found in Lenin's *What Is To Be Done?* had been expressed by Ogarev half a century before the publication of that influential blueprint for revolution. Ogarev was one of the earliest pioneers in Russian revolutionary thought, and it was he who formulated a definite theoretical system for creating a centralized organization of professional revolutionaries. The latter concepts were applied in the 1860's in creating the first Land and Liberty organization, the very name of which was borrowed from Ogarev's writings. Finally,

Ogarev's ideas, as we will see, were also influential in reviving the concept of the Zemsky Sobor in the 1860's. These, then, were the members of the Kolokol Group with whom Vasily Kelsiev became associated in London.[28]

# CHAPTER II

# A DISSENTER DISCOVERS HIS KIN

Herzen and Ogarev described their publishing facilities in London as "The Free Russian Press," and in choosing materials for publication they consciously strove to maintain the spirit implied in that description. It was partly because of the general integrity of the information they published that their periodical enjoyed high respect among Russians of all classes, including Tsar Alexander II himself. *The Bell*, of course, was not permitted to circulate openly in Russia, but was widely distributed there nonetheless. Because of the popularity of their periodical the London publishers received a great deal of information from inside Russia, both from members of the anti-tsarist radical intelligentsia and from individuals seeking to publicize personal grievances. The information was usually delivered to London by Russians travelling abroad legally, and some was of a confidential nature, indicating collaboration with *The Bell* of persons highly placed in the Russian government.

From such diverse sources, over a period of several years, there had accumulated in Herzen's residence a substantial collection of miscellaneous materials pertaining to the history and the social status of the Russian religious Dissenters or Raskolniks. One day, late in 1859, Herzen nonchalantly suggested to Kelsiev that he might look through some of these materials and see if any useful information could be derived from them for *The Bell*. Herzen attributed little significance to these papers and offered them to Kelsiev probably more for the purpose of evoking a reaction from that "nihilist with religious proclivities" than from any real hope of discovering valuable information in them. To the young revolutionary, however, that bundle of papers revealed the fiery message he had been searching for since the day when he lost the comfort of his family home and was cast out into the big alien world at the commercial school in St. Petersburg.

Kelsiev read the manuscripts throughout the night and in the morning felt as if he had spent that night in the mysterious macabre and enchanting unreality of the tales of Hoffmann, Poe, and *The Thousand and One Nights.*

> The Emasculates, with their mystic rites, their choruses, and their harvest songs so full of poetry; the Flagellants, with their queer beliefs; the solemn types of the Priestless; the intrigues of the leaders of the Old Believers; the existence of Russian villages in Prussia, Austria, Moldavia, and Turkey—all of this was startlingly revealed to me during that night. One sect passed after another; images rushed before me one after another as if in a magic lantern. I read, read, and reread; my head was turning; I was gasping for air. I would have murdered anyone who might have interfered with my reading. I would not have released those writings from my hands even for the price of the whole of California. Like a madman I ran out of the house at about noon, in order to refresh my head, which was no longer able to digest everything I'd read, and in order to share my ecstasy with Herzen, Ogarev, Chernetsky (our printer), Truebner, and the first person I should meet. They, of course, looked at me with bewilderment, without understanding the reason for my rejoicing; and from my explanations about the beliefs of our Dissenters they concluded only that the latter were absolute fools. In other words, no one understood me.
>
> "Nonsense!" they were telling me, "the Raskolniks are fools! . . ."

But I knew otherwise. These clumsy peasants, these bearded merchants, scorned and laughed at

by Europe and by our educated people; these ignorant barbarians, sunk in primitive materialism, all
of a sudden were elevated in my estimation. . . .
The Raskolniks bring honour to the Russian people,
proving that the Russians are not asleep, that every
sensible peasant wants to examine for himself the
tenets of his belief and to think for himself about the
essence of reality. The Raskolniks are proving that
the Russian man is searching for truth; and whatever
truth he finds, he would follow it fearing neither the
fire, nor the cave with the exit blocked, nor emasculation, nor even human sacrifices and cannibalism. In
the West the simple people have become blind.[1]

Herzen's writings confirm Kelsiev's account of the state
of inebriation the latter experienced from reading about the
Raskolniks. According to Herzen, Kelsiev undertook the task
of editing the government reports on the Raskol with a passion. These were the best days in Kelsiev's life, Herzen observed, for in the Raskol Kelsiev sensed the presence of simple
folk-socialism attired in evangelical garb. He worked with
devotion, and in the evening would come running to Herzen
to point out some social ideas held by the Dukhobors or the
Molokans or something purely communistic in the teachings
of the Theodocians. Kelsiev was delighted by the Sectarians'
wanderings in the forests and was ready to make it his life's
ideal to wander with them. Herzen sensed that Kelsiev was
tormented with emotional anguish and restlessness and was
a wanderer at heart—"a wanderer both in spirit and in practice."[2]

The writings which transported Kelsiev to the world of
Hoffmann had been collected by members of the secret government committees which held the Raskol population under
close surveillance during the reign of Nicholas I (1825-55).
These government reports contained a variety of specific information: testimonials of individual Raskolniks, statistical
studies of the numerical growth of the sects, a history of
the Castrates, conclusions and recommendations made by the
officials compiling the reports, and many documents of a

miscellaneous nature. Subsequently Kelsiev published these reports in four volumes, expressing in the editorial commentaries his own conclusions regarding the Raskolniks' revolutionary potentialities.[3]

The origin of the Raskol or Dissenting movement described in the government reports which Kelsiev read in London goes back to the seventeenth century. Whereas in Western Europe the protestors were the reformers of the church, in Russia the reformers were the established authorities of the church and the protestors were the defenders of the existing ways. The reforms which brought about the major schism or *raskol* which produced the Dissenting movement were administered by Patriarch Nikon, who headed the Russian Orthodox church from 1652 to 1658. The year which formalized the existence of the Raskol as a distinct religious body was 1666. In that year a church council excommunicated the opponents to the Nikonian reforms and thereby officially acknowledged their collective existence.

In reality the reformers were the schismatics, for it was they who had deviated from the faith the Russians had worshiped since the days of their Christianization. However, since they were supported by the state, the reformers triumphed over the defenders of the old faith and proclaimed the latter as schismatics or *raskolniks*. As prejudicial as the original use of the term "Raskol" has been, however, an historian writing three centuries after the origin of that usage has little choice but to adhere essentially to the established convention. Nonetheless, since over these centuries the Raskol became fragmented and since its subdivisions and the various sects which separated from the main church at later times have been confused with the original movement, it is necessary to clarify the denotative relationship of various terms applied to these dissenting elements.

The term "Raskol" or "Dissenting movement" and its derivatives will in the present context be used to designate both the adherents of the pre-Nikonian Orthodox church who were proclaimed schismatic by the Church Council of 1666-67 and all those who dissented from the officially recognized Orthodox church either before or after 1666, but who, as a formal religious body, existed after 1666. In order to distinguish between the adherents of the old Orthodoxy and the sects which deviated from both the old Orthodoxy and the reformed Orthodox faith, the term "Old Believers" will be used to designate the former and the term "Sectarians" to designate the latter. Schematically the denotative meaning of these terms may be represented as follows:

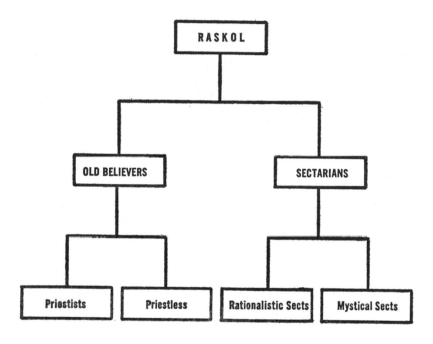

The changes which brought about the schism involved mainly the forms of worship. In making the sign of the cross, for example, Patriarch Nikon required that three instead of two fingers were to be used. To a modern reader such a change might appear insignificant, but one must remember that the forms of Christian worship are not arbitrarily devised conventions but symbolic representations of the essential elements of the faith. Thus, to an Orthodox Christian the two fingers used in making the sign of the cross symbolize the double nature of Christ, and the three fingers symbolize the Holy Trinity. By changing the form, therefore, Nikon in effect was tampering with the very essence of the Orthodox faith. He also changed the practice of using five consecrated loaves at the offertory to seven and of saying two hallelujahs to three. One loaf instead of an unspecified number of loaves were to be used at the altar, and in consecrating a church the procession was to be moved against rather than with the direction of the sun. Many textual changes were also brought in; some practices of worship were outrightly abolished; the spelling of the name Jesus was changed from Isus to Iisus; and the form of addressing God in the Lord's prayer was altered.

Although the concentration of a relatively large number of changes in a brief period of time seems to have been an important reason for the opposition to the reforms, the general conditions producing the schism, however, where manifold. Among the immediate and relatively simple factors evoking opposition toward Nikon and his reforms were Nikon's arrogance in enforcing the changes, his defiance of his former associates in the so-called Circle of the Zealots of Piousness, and his Achillean nine-year period of sulking following his defiant abandonment of the Patriarchate in 1658. Of the more complex reasons for the schism one must recognize the fact that the church reforms were enacted at a time when there was a multifarious intrusion of foreign influences into Russia. In fact, the Old Believer opposition was the first major reaction on the part of Russian society against the Western-oriented modernization.

The modernization movement had begun long before the appearance of the Old Believers. Under Ivan III (1462-1505) it was already a disturbing element, and following the Time of Troubles (1598-1613) modernization rapidly began to assume a dominant position in the general dynamics of the Russian state. By the seventeenth century the Mongols were defeated, but compared to the West, victorious Russia herself appeared to be primitive. The Russians feared the technologically superior West, yet there was nowhere to turn except westward. The north was frozen, the east was a cultural vacuum, the "Busurmans" ruled in the south, and the homeland was dark with ignorance. A Western-oriented modernization, therefore, was the policy that the new Romanov dynasty chose for Russia. In spite of the fact that these early developments have been overshadowed by the subsequent and more dramatic importation of Westernism by Peter I (1682-1725), a prominent nineteenth-century Russian historian, Sergei M. Soloviev, for example, was well aware of the extent to which Westernization had been a part of Russian life before Peter's reign. According to Soloviev, the first three Romanovs (1613-82) carried out significant reforms based on Western models. A standing army was created in Russia during that time, and its creation necessitated significant changes in the manner of life of the old military class, which in turn affected the entire social structure of Russia. Shipbuilding was begun, and attempts were made to reorganize the economic system. Foreigners were granted special privileges for establishing factories and industrial plants in Russia. In its foreign relations Russia began to be more and more oriented toward the West. The government began to emphasize the need for a broader educational system. New customs appeared both at the court and in the private homes of the noblemen. The relationship between the church and the state was defined, and individuals appeared who were interested in spreading the spirit of modernization to the population at large.[4]

Although in their essence the Nikonian reforms constituted innovations borrowed from the Greek Orthodox church, when viewed against the background of the general modernization that was taking place at the time, these reforms appear to have been a part of that drive. Furthermore, in the seventeenth century many Russians believed that the Greeks had been "Latinized" or Westernized as a result of their compromise with the papacy at the Council of Florence in 1439. In the light of the latter assumption Hellenization of the Russian church was regarded by these Russians to be tantamount to Westernization of it.

An important authority on the history of the Raskol, Kapterev, advanced a thesis that although many Russians in the seventeenth century did regard the Greeks to have been Latinized, the Russian rulers and the church hierarchy did not share this belief.[5] This may have been true of the first Romanov, but Tsar Alexis (1645-76), during whose reign the Nikonian reforms were promulgated, appears to have believed that the Greek church had been subject to Latin influences. In fact, Alexis sent an envoy, named Arseny Sukhanov, to the Orthodox East in 1649 and again in 1653 in an attempt to determine the extent to which Western influences had permeated the Greek church. Sukhanov argued with his Greek hosts defending the alleged purity of Russian Orthodoxy and insisted that their faith was polluted with "Latin heresy." His conclusions to that effect were transmitted in writing to the Tsar. Yet, despite the fact that he had this information, Alexis allowed Nikon to carry out his changes. In any event, the significant point of this entire problem is the fact that the Old Believers regarded the reforms as foreign innovations and that their reaction to these innovations, as Kliuchevsky noted, was a "pathological symptom" of the xenophobic feelings provoked in seventeenth-century Russian society by the spread of Western ideas.[6]

Ethnically the early Old Believers were predominantly of Great Russian stock, and their devotion to what they regarded to be the ancient Russian ideal was as intense as their devotion to the old Orthodoxy. They opposed the changes in religious texts and the innovations in ritual effected by the Nikonian reforms. They were distressed by the increased centralization of the administrative organs of the church. And they in fact viewed the reforms as a deliberate attempt to subvert the Orthodox religion and to humiliate Russia's historical traditions.[7] As the struggle against the reforms of the church was by necessity an opposition to the existing state authority, the Raskol assumed a political role. This, however, is not to say, as some of the nineteenth century writers (such as Shchapov, for example) contended, that the Raskol was primarily a political movement. On the contrary, in its origin the Raskol was a religious movement even though, by virtue of its opposition to a political entity, it assumed political connotations.

The depth and the intensity of the resentment these changes generated is effectively captured in the testimony of a Raskolnik. Recorded in 1855, this testimony was among the documents in the government reports published by Kelsiev.

### The Testimony of a Theodocian

On the ninth day of September, 1855, Lokhvitsky, a secret government official, and Archimandrite Ambrosius, abbot of Suzdal Spaso-Efimiev monastery, fulfilling a secret written order issued by His Excellency, the Governor of the Province of Vladimir, dated the thirty-first of August, Number 406, arriving in the cell of prisoner Raskolnik named Petr Poliakov, entered into a discourse with him on matters pertaining to the Orthodox church, the sacraments, the ritual, the clergy, and on matters pertaining to the government and the laws. During this investigation, Raskolnik Petr Poliakov made the following testimnoy:

> My name is Ivan Mikheev Ermakov. I served with the cossacks, then in the navy, and when I ran away from the service, a certain scribe made a passport for me, and I acquired the name of a retired noncommissioned officer, Petr Poliakov. I am seventy-one years of age. I consider myself to be of the orthodox faith, because I belong to the ancient church as it existed before it was perverted by Nikon.

I have never been on trial for anything. I write poorly, but I know how to read.

Before the time of Patriarch Nikon the church was orthodox and holy. From the time of Nikon, however, the clergy have violated the Christian faith, and your church, which you call Orthodox, is profaned, for on its throne sits a double-lettered *Iisus* [Jesus], who is a devil and an Antichrist. I, on the other hand, respect the ancient church, which existed before Nikon, and today's church I curse and never attend. I also hate and despise the Edinoverie church [the government-sponsored Old Believer church] and its clergy, for on its throne sits Satan himself.

I recognize the symbols of your faith with the following exceptions: I do not believe in the double-lettered *Iisus*, for he is an Antichrist; I believe in the singular, true *Isus*; in the teachings about the Holy Spirit and in the eighth part of your church symbols you have omitted the word "true" and have written "life-giving," whereas I believe in the *Holy Spirit, true life-giving Lord*. I recognize only one of the sacraments of your church, that is baptism by triple immersion in water. I do not recognize the other sacraments of your church to be true and sacred, because they do not bring blessings to the one who receives them, but rather they lead him into the chasm of hell and defile him. I recognize only those saints who were canonized by our ancient pre-Nikonian church. The new saints, such as Dimitry of Rostov, Innokenty of Irkutsk, Feodosy of Totemsk, Mitrofan of Voronezh, and other such users of tobacco, I do not recognize, and I curse them. The making of the sign of the cross with three fingers, as your church practices, I reject completely, for it is the way of the serpent; instead, I make the true sign of the cross—with two fingers. The rituals performed in your church, by your sly, apostate clergy, are loathsome and blasphemous. I absolutely do not recognize and do not tolerate your Synod or the clergy of your church, for they are loathsome blasphemers. They are the persecutors and the torturers of us, who are of the true faith, and they have made the tsar a victim of their devilishness and cunning.

I do not recognize Alexandr Nikolaevich as *emperor*, but I do recognize him as *tsar*. The imperial title and the state emblem of the two headed eagle were borrowed by Peter the Great from the impious satanic Roman pope. The title "emperor" means Perun, Titan, or Devil; the state emblem of the two-headed eagle is also satanic. Neither man, beast, or bird has more than one head; only the devil has two heads.

I will recognize the Tsar and the whole royal family as pious and of the true faith only when they begin to believe in the true *Isus* and reject *Iisus*, the Antichrist.

I will recognize the Tsar and the whole royal family only when they will free us—us, who believe in the ancient church and who suffer in prisons because of your false clergy who make the sign of the cross with three fingers and who are [therefore] pinchers and who have profaned both the church and the faith. I do pray for the well-being and for the long life of the Tsar and the whole royal family, but God does not accept my prayers for those who do not gratify and protect us—the sufferers and true believers—and who help the loathsome, ungodly Greeks and who pray for the supporters of the Greeks, which means that they are sinning before God. It is better not to pray for them.

The civil laws are created by the government officials and not the tsar. They are signed by the tsar, because he is afraid for his own life. Because of this, I regard those laws to be false and illegal, and I recognize only the Hundred Chapters of Ivan the Terrible.

I recognize only those civil authorities who have been appointed by the tsar and not the emperor.

We, who are of the true faith, do not have any officials over us now, but in former times we had the
boyars and the *voevodas*. Your Senate, on the other
hand, is a committee of the devil.[8]

Opposition to Nikon and his innovations arose almost
immediately following his election to the Patriarchate in
1652. With his election the small but influential Circle of the
Zealots of Piousness [*Kruzhok revnitelei blagochestiia*], organized in the 1640's for the purpose of instilling greater
piousness into the Russian clergy, split into two factions. On
the one side stood the members constituting the provincial
wing of the Circle and headed by Archpriests Ivan Neronov
and Avvakum Petrov (c. 1620-82) ; on the other side was the
Moscow faction which included Nikon and the Tsar's confessor, Archpriest Stephen Vonifatiev. The latter group was
supported by the Tsar and his close advisers, including his
authoritative chamberlain, Theodore Rtishchev. When the
two factions clashed, Nikon's group gained the initial victory:
Neronov was forced into submission and Avvakum was exiled to Siberia. Avvakum's exile, however, proved to be a
positive factor in the emergence of the Old Believer movement, for his sufferings in the name of the old faith served
to inspire those who sought to remain true to that form of
worship.

Avvakum's role in the formative years of the Raskol was
of central importance. He was not only the father of the Old
Believer church but also seems to have personified the movement. As a collective body the Raskolniks appear to have
imitated the woeful life he led. At least a limited understanding of Avvakum's life and character, therefore, is essential
for gaining an insight into the Raskol's collective character
in the early period of that movement's existence.

In many ways Avvakum was similar to his chief protago-
nist, Patriarch Nikon. They were both of peasant origin and
both were self-educated men. If Nikon slept on a rafter under
the church bells in order not to miss matins, Avvakum burned
his own fingers over a candle to punish himself for sinful
tendencies. Both of these religious zealots regularly "con-

versed" with angels and in their daily lives made little distinction between the miraculous and the mundane. They both yearned for power and both despised those who were morally weak. Each seems to have possessed an extensive knowledge of the Scriptures and each in turn failed to acquire the virtue of forgiveness. Thus, if Nikon exiled Avvakum to Siberia, Avvakum repeatedly expressed a desire to wreak vengeance upon Nikon.[9]

Accompanied by his wife and children, Avvakum spent some ten years in Siberian exile (1653-63). He was attached, in a punitive role, as a chaplain to a military detachment which was sent on foot from European Russia to the land called Dauria on the left bank of the Amur River in the Far East. The hardships he endured at the hands of the brutal commander of the expedition (A. F. Pashkov) were masterfully described in Avvakum's autobiography, which in itself has been recognized as an important literary work.

Then I was taken to Fort Bratsky [Avvakum wrote some ten years after the exile, while confined in a subterranean dungeon in northern Russia], thrown into jail, and given some straw. I remained there until St. Philip's fast, in a frozen tower. It is already winter at that time in this land, but God warmed me in want of clothing. I lay like a little dog on the straw. Some days they would feed me and some days not. There were a great many mice there, and I hit them with my biretta—the fools would not even give me a stick. I lay all the time on my belly, for my back was sore, and there were many fleas and lice. I wanted to cry out to Pashkov: "Pardon!", but God's will forbade it and ordered me to be patient. Later I was transferred to a warm house, and there I spent the winter in chains with the hostages and the dogs. [The hostages were from native tribes, kept by the Russians to secure the payment of tribute.] My wife and children had been sent far from me, some twenty versts away [1 v. = .66 mi.] And all that winter she was plagued and rebuked by her

servant Xenia. My son Ivan, a small lad, came to stay
with me for a while after Christmas. Pashkov had
him thrown into the cold cell where I had lain. He
spent the night there, poor dear lad, and almost
froze to death. In the morning he was sent back to
his mother. I did not even see him. He reached home
with his hands and feet frozen.

Avvakum, the combatant, had a keen aesthetic sensitivity, and in the midst of his sufferings he remained perceptive
to the natural beauty of the world. His autobiography sparkles
with lyricism praising what he called the beauty of God's
creation.

During the crossing [of Lake Baikal] the wind
fell, and we had to use our oars. In that place the
lake is not very wide, only eighty to one hundred
versts or so. When we reached the other shore, a
storm began to blow up, and we barely managed to
land because of the waves. From the shore rose steep
hills and sheer cliffs. I have dragged myself twenty
thousand versts and more, but never have I seen such
high mountains. Their summits are crowned with
halls and turrets, pillars and gates, walls and
courts—all made by the hand of God. In those hills
grow garlic and onion, the bulbs larger than those
of Romanov onions [grown in Romanov-Boriso-
glebsk, presently Tutaev, district] and very sweet.
And there is also hemp, sown by God's hand, and in
the courts there are beautiful grass and sweet-smel-
ling flowers. There are wild fowl in great number:
geese and swans floating like snow on the lake. And
there are also fish: sturgeon and salmon-trout, ster-
let, omul and white-fish, and many other kinds.
This is a fresh-water lake, but great seals and sea-
hares live in it. I never saw the like in the great
ocean, when I lived on the Mezen River. And the
fish are abundant; the sturgeon and salmon-trout
are so fleshy that one cannot fry them in a skillet,

because there would be nothing but fat. And all this has been created by Christ for man, so that man might find pleasure in it and praise God. But man, who is enslaved by vanity—well, his days pass like a shadow; he leaps like a goat; he puffs himself out like a bubble; he rages like the lynx; seeks to devour like a serpent; at the sight of another's beauty he neighs like a foal; he is wily like the devil; having had his fill, he falls asleep without observing the rule of prayer. He puts off repentance until the day of Judgment. Pardon me, I have sinned more than any man.[10]

Whether as a sufferer, a believer, a combatant, or as a poet, Avvakum was passionately engaged in the mission of living.

As the long years of his exile wore on, news of his sufferings for the old faith began to reach Moscow and other parts of European Russia. By his defiance of his tormentors in the Siberian wilderness Avvakum inspired confidence in the adherents to the old Orthodoxy back home. The downfall of Patriarch Nikon in 1658 led the Tsar to hope that a compromise could be reached with Avvakum and his supporters. Avvakum was brought back from Siberia and in 1664 was cordially received by the Tsar. The two were personally acquainted, and there was even some talk in Moscow that Avvakum might be appointed to the position of the Tsar's personal confessor. The decade-long Siberian exile, however, had hardened rather than weakened the defiant defender of the old faith. In his autobiography Avvakum relates how upon his arrival in European Russia from Siberia he consulted with his wife as to the course of action he should now follow.

Then we reached the towns of Russia, and I became aware, concerning the church, that it prevailed nothing, but rather a tumult was made. I was saddened, and sitting myself down, I reflected: What am I to do? Must I preach the word of Christ or go into hiding? For I was bound to wife and children. Seeing my distress, Dame Avvakum came

up to me respectfully and asked: "What troubles
you, my lord?" And I told her everything in detail:
"Wife, what shall I do? This is the winter of heresy.
Shall I speak or be silent? You have shackled me."
And she replied: "God forgive! What say you,
Petrovich? Did you not read the words of the
Apostle: 'Art thou bound to wife, seek not to be
loosed. Art thou loosed from a wife, seek no wife.'
I and the children bless you. Continue to preach
the word of God as fearlessly as before, and be not
concerned about us. As long as God allows it, we
shall remain together, and if they separate us, then
do not neglect us in your prayers. Go, go to church
Petrovich, and continue to denounce the heretical
lechery!" [11]

Avvakum heeded his wife's advice and followed it with the
utmost zeal. He preached the message of the old faith, and
he cursed its enemies, the Nikonians.

The Tsar was tolerant for a time but finally became convinced of the impossibility of a compromise. Avvakum was
once again exiled. In 1666-67 he was tried before the Church
Council, was excommunicated and sent to a subterranean
dungeon in Pustozersk, in the northern province of Archangelsk. During the fifteen years he spent in the earthen dungeon Avvakum endured sufferings far exceeding those he
had experienced in Siberia. As if the punishment imposed by
his jailers was not sufficient, he tormented himself with fasts
and by discarding the clothing he wore in order to feel more
fully the effect of the frozen earth. He was more fortunate,
however, than several of his fellow-inmates, for each of them
had lost the tongue and a hand before being placed in the
dungeon. In his autobiography, Avvakum noted that he was
taken to prison without mutilation. "The verdict stated: 'Let
Avvakum be imprisoned in a wooden framework underground
and be given only bread and water.' In answer, I spat. I wanted
to starve myself to death, and did not eat for eight days and
more, until the brethren ordered me to eat again." All of this
he did in the name of the old faith, and he taught his follow-

ers to do likewise. "Take heed, you who listen to me," he
wrote from his living grave. "Our misfortune is inevitable,
we cannot escape it. If God allows scandals, it is that the
elect shall be revealed. Let them be burned, let them be
purified, let them who have been tried be made manifest
among you. Satan has obtained our radiant Russia from God,
so that she may become crimson with the blood of martyrs.
Well planned, devil! It pleases us, too, to suffer for our dear
Christ's sake." No sacrifice for the faith seems to have been
too great for the devout Archpriest. He did not seek a martyr-
dom only for himself but was just as willing to sacrifice his
wife and children. Thus when his two sons failed to live up to
his expectations, he mercilessly rebuked them for their weak-
ness. "At that time came the order that my own two sons,
Ivan and Prokopy, should be hanged; but they, poor wretches,
lost their heads and missed the chance to seize the crown of
victory; fearing death, they made submission. So with their
mother, they were imprisoned underground. There you are:
death in the absence of death! May you repent in your prison,
while the devil thinks of some other device." [12]

    When Avvakum's own chance "to seize the crown of
victory" arrived, he did not miss it. Both before and during
his imprisonment in the underground dungeon he was able
to send petitions to Tsar Alexis. In these petitions he denounced Nikon but refrained from attacking the Tsar. In one
of his petitions, for example, Avvakum implored the Autocrat
to spit on the Hellenic *Kyrie eleison* and begin to utter in the
language of his forefathers, "Lord, have mercy upon us."
"You are Alexis, a son of Michael, a Russian and not a
Greek," Avvakum pleaded with his master. "Speak your own
native tongue; stop destroying it in the church, in the home,
and in the proverbs. As Christ has taught us, thus ought we
to speak. God loves us not less than he loves the Greeks."
By 1681, however, after having spent twenty-eight years of
his life either walking across Siberia or bound in chains or
confined in the earth dungeon and being over sixty years old,
Avvakum was no longer able to control his emotions. In a
petition to the new Tsar, Theodore (1676-82), he made a
grave mistake by attacking the latter's deceased father. As in

the petitions to Alexis, he pleaded with Theodore to "quarter Nikon, the dog, and the Nikonians," but he also warned the young monarch that "God himself judges between me and Tsar Alexis, who is now being tormented." This, Avvakum explained, "I have heard from the Saviour, and it serves him right." [13] The latter remark proved to be fatal for the uncompromising defender of the old faith. Whereas Alexis had been personally acquainted with the Archpriest and had certain attachments to the old rituals, Theodore was educated by a Westernized Kievan monk, spoke Polish, and had no personal connections with any of the Old Believers. Offended by Avvakum's irreverence, Theodore ordered the defiant sufferer to be executed. On April 14, 1682 (o. s.) Avvakum was taken out from his icy dungeon and, along with three other Old Believers, was burned to death in a wooden framework. It has been said that he burned crossing himself with two fingers (a symbol of the old faith), and it may safely be assumed that he burned shouting curses against his enemies—the "polluters" of the Orthodox faith, the "destroyers" of Holy Russia. The chief "destroyers" of Holy Russia and of Avvakum, it might be noted—Alexis and Nikon—were by that time already dead, and Avvakum's executioner, Tsar Theodore, departed from this world only thirteen days following the death of his victim.

From the time of Avvakum's death in 1682 to the time when Kelsiev made his "discovery" of the Dissenters in London, the Raskol developed into an extremely complex religious movement. At the time of the Raskol's origin a bishop, Paul of Kolomna, had sided with the Old Believers, but he was immediately imprisoned and died mysteriously soon thereafter. The Old Believers, therefore, had no hierarchs with the authority for ordaining priests. The number of priests subsequently joining them was never sufficient to satisfy the need; and, to add to the Old Believers' difficulties, some of their members refused to accept the services of these "Nikonian" priests. This situation resulted in a major schism within the Schism. The Old Believer movement split into two branches: the Priestists [*Popovshchina*], who accepted the refugee priests, and the Priestless [*Bezpopovshchina*], who chose to remain "flocks without a shepherd." The former remained a relatively cohesive group, but the Priestless gave rise to a variety of sects and denominations. By the middle of the nineteenth century, therefore, there were three general divisions within the Dissenting movement: the Priestists and the Priestless denominations of the Old Believers and the Sectarians. In addition to the sects which separated from the Priestless, the Sectarians included sects which had no connection with the original Raskol. The Raskol as a whole, and especially the Sectarians, endured severe hardships as a result of persecution by the official church and the government and did not acquire legal status until after the Revolution of 1905.

From the government reports Kelsiev learned that ever since their appearance the Raskolniks had persistently defied the official church and the state. In his eyes their capacity for such a prolonged defiance was potentially a valuable revolutionary attribute. He learned, for example, that even before Avvakum's death there was violent mass resistance to the Nikonian innovations at the Solovetsky monastery. This important religious centre is located on the largest of the Solovki Islands in the White Sea, some one hundred miles south of the Arctic Circle. Its importance within the Russian church can be seen in the fact that its archimandrite was appointed directly by the tsar and the patriarch and was not subordinated to any intermediate ecclesiastical authority. Enclosed within a wall some thirty feet high and possessing eight turrets armed with cannons, the monastery served as a fortress protecting the entry to the port of Archangelsk. Its archimandrite administered the territory of the Solovki Islands and controlled extensive tracts of land along the seaboard. On that land the monastery owned saltworks, mica quarries, tanning cottages, potash works, and fisheries. The saltworks alone employed some fifteen hundred workers. At the time of the revolt there were probably three hundred monks and four hundred laymen living within the walls of the monastery. Among the laymen were political exiles, refugee cossacks, and local labourers.

In 1657 the monks of the Solovetsky monastery refused to accept the revised service books and in 1668 they deported

to the mainland the newly-appointed archimandrite, Joseph.
They then petitioned the Tsar to appoint their own candidate,
one Nikanor, as archimandrite. When the Tsar responded
with threats, they openly defied his authority, and their rebellion thus assumed the nature of an insurrection against the
state. Government troops blockaded the island, but the in-
mates of the monastery held out for nearly eight years. With
the aid of the local population the rebellious monks were
able to replenish their supplies and to evacuate to the mainland those who were unfit for fighting. They were finally
subdued, as a result of a betrayal by one of their brethren,
Theoktistus, who, having fled from the monastery, informed
the enemy of a secret passage. On the night of January 22,
1676 (o. s.) the government troops entered the monastery.
In the massacre that followed most of the monks were slain
outright. Nikanor and possibly twenty-seven others were
ceremoniously hanged or quartered. When a new community
of monks was brought in, there were only a few, possibly
fourteen, of the former residents to meet them.[14]

Claims have been advanced to the effect that the religious question was not the chief cause for the outbreak of the
insurrection at Solovki, for along with the monks there were
political exiles and military deserters there. A well-known
nineteenth-century historian, Kostomarov, for example, pointed
out that the reign of Alexis was plagued with a profusion of
uprisings, and that the Solovki revolt was merely one of many
such revolts. At the beginning of Alexis's reign, he indicated,
there were uprisings in Novgorod, Pskov, Solvychegodsk,
Ustiug, and in Moscow itself. Simultaneously with the Solovki
revolt there was, of course, a major insurrection in 1670-71,
led by the famous cossack, Stephen Razin.[15]

While recognizing the value of such claims, one nonetheless must be aware of the fact that many of the insurgents
at Solovki were men of religion, that religious problems were
involved there, and that the rebels did identify themselves
as defenders of the old faith. Following their defeat both the
Orthodox population of the maritime province and the Old
Believers at large regarded the Solovki monks as martyrs who
suffered and died for the old faith. The population of that

region, therefore, became receptive to the proselytism of the refugee monks who fled the monastery during the siege. These monks made significant contributions to the growth of the Raskol, and by the end of the century the northern maritime province had become one of the major strongholds of the Priestless branch of the Old Believers. Some forty years after the fall of the Solovetsky monastery a famous Old Believer theologian, Simon Denisov, wrote a popular tract, *Concerning the Fathers and the Sufferers of Solovki*, which further enhanced the symbolic significance of the rebellion. Denisov pictured the defeated monks as martyrs and described miracles which allegedly were related to the insurrection. He even claimed that Tsar Alexis died the very day the monastery had fallen, implying thereby that his death was a vengeance of God for the sufferings of the Old Believer monks. (In reality, Alexis died a week later, on January 29.) All of this tended to popularize the Old Believer cause in the north and to inspire its defenders throughout Russia. Seeking to find an element capable of challenging the autocracy, Kelsiev was elated by the bravery displayed by the Old Believers of the Solovetsky monastery.

The reports also mentioned the role the Old Believers played in the unrest among the streltsy in 1682. The streltsy, a special infantry corps organized by Ivan IV (1533-84), made themselves famous in Ivan's campaigns against the Tartar strongholds on the lower Volga. By the second half of the seventeenth century, however, like the Janissaries of the Turkish sultan, they had outlived their usefulness and had become prone to behave in a violent and undisciplined manner. During the succession controversy following the death of Tsar Theodore in April, 1682, when two factions were contesting for the throne—one representing Peter I and the other his half-brother Ivan—the streltsy of the Praetorian Guard took a stand against Peter and succeeded in placing Ivan on the throne along with him. Although it was with their aid that Ivan's sister Sophia became regent, they challenged her authority as well.

The chief instigator of the opposition to Sophia was Prince Ivan Andreevich Khovansky, the commander of the

unruly streltsy, who apparently desired the position of regent for himself. He was an Old Believer, and had he realized his political aspirations, the old Orthodoxy might have been restored in Russia. Knowing that many of the fourteen thousand guardsmen were either Old Believers or sympathetic to the old faith, Khovansky attempted to rally them in defense of that faith. He demanded that Sophia permit a theological disputation to take place in Red Square between the Old Believers and the representatives of the official church. He planned to convert this gathering into a massive protest against the newly-installed Regent. Sophia, however, sensed the danger and insisted that the disputation be held inside the Palace of Facets in the Kremlin, in order to preclude a massive public assembly. On July 5, 1682 (o. s.) an Old Believer priest, Nikita Dobrynin, led a shouting crowd of his coreligionists into the Kremlin and confronted the representatives of the government and the official church, including Regent Sophia and Patriarch Ioakim. In an atmosphere of high emotional tension the disputation rapidly degenerated into an incoherent polyphony of oaths and accusations emanating from the crowd of bearded champions of the old faith. The vaulted, thirty-foot high ceiling of the palace, built by Italian architects of the Renaissance, echoed curses against Nikon and calls for Sophia's resignation. After a momentary hesitation, Sophia answered the Old Believers' theats by reminding them that if Nikon had been a heretic as they were charging, so also had her father, Tsar Alexis. Her threat to appeal directly to the people and to remove the two youthful Tsars from Moscow served to pacify the unruly crowd. Although the Old Believers left the palace claiming a victory, their spokesman, Dobrynin, was apprehended and executed in Red Square. Prince Khovansky, too, perished at the hands of the vengeful Sophia, who managed to lure him and his son to her court outside of Moscow, where they were executed. Following Khovansky's death in September, Sophia subdued the mutinous streltsy and thus stifled another militant demand for the restoration of the old faith.

As in the case of the suppression of the Solovki monks, the outcome of the suppression of the streltsy was interpreted by the writers of the government reports as having strengthened the Dissenting movement. Her experiences with the streltsy led Sophia to issue a decree in 1685 aimed at eradication of the movement. In accordance with this decree, the Raskolniks who failed to recant were to be burned to death. The conversion of others to the old faith was proclaimed to be a crime punishable by death. New converts were to be punished by death if they failed to repent and by whipping if they repented. Similar punishment was to be administered to those knowingly protecting Raskolniks. Finally, those who unwittingly harboured Raskolniks were to be subjected to fines ranging from five to fifty roubles.

The effect of this decree on the Raskol population may be likened to the effect of a falcon's dive into a flock of flying doves: they scattered far and wide in many directions. They fled to the Volga and beyond; they settled in the marshy forests of the north; they joined the restless cossack population on the Don; and they spilled over across the frontier into Poland and the Ottoman Empire. In spite of the sufferings of individuals, the forced dispersion of the Raskol population resulted in a wider diffusion of the old faith, and the harshness of the persecution tended to win sympathy for the sufferers from the general population. The persecution also served as a lesson, albeit a bitter one, in the ways of survival.[16]

In 1689 Peter deposed Sophia and began to rule the country in his own right. The streltsy once again became involved in dynastic troubles, and once again they were on the side opposing the government. Upon assuming full authority over the throne, therefore, Peter was determined to secure his position against any future action on the part of the streltsy. His opportunity for dealing decisively with these archaic warriors arrived in 1698. Peter was abroad on his first famous excursion through Western Europe when he received news from home of renewed unrest among the streltsy. He abruptly terminated his quest for foreign ways by which he was planning to "civilize" his people and rushed to Moscow to instill civility in his undisciplined subjects by means less than enlightened. In 1705 the streltsy corps was disbanded, and with it the possibility of an Old Believer tsar being placed on the

throne of Russia vanished. The reports Kelsiev studied, however, interpreted even these events as having been beneficial
to the growth of the Raskol, for the exile of the surviving
streltsy to the Ural region and beyond strengthened the Raskol
in those areas. The Raskolniks' influence in the Ural region
had apparently become so strong that in 1722 Peter found it
necessary to restrict the practice of exiling them there.[17]

Another encounter between the government and the Raskolniks during the reign of Peter the Great occurred at the
time of the Don Cossack rebellion in 1707-08. The reports
revealed that Peter's suppression of this revolt resulted in a
mass exodus of the Old Believer cossacks across the frontier
into the Ottoman Empire. This information proved to be of
special significance for Kelsiev, for it was among the descendants of these refugee cossacks that he was destined to test
his theoretical conclusions concerning the Raskolniks' revolutionary potentialities.

In spite of his harsh treatment of the streltsy and his
difficulties with the Old Believer cossacks, in general, Peter
was less hostile toward the Raskolniks than his predecessors
had been, for he had little interest in religious matters as
such. Nonetheless, the Old Believers' involvement with the
streltsy and their hostility toward his innovations prevented
the first "secular" tsar of Russia from extending legal recognition to the Dissenting movement. Although he refrained from
enforcing the harsh provisions of Sophia's decree of 1685, he
imposed on the Raskolniks special taxes and restricted their
freedom of movement. They were, for example, barred from
living in the cities, were required to wear a distinct marker
of yellow cloth on their outer garments, and were obligated
to pay double taxes—the special tax being payment for the
beard.

By their emphasis on the Raskolniks' ability to thrive in
the face of persecution the reports continuously reinforced
Kelsiev's growing assumption that the Raskol was a potential
revolutionary element. The officials compiling the reports
went into great detail in describing the gruesome methods by
which some of the Raskolniks had perpetrated self-mutilation
or self-annihilation, allegedly in an effort to avoid compromis-

ing with the state. They compiled accounts of the examples of self-immolation by the Raskolniks, and they indicated that suicide through fasting was a rather common practice among them. Some Raskolniks, according to the reports, committed suicide by barring themselves in caves, others by chaining themselves to trees deep in a forest or by having their hands caught in the split trunk of a tree. To Vasily Kelsiev, who was seeking a political cause to which to devote his own life, such information was of great significance, for both the compilers of the reports and he interpreted these acts as examples of defiance of the existing authorities.

Kelsiev was amazed by the Raskolniks' ingenuity in outwitting their opponents and by their ability to defend their beliefs at the theoretical level. With the hope of discrediting the Old Believers, Peter I, for example, encouraged the Orthodox clergy to engage in theological disputations with them. To his dismay, however, he discovered that the Orthodox clergy were no match for the Old Believer theologians. On one occasion the church officials resorted to a method similar to that used in acquiring the "Donation of Constantine." In an attempt to present the Nikonian innovations as being based on early practices of the Russian church, the church officials tampered with some old parchments. The text of the resulting "proof" was widely distributed in order to enable the provincial clergymen to rely on it in their disputations with the Old Believers. The Old Believers, however, did not have to wait long for their Lorenzo Valla to appear. He appeared in 1720 in the person of a certain Deacon Alexander, the founder of the Deaconotive sect. Employing philological methods, Alexander, in his *Otvety* [*Replies*], proved fully and conclusively that the document had been forged. Thereafter, his *Replies* served to strengthen the Old Believers' theological position. To Kelsiev this example was another proof that neither force, oratory, nor forgery enabled the government to subdue the resolute Raskolniks.[18]

Kelsiev learned that during the reign of Catherine II (1762-96) a marked change in government policy in favour of the Raskolniks was initiated. In 1762, for example, a law was enacted permitting the Raskolniks who had fled abroad to return to Russia and to settle in specified areas of the Empire. The special tax which Peter I had imposed on the Raskolniks was abolished by decrees issued in 1769 and 1792. Catherine allowed the Raskolniks to reside in the two capital cities, Moscow and St. Petersburg. The latter provision proved to be of a lasting consequence for the Old Believers, for during the time of the plague in 1771 they founded hospitals and charity homes in Moscow and through the work of these institutions gained many new converts. Some of these converts were wealthy, and those who contacted the plague usually bequeathed their worldly possessions to the Old Believer church. As a result of these activities two permanent religious centres were developed in the suburbs of Moscow: the Preobrazhenskoe and Rogozhskoe Cemeteries. These centres included Old Believer churches, charity homes, and hospitals. In 1785 the Old Believers also were granted the right to hold office in municipal governments. Catherine's tolerance toward the Raskolniks appears to have been especially notable in view of the fact that during her reign occurred the most violent peasant uprising in the history of Russia, led by Emelian Pugachev, among whose followers were many Raskolniks.[19]

The tolerant policy toward the Raskolniks initiated by Catherine II continued under both Paul (1796-1801) and Alexander I (1801-25). With the ascension of Nicholas I, however, a more restrictive policy was initiated. Once again the Raskolniks were deprived of the civil rights, which they had gained during Catherine's reign, and were forbidden to repair existing places of worship or to build new ones. The business activities of all the Raskolniks were severely circumscribed, and the children of those Sectarians who did not recognize the validity of baptism were declared illegitimate. Since the laws aimed to affect the Raskolniks adversely were usually secret, there was an obvious correlation between the number of such secret decrees and the harshness of the anti-Raskol policy of the ruler during whose reign such decrees were promulgated. On the basis of this evidence, Nicholas's reign appears to have been one of the most oppressive periods in the history of the Raskol. Whereas during the thirty-three years of Catherine's rule only eight secret decrees relating to the Raskol were enacted and during the twenty-four years of Alexander's rule fifty-nine decrees, in the thirty years of Nicholas's administration the number of such decrees was 495.[20]

Nicholas, as has been noted, was the Tsar responsible for the establishment of the secret committees from whose reports Kelsiev derived his information about the Raskolniks. These committees were organized to conduct an extensive surveillance of the Raskol population, and by the end of Nicholas's reign there was at least one such committee in every province in which the Raskol was known to be relatively strong. The cities in which such committees were located included Moscow, St. Petersburg, Petrozavodsk, Tambov, Chernigov, Tver, Saratov, Viatka, Irkutsk, Ekaterinburg, Kharkov, Kostroma, Tobolsk, Ufa, Mogilev, Nizhnii Novgorod, Simbirsk, Archangelsk, Samara, Yaroslavl, and Kursk. There was also a special committee to evaluate the reports of the provincial committees, and all of the committees were under the supervision of the Ministry of Internal Affairs, with frequent interference from the Third Section. In addition to the specially-appointed government officials, a committee usually included the governor of the province, the bishop, a representative of the State Senate, and the chief of gendarmes of the province.

The overall task of these committees was to compile information pertaining to the Raskol's numerical strength, the density and distribution of its population, its social stratification, the location and the number of its places of worship, its leadership, the relationship between the Raskolniks and the local officials, etc. The ultimate purpose of this detailed investigation seems to have been nothing less than finding means for the eradication of the movement. To Kelsiev, however, the information contained in the reports was most encouraging, especially the statistical data pertaining to the numerical strength of the Raskol. He discovered, for example, that in the province of Kostroma there were, according to the official census of the population, 20,587 Raskolniks, but the reports of the secret committee working in that province showed that there were at least 48,072 Raskolniks and 57,571 active supporters of the Raskol. In the province of Nizhnii Novgorod, to cite another example, only 23,323 Raskolniks were officially registered in 1854. An additional 62,414, however, were discovered by Orthodox priests through confession, and the secret committee of that province estimated that the total number of Raskolniks living there in 1854 was 170,500.[21]

The committees reported that in some provinces there were as many as six, eight, or even ten times as many Raskolniks as the official figures revealed. According to the official census figure, the total population of the Raskol in 1852 was 700,000. The Raskolniks themselves, however, boasted that their number totalled 9,000,000. The government officials who analyzed the data collected by the secret committees were inclined to regard the latter figure as a more accurate estimate of the actual Raskol population. The practice of counting the Raskol population was initiated under Peter the Great, but for more than a century thereafter the government was unable to derive an accurate estimate of its number. The difficulties were caused by several factors, including the general inefficiency of the administrative system, the Raskolniks' ingenuity and cunning, and the interest of local officials in protecting the anonymity of Raskolniks in order to insure for themselves a permanent source of revenue through bribery. Because of the extensiveness of the surveillance system which Nicholas I had established and because of Alexander II's determination to know the actual state of affairs in his Empire, by 1863 the government was able to arrive at a relatively accurate estimation of the Raskol population. According to the information released by the Ministry of Internal Affairs in that year, there were 8,220,000 Raskolniks in the Russian Empire. Of these, 5,000,000 were Priestists, 3,000,000 were Priestless, and 220,000 were Sectarians. The latter figure was further subdivided into the Molokans and Dukhobors numbering 110,000 and the Khlysty and Castrates also numbering 110,000. Although this estimate was more realistic than any previous government's count of the Raskolniks, those who studied the Raskol were inclined to regard even this revised figure as being too low. Subsequently other estimates were advanced, which placed the figure at 13,000,000 in 1880 and as high as 20,000,000 by 1900. In the light of these varying estimates it seems reasonable to assume that at the time of

Kelsiev's encounter with the Raskolniks in the 1860's their total population numbered approximately 10,000,000. This would mean that during that period nearly fourteen per cent of Russia's population of 73,000,000 were Raskolniks.[22]

The reports do not include a systematic study of the social stratification of the entire Raskol, but a general impression of the class distribution may be gleaned from the information available for the province of Yaroslavl. In that province the following distribution of the Raskol population was found to exist in the 1850's: 86.9 per cent were peasants, 12.2 per cent were petty bourgeoisie, and 0.9 per cent were retired professional military personnel. With the exception of the nobility, which is not represented here, this distribution approximates the social stratification of Russia's population at that time.[23]

The general conclusion that the writers of the reports reached concerning the Raskol's political nature was that the Priestists were the least dangerous to the government, since they differed from the Orthodox church only in their usage of pre-Nikonian rituals and service books. The Priestless, on the other hand, were depicted as being politically more dangerous, for they did not pray for the tsar and some of them regarded the monarch as an incarnated Antichrist. They were the second largest group of the Raskol, numbering at least three and possibly five million in the 1860's. In addition to being the prime source from which various lesser sects had emerged, the Priestless were split into four major branches: the Pomortsy, Feodosievtsy, Filipony, and Stranniki (that is, Maritimers, Theodocians, Philiponites, and Wanderers). With the exception of the Theodocians, all groups were hostile to the government, and the Wanderers were depicted in the government reports as being the most defiant.

The Wanderers emerged as a group in the second half of the eighteenth century under the leadership of an army deserter, a peasant by origin, named Efimy or Euphemius (d. 1792). The sect was centred in the large village of Sopelki, some fifteen miles from Yaroslavl, on the Volga, north-east of Moscow, and by the middle of the nineteenth century it had spread along the entire length of the Volga, to Siberia, and was known as far north as Archangelsk. Euphemius based his teachings on the Apocalypse, proclaiming that the Antichrist had revealed himself in 1666 in the person of Nikon and had later assumed the form of Peter the Great. Because of the special significance of the year 1666 in the history of the Raskol, Euphemius regarded 666 as an apocalyptic figure. He employed this figure to "prove" the satanic origin of those whose name or title spelled in Slavonic letters (which were used as numerals) would add up to the sum of 666. According to Euphemius, the name Nikon, for example, or at least its Greek form Nikityos, marked its bearer as an incarnated Antichrist, for the numerical value of its Slavonic letters produced the "satanic" sum. Euphemius uncovered Peter's diabolic nature in the latter's newly-adopted title "emperor." To achieve the desired results, Euphemius used a rather dubious, allegedly the old Roman, spelling of the word: *iperator*. He added credence to his pronouncement against Peter by pointing out that the Tsar's two titles, "tsar" and "emperor," were two horns—and who has ever seen a horned man? Later Euphemius decided that all Russian rulers who used two titles were of a common species with Peter.[24]

Having assumed that an Antichrist was occupying the throne of Russia, Euphemius concluded that Russia was a fallen Babylon, and true Christians, therefore, must avoid all contact with the state. Initially, the Wanderer sect consisted exclusively of those who were re-baptised and had agreed to live in accordance with the teachings of their founder. They abandoned their homes, families, and property, renounced all association with the state, and became wanderers in the true sense of the word. This harsh form of existence, however, was not conducive to the sect's growth and perpetuation. A compromise was made, by which some members became *zhilovye* or sedentary Wanderers. The latter remained in their homes and ostensibly led lives indistinguishable from the ways of their Orthodox neighbours. Their duty was to provide food and shelter for the true Wanderers, and they fulfilled their requirement of wandering by being carried out from their homes into their fields or orchards on their deathbed.

The officials of the secret committees complained in their

reports that the immoral behaviour of the Wanderers encouraged other Russians to desert their families. An official from the province of Yaroslavl, for example, reported that some male Wanderers shared their mistresses, some of whom were under fifteen years of age, with their coreligionists. He reported that abortion, abandonment, and even the murdering of illegitimate children were rather frequent among the Wanderers. He also charged that the Wanderers harboured deserters and criminals. It is difficult either to refute or to validate these allegations, but a Wanderer's testimony, included in the reports, does indicate that the re-baptized Wanderers were contemptuous of marriage as an institution. Since, according to the Wanderers' interpretation, all Russian laws were issued by the Antichrist, marriage was sinful. Kelsiev, in any case, did not hesitate to pass judgment on the accusations made in the reports. In his editorial notes to the reports he refuted the officials' allegations concerning the criminality of the Wanderers and expressed a feeling of admiration for their egalitarianism and their total rejection of the state.[25]

The special committee which analyzed the information collected by the provincial committees classified the Sectarians as being politically far more dangerous than either the Priestist or the Priestless subdivisions of the Old Believers. In spite of the fact that the officials of the special committee were aware of the diversity existing within the Raskol as a whole, they advised the government that from a political standpoint the Sectarians and the Priestless should be regarded as a unified force. In view of the fact that the Sectarians were divided into some one hundred and thirty sects, with each sect believing that it alone possessed the true faith, the credulity of the committee's conclusion tends to resemble the validity of Euphemius's proof of Peter's satanic nature. Nonetheless, to Vasily Kelsiev, in his search for an anti-governmental force, the committees' word was like an oasis to a man in a desert. He agreed with the government officials concerning the political potential of the Raskolniks and saw in them "a great guarantee of the future development of Russia." Because of their restlessness and in some cases rather bizarre forms of behaviour, Kelsiev came to regard the Sectarians as the most active guarantor of that future.

Both in their origin and in their religious character the Sectarians were a multifarious group. Some of the sects drew on Finnish pagan cults for their beliefs, some on Judaism, others on Protestantism, but the majority of them evolved their beliefs from the Orthodox faith as the result of an intense quest generated by the Nikonian innovations. Although at least one of the sects—the followers of a certain Priest Kapiton—emerged as early as the 1630's, most of the other sects seem to have developed in the eighteenth century. By the 1860's according to the Government's estimates, the Sectarians numbered some 220,000 adherents, but according to informed non-governmental sources, their number was as high as 2,000,000.[26]

The behaviour of the Sectarians ranged from the innocent nude processions of the Worshipers of Cupid [*Kupidony*] to the hellish mass immolation of the self-burners. The Molokans, at least according to the government reports, advocated universal anarchism. The Dukhobors were pacifists who refused to acknowledge any loyalty to the state. The Stranglers [*Dushilchiki*] believed that salvation was possible only through a violent death. They, therefore, murdered their co-believers in order to assure them of eternal bliss. The Jumpers [*Skakuny*] expressed their scorn of all worldliness by rhythmic nocturnal dancing. Under the direction of their prophet, the Jumpers, dressed in loosely-flowing white garments, would jump up and down as they moved around in a circle. The prophet counted the cadence. The tempo would be increased steadily until the vertical and horizontal movements of the dancers resembled the billowing waves of a stormy sea. When the desired state of spiritual inebriation was reached, the exhausted dancers would fall to the ground, and the ceremony would culminate in an erotic orgy. The Worshipers of Napoleon [*Napoleonovshchina*] lit candles and worshiped before the bust of the Corsican invader of Russia. The Montany believed that any act was morally justifiable as long as it promoted their cause. The Paternalists [*Otsovshchina*], drawing their own interpretation of the biblical injunction "whatsoever a man soweth, that shall he also reap" (Galatians 6:7), accorded the father first claim to sexual relations with his daughters. Both the compilers of the reports and Kelsiev tended to interpret most of this behaviour as an expression of the Sectarians' defiance of the established order.[27]

The government reports which Kelsiev published in London included a history of the Emasculates [*Skoptsy*] written by Nicholas I. Nadezhdin (1804-56), the editor of the journal *Telescope*. Nadezhdin described the practices of this unique sect in great detail and warned the government that the Emasculates were politically dangerous. Although in his commentaries Kelsiev remarked that the Emasculates were "fanatical degenerates," he, like Nadezhdin, was overwhelmed by the strangeness of their practices and tended to ascribe their characteristics to the entire Raskol population. Although the Emasculates as such were a relatively small sect, Kelsiev's inclination toward projecting their image on the entire Raskol, makes it necessary for us to delve into the background of this sect in some detail.

The history of the Emasculates is a maze of facts and fiction. The sect itself was founded in the second half of the eighteenth century by a peasant named Kondraty Selivanov, who came from the province of Orel, in central European Russia. Its roots, however, lie deep in the past. Nadezhdin suggested that the very concept of mass emasculation was introduced to Russia from Byzantium, where eunuchs were an important element in society. A well-known analyst of sectarianism, Vasily Rozanov, on the other hand, believed that the Russian Emasculates had based their teachings on Matthew 19:12, in which they interpreted the pronoun "it" to mean emasculation: "For there are some eunuchs, which were so born from *their* mother's womb: and there are eunuchs, which were made eunuchs of men: and there be eunuchs, which have made themselves eunuchs for the kingdom of heaven's sake. He that is able to receive *it*, let him receive *it*." According to another writer on the Raskol, the Russians were exposed to a religious eunuch soon after the Christianization of Russia. A certain Bogomil named Adrian came to Russia in 1004 and attempted to preach a religion which called for the emasculation of its believers. Adrian was excommunicated and imprisoned, and from that time until the eighteenth century no instance of religious emasculation has been recorded in Russia. As a sect, the Emasculates evolved from the Flagellant sect [Khlysty], and the earliest known official confirmation of their existence was made in 1772, when the government ordered an investigation of this "new heresy." [28]

Selivanov's life is shrouded in legend. It is known that in 1775 Catherine II exiled this Orel peasant to Siberia for having emasculated a number of his followers who worshiped him as a god. He was sent to Nerchinsk, beyond Lake Baikal, but for some reason stopped short of his destination at Irkutsk. Although his followers sent emissaries to Siberia to arrange his escape, it is not known under what provisions he appeared in Moscow in 1795. Upon his return from Siberia, Selivanov claimed not only to be a redeemer but also the Tsar Peter III, Catherine's husband, who was deposed and murdered by his wife's paramours in 1762. Following Paul's ascension to the throne in 1796, Selivanov moved to St. Petersburg and in 1797 appears to have had an audience with that monarch. He had allegedly repeated before Tsar Paul the claim of being Peter III, the Tsar's father, and offered to initiate him into the Emasculate sect. Paul had Selivanov placed in an asylum, where he remained until 1802. Alexander I, who inclined toward religious mysticism, freed Selivanov, and for nearly two decades the self-proclaimed deity reaped a bountiful harvest of converts. According to Nadezhdin, by the 1840's there were probably 300,000 Emasculates in Russia. Many of them were wealthy and some even millionaires.

Alexander had favoured Selivanov to such an extent that he prohibited the police from entering the premises in which Selivanov conducted his ceremonies of spiritual inebriation or *radeniia*. Some of the highest aristocrats were among Selivanov's visitors, and in 1805 the Tsar himself apparently honoured the chief Emasculate with a personal visit. Selivanov's good fortunes were terminated, however, when the Governor-General of St. Petersburg, Count Miloradovich, discovered that two of his own nephews were among the regular visitors at Selivanov's rites and that Selivanov had castrated several members of the Guard. Miloradovich petitioned the Tsar for Selivanov's arrest, and, after some hesitation, Alexander acquiesced. In 1820 Selivanov was sent to the monastery of Euphemius in Suzdal, north-east of Moscow. There he continued his religious activities, distributing his own hair, bread crumbs from his table, and other relics venerated by his followers as sacred objects. Like Avvakum, Selivanov left some autobiographical writings. In spite of the efforts of his followers to gain his freedom, he died in 1832 in his relatively pleasant confinement.

To his followers Selivanov was much more than an emasculated peasant from the province of Orel. They came to believe that he was the son of the virgin Empress Elizabeth (1741-61) and was conceived by the Holy Ghost. Elizabeth, so the legend goes, was empress for only two years. She was succeeded by one of her doubles and went to the province of Orel to live among the Emasculates under the assumed name of Akulina Ivanovna. (And, indeed, there was a pious peasant woman by that name living in the province of Orel at that time.) Before abandoning the throne, however, Elizabeth had her son, Peter, emasculated. When Catherine married Peter and discovered that he was an emasculate, she plotted to murder him. Having been warned of the plot, Peter exchanged clothes with one of his guards and fled from the palace. The guardsman, who was also an emasculate, was taken to be Tsar Peter and executed. Although Catherine discovered the error, she publically announced Peter's death. Initially Peter fled to Western Europe but later went into voluntary exile in Siberia. Following Catherine's death, Tsar Paul, the son of Catherine and Peter, brought his father (actually, Kondraty Selivanov) to Moscow and asked for his blessing. (There is no explanation of Peter's fatherhood in light of the fact that, according to the legend, he was emasculated at an early age.) Peter insisted that he must withhold his blessing until after the Tsar had been castrated. Paul became offended and had his father confined in a church, where he remained until Alexander set him free. Alexander, however, soon discovered that Selivanov's followers were not living in accordance with the teachings of their founder and, to punish them, exiled Peter or Kondraty Selivanov to a Suzdal monastery. The legend ended with a ringing prophecy. The Emasculates believed that their Christ, Tsar Peter III, would return in a triumphant march. His great army of Emasculates, commanded by none other than Napoleon Bonaparte, who was the second son of the virgin Empress, would follow him into Moscow. The ringing of the bell in the Cathedral of the Enunciation [*Uspensky sobor*] would signal the assembling of "millions and billions" for the judgment. Peter would ascend the throne, and the kings of all lands would pay him homage. The Castrate missionaries would then go out into the world and cleanse the whole human race through castration.

According to the government reports, the Emasculates maintained a peculiar form of organization. The sect was divided into "ships," with each "ship" commanded by a "skipper." The "skipper's" authority over his "crew" was absolute. The government officials warned their superiors that this system of organization was readily adaptable for revolutionary purposes. What is more, the Emasculates did not recognize the existing government and were waiting for Tsar Peter III to return to his throne. Nadezhdin cautioned that although all of this might appear rather naive, Pugachev's personification of Peter III had shown that the Russian people were prone to take such legends seriously.

Nadezhdin was a prominent intellectual, and his conclusions about the Castrates therefore had an especially strong impact on Kelsiev. The son of a Riazan priest, Nadezhdin was a literary critic, an ethnographer, historian, and for a time a professor at the University of Moscow, lecturing on the theory of fine arts, archeology, and logic. It was in his journal, *The Telescope*, that Chaadaev's controversial "Philosophical Letter" was published in 1836. In the 1840's he was affiliated with the Ministry of Internal Affairs, editing the *Journal* of that Ministry and conducting extensive studies of the Raskol. His history of the Castrates (*Izsledovaniia o skopcheskoi eresi*, appearing in Kelsiev's *Sbornik*, vol. III) is probably the only extensive description of that sect. It was written for the use of the government and was first printed in a limited number of copies in 1845. Kelsiev was well aware of Nadezhdin's prominence and found it unnecessary to question the credibility of his conclusions.[29]

These, then, were some of the characteristics and the historical background Kelsiev learned about the Raskol in the secret government reports. Although the information those reports contained is diverse and rather extensive, by no means does it constitute an exhaustive history of the movement. Kelsiev, however, was not interested in historical accuracy or completeness. He was in need of the means by which he could express his own political restlessness in some definable terms, and that information proved to be precisely the catalyst required for the congealment of his hitherto chaotic political nascency.

For Kelsiev, the discovery of the Raskolniks was a discovery of a kinfolk which had been waiting for him to lead them to freedom. This was the vision he seems to have entertained in the light of his own mystical predilections and in the light of the emphasis the government officials had placed on the Raskol's political significance. The possibility that the officials who compiled the reports may have exaggerated the political danger of the Raskol in order to please the Tsar who, after all, had ordered them to uncover such a danger, was not admitted in Kelsiev's reflections on the subject, for such a grain of uncertainty would have been disturbing to his projected expectations. Thus, if the officials had not fully convinced their superiors of the immediacy of the Raskol's political threat, they did convince the imaginative Vasily. He was impressed by the viability of the Raskol in the face of persecution, and he was especially responsive to the information stating that the Raskolniks were organized into cells and maintained secret printing presses. Being a rebel and a wanderer at heart, not unlike the Wanderers of the Raskol, Kelsiev felt a certain affinity for the "apocalyptic nihilists," for, as he had learned in the reports, they had had two centuries of experience in the ways of a negative existence. To illustrate the extent of negativism of which some Raskolniks were capable, it might be useful to cite a tract which the Raskolniks of Saratov enjoyed copying and memorizing in the nineteenth century.

Sin—died
Truth—vanished
Reality—became hoarse
Conscience—is lame
Credit—is bankrupt
Faith—has remained in Jerusalem
Hope—is anchored on the bottom of the sea
Love—is sick with a cold
Innocence—is on trial
Virtue—is begging
Good deed—is under arrest
Helpfulness—is deaf
Advice—has become insane
Honesty—is dying of hunger
Meekness—is down with a fever
Sincerity—has been murdered
Justice—is on the run
Righteousness—has abandoned the world
Bliss—has been taken to heaven
Honest work—is living on charity
Reason—is in penal servitude
Law—has been denied the means of existence
Endurance—is the only thing which remains, and
        even it soon will break.
Amen.[30]

The words in the left column were printed in red.

# CHAPTER III

# A JOURNEY FROM LONDON TO MOSCOW

Kelsiev was not the only intellectual of his day to discover the religious Dissenters and to express enthusiasm for their potential political importance. In fact, during the three decades from the 1840's through the 1860's many members of the Russian intelligentsia became interested in that religious movement.

During the eighteenth century the historical significance of the Raskol had fallen into obscurity. This was in part due to the general immaturity of historical studies in Russia and in part because of the government's attempt to minimize the importance of the Raskol. During the reign of Nicholas I, however, the government inadvertently aided in popularizing the Raskol by establishing committees to study the phenomenon. Although the secret committees were created in order to obtain the data needed to formulate an effective policy for the ultimate eradication of the Raskol, some members of these committees became genuinely interested in the religious movement as an historical and social element. Of these, Ivan P. Liprandi (1790-1880) deserves mention. The son of a wealthy Italian immigrant, Liprandi directed the Special Committee investigating the Raskol. Based largely on materials obtained by the subordinate committees, he published a valuable historical study (*Brief Survey of the Russian Schism, Heresies, and Sects*) which is especially useful for information on the Raskol's political character. Another well-known participant in Nicholas's anti-Raskol activities was Paul I. Melnikov

(1819-93). He served as an investigator of the Raskolniks in his native province of Nizhnii Novgorod (Gorky) on the Volga. Melnikov studied Slavic languages at the University of Kazan, taught history in a gymnasium, and became a well-known novelist, writing under the pseudonym of Andrei Pechersky. He applied his knowledge of the Raskolniks by writing about them in his novels and thereby aided in popularizing them as a movement. Through his official and personal investigations, Melnikov became such an authority on the movement that even many Raskolniks considered him to be its official historiographer.

In addition to the reports which the secret committees compiled, Nicholas's government made several attempts at producing a coherent history of the Raskol. As has been noted earlier, Nadezhdin's history of the Emasculates was written at the government's request. In 1852 the Ministry of Internal Affairs also planned to provide funds for writing a definitive history of the Raskol as a whole. With the outbreak of the Crimean War in the following year, however, the latter project was cancelled. In 1855 the Holy Synod directed the theological seminaries and academies to use Makary's *History of the Russian Raskol*, published in the previous year, as the standard text on the subject. That text deals primarily with problems of religious dogma and was therefore unsatisfactory for use by the government officials, who were more interested in the Raskol's social and political role. Determined to have a comprehensive history of the Raskol, in 1857 the Ministry of Internal Affairs took measures to produce such a text. The Ministry was headed at the time by Sergei S. Lanskoy, who commissioned Melnikov and another historian, A. I. Artemiev, to undertake the task of producing an authoritative study of the Raskol. Other authorities on the Raskol, including well-known Professor Nicholas I. Subbotin, were instructed to assist the two writers. Moreover, the Ministry placed at their disposal the archival materials located in the Imperial Public Library, the Rumiantsev Museum, and in the Ministry's own depository. Although Melnikov succeeded in publishing three volumes of documents, the actual history was not written. Before the writers commenced their work on the text, Lanskoy was replaced by Peter A. Valuev in 1861, and because of financial considerations, the latter cancelled the project. Thereafter the government made no further effort at producing a history of the Raskol.

The government was more successful in founding an anti-Raskol journal, however. This was the *Pravoslavnyi sobesednik* or *Orthodox Interlocutor*, which the Holy Synod began publishing at the Theological Academy of Kazan in 1855. The government supplied its editors with abundant materials on the Raskol, including some of the information collected by the secret committees. Contrary to the government's intentions, however, the articles published in this periodical served to stimulate a wider interest in the Dissenting movement. In 1857, *Pravoslavnyi sobesednik* published an article which discussed the political significance of the Raskol. The author of this anonymously printed article was Afanasy P. Shchapov, who soon thereafter became well known for his revolutionary speeches in which he advocated the idea of regionalism or *oblastnost*. Couching the essential message in phrases superficially reflecting the prescribed tone of hostility toward the Raskolniks, Shchapov depicted them as the leading surviving element of *zemstvo* or folk democracy. The implication was that, politically, Raskol was antithetical to the autocratic centralism of the government.

Shchapov acquired some of the information for that article from the government reports, and his basic premise that the Raskolniks were an element representing *zemstvo* democracy was in accord with the assumptions expressed by the officials who compiled the reports. There was, of course, a fundamental difference in the purpose for drawing their respective conclusions: the civil servants stressed the political nature of the Raskolniks in order to justify the persecution of them, whereas Shchapov emphasized it in order to discredit the government. Shchapov developed these ideas further in his master's thesis (*Russkii raskol staroobriadstva*) which he published in 1858. Together with Kelsiev's publication of the government reports, Shchapov's writings played an important role in projecting the image of the Raskol as a viable political element. So it was that the government's efforts in studying the Raskol for the purpose of eradicating it served to enhance the Raskol's historical significance. The Raskolniks now came to the attention not of the undisciplined illiterate streltsy but of the "Pugachevs of the universities." [1]

From Kelsiev's editorial notations to the government reports it is evident that he and other members of the Kolokol Group were acquainted with Shchapov's thesis. Even more significant, however, was the fact that some of the ideas Herzen had independently expressed on the Raskol's political nature were in many ways similar to those expressed by Shchapov. There is some indication that during his exile to Viatka in 1835-37, Herzen became familiar with the life of local Raskolniks. It is also likely that early in the 1840's he had personal contact with a wealthy and socially prominent Raskolnik, Kuzma T. Soldatenkov, since both men frequented the home of a certain Evgeny F. Korsh. In 1843, Herzen met August von Haxthausen, a Prussian official who came to Russia to study the life of the Russian peasantry. Although Herzen mentions the fact that he was interested in Haxthausen's views concerning the peasant commune or *obshchina* without saying anything about the Raskol, it is unlikely that this Prussian traveller, whose pioneering study of the Russian peasants' way of life includes revealing descriptions of life in the villages populated by various Raskolniks, did not discuss the Raskolniks with Alexander Herzen. In any event, the extent to which Herzen's political thought was influenced by his concern with the Raskol is evident from many of his writings published after his migration to Western Europe in 1847.

Herzen's high regard for the potential political role of the Raskolniks is revealed in his theory of peasant socialism, in which he assigned the Raskolniks an important function in a future socio-political reorganization of Russia. This theory of socialism is Herzen's most important contribution to Russian political thought. In it he advocated a fusion of Western socialist ideas with the institution of the Russian peasant commune. In a broad historical sense it represented an attempt to reconcile two opposing tendencies existing within the Russian intelligentsia: Westernism and Slavophilism. His views regarding the method by which this fusion would be effected did not remain constant, but initially he thought that the fusion would result from a revolution in which the peasants, including the Raskolniks, would play a dominant role. The failure of the mid-century West European revolutions had led Herzen to conclude that the West was incapable of implementing a socialist system, for all of its classes were essentially bourgeois in outlook. The lower classes, he believed, were simply bourgeoisie without property. Socialist theories, therefore, even though they were formulated in the West, were alien to the mentality of Western societies. Having postulated the impossibility of socialism in the West, but remaining loyal to the socialist ideal, Herzen pursued the corollary of applying socialist theories elsewhere. Quite naturally, he chose Russia to be the experimental garden. He rebuked the Slavophiles for their allegedly mystical views on the peasant commune, yet his own Rousseauistic idealization of it was expressed in such melancholic language that at times he seemed vulnerable to his own reproofs. Because he idealized the peasant commune, he came to believe that of all the Russian peasantry the Raskolniks would be the most receptive to socialistic ideas, for they had preserved the commune in its purest form.

The Raskolniks, Herzen thought, had maintained the ancient commune in a more active state than had the rest of the peasant population. Although it was true, he reasoned, that some of the sects held rather absurd beliefs, the Raskolniks in general were "well-ordered and energetic." He admired their ability to stand firm in their beliefs and increase in number in the face of persecution. Some of the sects, he noted, were communistic in organization, and it seemed feasible to him that a populist movement could emerge from one of the Raskol's *skity* or hermitages. Such a movement, he thought, would be nationalistic and communistic in character and would readily spread and join a revolutionary movement imbued with Western socialist ideas.

Herzen believed that the future of Russia belonged to the *muzhik* or peasant. Defending the Russian peasantry against attacks made by a French nationalistic historian, Jules Michelet, Herzen argued that although the Russian peasants were at times treacherous in their dealings with their masters, they lived in a state of harmonious brotherhood with one another; and this, he emphasized, was especially true of the Raskol peasants. The Raskolniks, he felt, had repeatedly demonstrated their mutual loyalty, self-sacrifice, and group solidarity in the face of severe persecutions. Since the peasant commune was to him the basic element which made Russia the only fertile ground for planting the seeds of socialism, the commune in its purest form, that of the Raskolniks, was the choicest plot in that ground. Whereas the Orthodox masses, he claimed, respected the tsar and the official church, the Raskolniks opposed them both. Herzen dramatized the revolutionary potential of the Raskolniks by saying that within their midst one could hear an ominous growl against governmental oppression, and that at times "in these dead and inaccessible seas their growling sounds like a menacing roar, heralding terrible storms." The fact that such a prominent thinker as Herzen entertained such strong ideas concerning the Raskol's revolutionary potential adds considerably to the respectability of Kelsiev's enthusiasm for the religious Dissenters.[2]

Like Shchapov and Herzen, Kelsiev regarded the Raskol as a carrier of the seeds of folk democracy. He interpreted the Raskolniks' opposition to the state as a continuation of the cossack struggle against encroachment by the central government upon the traditional regional autonomy of the Russian people. In the commentaries on the reports he described the Raskol as a movement which, although incapable of articulating its political aims, is capable of suffering for the kind of life it desired. The Raskolniks, he claimed, desired complete religious freedom for all denominations. They considered the payment of taxes to the central government to be a crime. At the same time they maintained a high respect for the elected elders and preceptors. On the basis of these assumptions he concluded that it would not be long before the Raskolniks would start thinking about the means by which to establish elective local and provincial administrations. Whenever possible the Raskolniks, he thought, avoided being tried in the government courts. To him this meant that they were "only a step away from becoming aware of the need for a court of arbitration and for a jury to deal with criminal cases." The Raskolniks, he went on to say, disliked the practice of carrying passports and the practice of being restricted to a place or a social class, and they were demanding full personal freedom. They hated the police and demanded an end to the arbitrary conscription of the serfs. On the other hand, they had no objection to a military force comprised of free men. On the basis of his reading in the government reports of various religious tracts written by the Raskol theologians, Kelsiev concluded that the Raskolniks in general were not opponents of learning and that they were much better educated than the general Orthodox population. He also came to regard the Raskolniks as being better disciplined and more resourceful than the Orthodox population. He noted that the diminution of independence of the cossacks coincided with the growth of the Raskol, and he decided that the cossacks had failed to maintain their democratic organization and their independence only because they had failed to evolve a viable revolutionary programme. Their democracy, he contended, was self-contained and frozen. Using the cossack experience as a lesson, he concluded that the Raskolniks, like the cossacks, lacked an integrated revolutionary programme, and he assigned the responsibility for providing such a programme for them to the revolutionary intelligentsia in general and more specifically to himself.[3]

Kelsiev was favourably impressed by the fact that the Raskolniks were primarily Great Russians. He attributed this to what he called the "deterministic tendencies" within the Russian historical character. Like Bakunin, he believed in the latent revolutionary capacity of the Great Russians and claimed that once a Russian adopts certain principles, he will make them into an orthodoxy and, if necessary, will defend them with his life. To dramatize the strength of his own and the Raskolniks' determinism in order to illustrate the alleged nature of the historical conscience of the Russians in general, Kelsiev drew on an old Novgorod *bylina* or epic. He cited a passage about a folk hero—a dare-devil, a rowdy named Vasily or Vaska Buslaev. "Tired and worn by life, Vaska one day decided to go to Jerusalem to pray. On the way there, however, he came upon a magic stone bearing an inscription which said that one must not pass beyond the stone lest he would fall and be killed. Vaska Buslaev's soul could not withstand the temptation: he jumped over the magic stone, knowing that he would be killed—and was killed." Kelsiev concluded the tale by saying that "we, too, know that our task is dangerous, but the Russian man has to search for truth." Vasily Kelsiev's search for truth, as we will see, had indeed much in common with Vasily Buslaev's fatal leap over the magic stone.[4]

In November 1861, when Kelsiev was preoccupied with publishing the government reports on the Raskol, there appeared in the British capital a Russian Old Believer. He stayed at a fashionable hotel in Piccadilly. A few days following his arrival he wandered into the store of a Polish bookseller named Tchorzewski and expressed a desire for communicating with the publishers of *The Bell*. Tchorzewski was affiliated with the Russian publishers and, in fact, was engaged in selling their publications. He hurriedly notified Kelsiev about the mysterious Russian visitor, and the following morning the ebullient revolutionary met a calm, cautious Old Believer in the lobby of the latter's hotel. The Old Believer, according to Kelsiev, was "a man of about thirty years of age, not very tall, with a pock-marked face, lean, with a thin Russian beard." Kelsiev at first was cautious in talking with the stranger, lest the latter be an agent of the Russian police, but arranged for another meeting with him nonetheless. They met again in the afternoon of the same day, and during the three-hour long discourse that followed Kelsiev was pleased to learn that his guest was a very pleasant fellow, lively and cheerful, and "remarkably intelligent." From a few words, Kelsiev observed, the Old Believer could grasp any kind of question, always answering it in detail and yet concretely, considering it from all sides and picking it to pieces. One characteristic of his mind was especially striking to Kelsiev: "he never gave a direct answer, no matter what one might ask him." Instead, he approached each question from a distance, as if stepping back from the object of his attention in order to gain a perspective. Only after some twenty or even thirty minutes would one begin to realize that the Old Believer was explaining precisely what was expected of him. In the process he would bring out the pros and cons of the issue, elucidate them in the most vivid manner, and on the basis of the information thus revealed would draw a firm conclusion. "What power of intellect, what dialectical abilities this man possesses!" Kelsiev marvelled. "Even though he has no formal education and was brought up exclusively on the reading of religious books." From the time of their first prolonged conversation, Kelsiev became favourably disposed toward his new acquaintance and persuaded him to move into a room located in the same building where Kelsiev and his family were living.[5]

Kelsiev's eloquent, bearded neighbour introduced himself as Polikarp Petrov, a merchant by trade and "an ordinary" Old Believer by faith. He travelled with a Russian passport, allegedly on commercial business. During the six weeks Polikarp spent in London, he and Kelsiev had sufficient time to have prolonged discussions on many subjects. Their discussions revolved primarily around the religious and political problems of the Raskol. In the political sphere they considered the feasibility of moving the Priestists' prelacy from its location in the Hapsburg Empire to London. Polikarp assured Kelsiev that *The Bell* was well known among the Raskolniks in Russia, and he thought that there was a real possibility for the London revolutionaries to gain some financial aid from the Old Believers. At the same time, Polikarp cautioned Kelsiev against becoming excessively optimistic about prospects for any extensive cooperation between the revolutionaries and the Raskolniks. He advised Kelsiev that the religious differences existing among various sects and denominations of the Raskol would preclude any unified political effort on their part. The elements which might cooperate with the London revolutionaries, he thought, would probably do so not so much because of their political predilections but in order to use the London publishing facilities to polemicize with the other elements of the Raskol. In spite of Polikarp's reservations, however, Kelsiev was encouraged by their discourses and continued in his resolve to achieve collaboration with the Dissenting movement.[6]

Herzen, too, enjoyed lively discourses with Polikarp and described him as a person who seemed to have "spent his entire life among literary men." Herzen's interest in the Raskol was particularly aroused when Polikarp mentioned that the only Russian, in addition to Bakunin, who attended the Pan-Slav Congress held in Prague in 1848, was an Old Believer named Olimpy Miloradov. Bakunin confirmed Polikarp's information, and, according to one writer, Herzen became so enthusiastic that he "practically called himself a Raskolnik." Polikarp's reference to Miloradov's appearance in Prague was based on fact. Miloradov was an Old Believer monk who played an active role in establishing the Priestists' hierarchy in 1846 at Belo-Krynitsa, in Austrian territory. In 1848 he came to Vienna with a petition to the Austrian government for reopening the Priestists' see at Belo-Krynitsa, which was closed on demands from the Russian government. With the outbreak of the revolution, he apparently travelled to Prague, and at the Pan-Slav Congress held there denounced both the Austrian and the Russian emperors. In the 1860's, when Kelsiev's activities had stimulated a wide interest in the Raskol, Bakunin attempted to communicate with Miloradov but without any success.[7]

One can readily doubt that the serious-minded Herzen would have allowed his enthusiasm to lead him so far astray as to call himself a Raskolnik; on the other hand, there is little reason for questioning the accounts of Bakunin's ostentatious display of blatant hypocrisy before the sensitive Old Believer visitor from Russia. According to an account based on Polikarp's own observations, on one occasion he was interrupted during his evening hour of solemn prayer by the sound of a man noisily coming up the stairs and singing at the top of his voice the canticle, "Lord, when Thou was baptized in the Jordan." Polikarp's door was flung open, and, in a state of utter astonishment, the Old Believer saw the smiling face of a singing stranger accompanying Kelsiev. He was Michael Bakunin, a stranger to Polikarp, though not a stranger to the world, for he had just recently arrived in London by way of Japan and San Francisco after an escape from Siberia. With

some discrepancies in detail the same incident was also recorded by Kelsiev.

Bakunin appeared. He had met with Polikarp before, at the Herzens. But in the presence of Herzen,
the principal, who held him in leash, it was not
possible for Bakunin to spread his wings, as he did
with me, and to show his talents. I remember how he
came up to my study, singing as loudly as he could
some kind of trope—this was the *captatio benevo-
lentiae* of the Old Believer. Then with excessive
sweetness he began to beg Polikarp to explain to him
for his edification the difference between the old
faith and the Orthodox religion, implying that he
himself would have no objection to becoming an
Old Believer if Polikarp could convince him of the
correctness of the old faith. Polikarp could not help
but understand the real meaning of this crudely-
devised snare, but, being an extremely delicate man,
he went into explanations of the old Russian rituals
and of Nikon's reforms. Bakunin gasped, expressed
amazement at Polikarp's information, nodded agree-
ably to some of his assertions, revealed a state of in-
dignation at the Nikonian innovations, and finally,
exhausted by his own shameful comedy, began to
ask Polikarp to give him lessons in Russian history.

Bakunin had apparently continued in this vein for several
hours, converting Russia to the old faith and placing on its
throne an Old Believer tsar. This quixotic encounter culminated with Bakunin's invitation to Polikarp to evening tea
at the residence of the volatile anarchist.[8]

The jovial atmosphere of that evening's gathering proved
to be another test of Polikarp's endurance. He found Bakunin's diminutive quarters filled with smoke, which was offensive
to him, for to the Old Believers tobacco is an "accursed weed."
The revolutionaries gathered there shouted sharp phrases
about politics, about humanity, revolutions, monarchy, and
equality. "Everyone spoke, no one listened. They burned with

emotionalism and expressed the most extreme views in a most fervent manner. All that Polikarp could do was to throw up his hands and exclaim now and then with astonishment: 'The fate of the world is being decided here! Yes, the fate of the world.' " Kelsiev readily perceived Polikarp's discomfort caused by the improprieties of his host, but it was only later that he realized how deeply the Old Believer had been disturbed by the revolutionaries' nonchalant discussions of issues which to him were of the utmost importance. Soon after the eventful meeting, which took place on January 5, Polikarp departed from London and returned to Russia. According to an account written with Polikarp's collaboration, he failed to achieve his objectives in London and left there with a heavy feeling of dismay.[9]

Two months following Polikarp's departure from London, Kelsiev reversed roles with him and travelled on a secret mission to Moscow. In Russia he learned the true identity of the Old Believer visitor to London. Polikarp Petrov was not a merchant but an Old Believer bishop. His full name was Polikarp Petrovich Ovchinnikov (1827-1907), but he was better known by his ecclesiastical name, Pafnuty of Kolomna. Pafnuty was an influential figure among the Priestist Old Believer hierarchs. He had become a bishop at the age of thirty-one and for several years served as the real power behind the Priestist Bishop of Vladimir, Anthony, who claimed the senior position in the Priestist church of all Russia. Pafnuty was a young zealot who, upon becoming bishop, set out to invigorate the Priestist church and to reform its hierarchy. His small following of youthful reformers became known as Pafnuty's Brotherhood, and in many ways it resembled the Circle of the Zealots of Piousness of the Nikonian period. Pafnuty and his Brotherhood complained of the general supineness of the Belo-Krynitsa prelacy, headed by the lethargic, incompetent Metropolitan Cyril; they sought to establish facilities for printing the pre-Nikonian service books; and they demanded higher qualifications for the clergy. To accomplish this task, Pafnuty advocated closer cooperation with the official church and the government, hoping to win thereby legal recognition of the Old Believer hierarchy. In July of 1860, Pafnuty de-

fied Anthony's authority in protest against the latter's mach-
inations in claiming for himself the position of seniority
over the Old Believer hierarchy within Russia. Following this
break with his superior, Pafnuty spent five years in voluntary
seclusion, interrupting it only for his visit to London. In 1865,
together with three of his followers (Onufry, Ioasaf, and Filaret), Pafnuty abandoned the old faith and joined the *Edinoverie* or Uniate branch of the official church. Pafnuty's ecclesiastical career did not end here, however. Having spent over
a decade polemicizing against his former co-religionists on
behalf of the official church, he returned to the old faith and
lived to see the day when the Raskolniks gained legal recognition in Russia, following the Revolution of 1905.[10]

The attention devoted to the Raskol in *The Bell* was one
of the factors which attracted Pafnuty and his supporters to
the London revolutionaries. In the initial issue of *The Bell* its
editors outlined the aims of their anti-tsarist publication, and
one of their commitments was to publicize the details of the
government's persecution of the Raskolniks. They fulfilled
this promise, for news about the Raskolniks was seldom absent
from the pages of their widely-circulated publication. This
news ranged from reports of bribery involving the government
officials and the Raskolniks to inflamatory accounts of armed
conflicts. In describing the suppression of the peasant uprising
which occurred at Bezdna on April 12, 1861, for example,
Herzen appealed to the Raskolniks with the words "Strength-
en yourselves in spirit and always remember the cry with
which the Bezdna victims died: Liberty! Liberty!"[11] Moreover, the general popularity of *The Bell* and its influence in
Russia had attracted wide attention among the inquisitive
Raskolniks. Some of their leaders, including Bishop Pafnuty,
came to believe that the London revolutionaries were genuinely
devoted to securing religious freedom for the Raskolniks. The
influence of *The Bell* among the Raskolniks was further enhanced by Kelsiev's publication of the government reports
on the Raskol. Many Raskolniks, thus, came to believe that
the publishers of *The Bell* represented a force sufficiently for-
midable to influence the Russian government's policies.
When in 1859 the government threateningly rejected Pafnuty's

petition for legal recognition of the Priestist hierarchy and when the following year he broke with Bishop Anthony, Pafnuty decided to take the drastic step of communicating directly with the Kolokol Group.

As one writer expressed it, Pafnuty went to London to "smell out" the real character, the aims, and the general reliability of the Kolokol Group. He apparently went there to determine the feasibility of moving the Priestists prelacy to London. He also hoped to enlist the aid of the Kolokol Group for the establishment of a seminary in London and wanted to make arrangements for the use of their printing facilities. The Moscow Priestists who sponsored his mission to London were prepared to provide the necessary financial support for these projects.[12] None of these aims were, of course, realized.

It would be a simplification of the problem to attribute the failure of Pafnuty's mission solely to Bakunin's ostentatious joviality, yet the irresponsible behaviour of the famed anarchist and of his companions did aid in removing the veil through which Pafnuty visualized the London revolutionaries before he had met them. Prior to his visit to London, Pafnuty, undoubtedly, imagined them to be men of authority, dignity, and wisdom, for they were the same men who wrote authoritatively, seriously, and at times wisely about problems which were of concern to the Old Believers. Yet, as he listened to Bakunin's sardonic singing, as he observed the wild gesticulations of his friends, and as he smelled the heavy odour of smoke at their gathering, Pafnuty came to recognize the drastic disparity existing between them and the revolutionaries of his imagination. He did retain a favourable impression of Herzen, but he complained that during his six weeks in London, he was able to speak to Herzen on only four occasions. He felt that this was because Herzen's residence was usually filled with "free thinkers," and, therefore, Kelsiev deliberately kept him away to preserve a favourable image of the Kolokol Group. It is also possible that because they were not aware of Pafnuty's real identity, the revolutionaries offended the strongly egocentric Bishop by failing to treat him in the manner warranted by his rank. In any case, in failing to win Pafnuty's trust, the London revolutionaries missed a singular opportunity for establishing close relations with the dominant group of the Old Believers.

Pafnuty's disenchantment with the London revolutionaries did not immediately manifest itself with sufficient vividness to be fully perceived by Kelsiev. On the contrary, Pafnuty's departure from London was ostensibly cordial, and the confidence he expressed in the possibility of providing some financial support for the periodical Kelsiev planned to publish led the latter to think that this was indeed the beginning of permanent relations between the revolutionaries and the Old Believers. "I told him," Kelsiev explained later, "that I would go to Moscow myself in order to get things moving, and he said that this would not be such a bad idea. Then, having elicited from him a promise to write me ... from Moscow, I accompanied him to the station. We embraced, and the train began to move." [13] Thus, heartened by Pafnuty's visit, Kelsiev decided to undertake a clandestine journey to Moscow.

Leaving his ailing and impoverished wife and an infant daughter (born after the death of their first child) in the slums of Fulham, Kelsiev went to Berlin, where he obtained a Russian visa, and on March 2, 1862 crossed the border of his beloved though hostile homeland. A wig, an illegal Turkish passport, and the assumed name of Vasily Jani were the devices which aided Kelsiev in concealing his true identity from the Russian police during the six weeks he spent in St. Petersburg and Moscow. Writing after his break with the revolutionary movement, he explained the reasons for his journey in a rather instructive way. After he had discovered the Raskolniks, a trip to Russia became his favourite dream, and with Pafnuty's visit to London that dream simply captivated him. He was suffering from a depressing nostalgia for the homeland, he claimed, and was ashamed of his ignorance of the real concerns of the Russian people. Neither from Herzen nor from Ogarev was he able to learn just what was needed for Russia and how this could be achieved. He had little understanding of peasant concerns and the general economic problems and felt that he needed to know more about them. What is more, there was no real agreement on these problems among his colleagues in London. On the other

hand, such issues as freedom of speech, public trial, abolition
of corporal punishment, freedom of religion, and the natural
division of provinces on the basis of historical and ethnic
lines were exciting and meaningful to him. But the main thing
that was impelling him to go to Russia was his desire to see
for himself the extent of the revolutionaries' influence there
and the desire to determine the possibility for cooperation between the revolutionaries and the religious Dissenters. Together with these was the fact that, having heard again and
again from youthful visitors from Russia that the preparation
for a revolution there was progressing at such a rapid pace
that the people were becoming more and more sympathetic
to the cause, he decided "either to prevent the explosion, or,
if that was already too late, direct it somehow in a more sensible way." [14] When one considers the fact that Kelsiev made
these explanations in a confession addressed to the tsar, one
may exercise some caution in accepting the truthfulness of his
reference to the "explosion," but otherwise these explanations seem plausible enough. He was homesick, he wanted
to assess the general revolutionary situation, he was a Vaska
Buslaev at heart, and, above all, he was determined to develop
a permanent relationship between the revolutionaries and the
Raskolniks.

Kelsiev spent over a week in St. Petersburg, four weeks
in Moscow, then returned to St. Petersburg, and from there
crossed the border and went to East Prussia. Among the
members of the revolutionary intelligentsia whom he met
in Russia were Andrei I. Nichiporenko (1837-63) and Nicholas A. Serno-Solovievich (1834-66).

He had been acquainted with Nichiporenko from the
time of their studies at the commercial school in St. Petersburg.
Legally Nichiporenko now served as a minor government
official and illegally as a correspondent for *The Bell*. He knew
of Kelsiev's pending visit to Russia, for the two met in London
only shortly before the latter's departure from there. Throughout Kelsiev's stay in Russia, Nichiporenko served as his chief
mentor, and it was through him that Bakunin arranged for
a certain Marquis de Traversi to transmit to Kelsiev a sum
of three hundred silver roubles for the latter's needs in his

daring venture. Although Kelsiev distrusted the talkative
Nichiporenko, he found him indispensable for contacting
other revolutionaries and some of the Old Believers.

Nicholas Serno-Solovievich was a well-known member of
the revolutionary intelligentsia of the 1860's. The son of a
nobleman, he graduated with a silver medal from the famous
Imperial Lyceum. For a time he served as a government official, but in 1861 resigned and opened a book store and a public library in St. Petersburg, both of which he used for the
advancement of the revolutionary cause. Serno had close
contacts with the revolutionaries in London and was one of
the organizers of the Land and Liberty revolutionary society.
In 1858 he created quite a sensation among the revolutionaries
when he approached the Tsar during the latter's stroll in the
garden at Tsarskoe Selo and handed him a manifesto calling
on the monarch to follow the ideas of the young generation.
In the writings of Kelsiev and of other contemporaries of
Serno's he is described as heroic, unreservedly honest, and a
noble individual. Kelsiev depicted him as a man who was
extremely intelligent and energetic, "always ready to do a
noble deed and one who passionately loved Russia"; while
according to Herzen, Serno-Solovievich was an unusually
noble individual who was "entirely devoted to the revolutionary cause." [15]

At that juncture in his revolutionary activities Kelsiev
was mainly interested in bringing about as wide contacts as
possible between the revolutionaries and the Raskolniks. The
ultimate purpose of these contacts was to be the creation of
an organized revolutionary force composed not only of leaders,
as it now was, but of leaders with masses. In immediate terms
he was interested in expanding the facilities for distribution
of the London publications inside Russia and to gain financial
support from the wealthy Raskol population for the revolutionary cause. He thought that the most effective way to attain
wide circulation of *The Bell* in Russia would be to arrange
for having it clandestinely printed within that country. This
was to be accomplished by smuggling the plates from
London.[16]

During his presence in St. Petersburg, Kelsiev stayed

with Serno-Solovievich. Since the latter was at that time preoccupied with organizing the secret society, which became
known under the name of Land and Liberty, Kelsiev attempted
to convince him of the possible advantages such a society
might derive from close cooperation with the Raskolniks.[17]
As a matter of interest it may be noted that the Priestist branch
of the Old Believers, which embraced about one-half of the
Raskol population, possessed an administrative organization
resembling the system evolved by the Land and Liberty society.
The administrative framework of these two bodies bear comparison. At the apex of each there were two governing centres: one inside Russia and the other abroad. The metropolitan
of Belo-Krynitsa, in the Austrian Empire, served as the head
of the Priestists, and their domestic centre was in Moscow.
In the case of the Land and Liberty society, the Kolokol Group
in London served as its foreign centre while the central committee was located in St. Petersburg. Under these administrative organs there were regional and municipal or county units
in both organizations. In addition to their foreign governing
centres, each organization possessed a strong low-echelon
branch outside Russia proper: the Old Believer settlements on
the Danube in the case of the Priestists, and an active group
of Russian officers in Poland in the case of the revolutionaries.
Finally, during its brief but vigorous existence, the Land and
Liberty society attempted to establish strongholds in Russia
coinciding geographically with the distribution of the Raskol
population. All of this is not meant to suggest that there was
actually a direct relationship between the two organizations
at these levels, but rather these facts are mentioned because
they lend some credence to the speculative plans Kelsiev discussed with Serno-Solovievich and other revolutionaries in
Russia.

Kelsiev's contacts with the Raskolniks were disappointing
in one important respect, but on the whole seemed promising.
The disappointment was related to Bishop Pafnuty's refusal
to meet him. Kelsiev learned of Pafnuty's true identity in
St. Petersburg and, unaware of the latter's adverse feelings
toward the revolutionaries, hastened to Moscow where Pafnuty
was presently residing. He travelled by train and was accom-

panied by Nichiporenko and a prominent Old Believer publisher, Dmitry Efimovich Kozhanchikov (d. 1877). It is likely that Kozhanchikov and another Old Believer publisher, Kozma Terentievich Soldatenkov, the son of a wealthy Old Believer merchant, financed, at least in part, Kelsiev's venture into Russia. Both of these Old Believers were attracted to the revolutionary movement by Kelsiev's publication of the government reports and by the concern the London revolutionaries were voicing for the Raskolniks on the pages of *The Bell*. In Moscow, Kozhanchikov remained with Kelsiev for four days, and it was with his aid that Kelsiev was able to meet some of the local Old Believers. Kozhanchikov's influence, however, was not sufficient for Kelsiev to gain an audience with Bishop Pafnuty. The Old Believers Kelsiev met timidly informed him that Pafnuty had recently departed for Kiev and would not return in time to meet him. From the tone of their voices and their mannerisms Kelsiev readily perceived the real meaning of their words.

According to an account appearing in a polemical article written with Pafnuty's collaboration, the Old Believer Bishop was indeed in Moscow at that time and was aware of Kelsiev's desire for an audience with him. There is curious mention in that article of a premonition Pafnuty allegedly experienced on the night of Kelsiev's arrival in Moscow. According to this statement Kelsiev appeared in such a frightful form that Pafnuty was awakened in terror of what his dream revealed. In the morning, when his assistant came to tell Pafnuty the surprising news of Kelsiev's arrival, the Bishop surprised him by informing him of the same news.[18] In any event, Kelsiev was both surprised and genuinely disappointed by Pafnuty's decision to avoid contact with him.

Kelsiev did establish an important link with the Moscow Priestist Old Believers. His chief contact among them was made through a merchant named Ivan Ivanovich Shibaev, who was the same age as Kelsiev. He learned of Shibaev from Bishop Pafnuty, during the latter's visit to London. Pafnuty described Shibaev as a person who was "always looking for something progressive to do." Writing after his own break with the revolutionaries, Kelsiev characterized Shibaev as one "who understood absolutely nothing about politics." Shibaev, he claimed, was under the impression that a revolution might occur in Russia at any moment, and that it would inevitably result in the restoration of the old faith. When Kelsiev suggested that the revolution had not yet been organized and that it could be effected only if the Old Believers were willing to help bring it about, Shibaev allegedly retorted that the Old Believers knew nothing about organizing revolutions and, besides, it was dangerous for them to have any dealings with the London "foreigners." Kelsiev went on to say in this obviously anecdotal tone that when he suggested to Shibaev that the Old Believers ought to contribute financially to the work the London revolutionaries were engaged in, Shibaev said that he was certain that in London there were "millions and billions" of roubles available to them.

Although the preceding account probably does illustrate to some degree Shibaev's political naiveté, it distorts the facts concerning the significance of his liaison with Kelsiev. Recording his initial impression of Shibaev, Kelsiev described him as "a young man, in a long frock coat, with trousers tucked inside his jack boots, with a large blond beard and light blue eyes. In appearance, he was nervous, gentle—he was a poet, a dreamer, a man capable of being attracted by everything that was mysterious and outside the ordinary." This description of him and Shibaev's career tend to confirm Pafnuty's remark concerning Shibaev's inclination toward "progressivism." When he was eighteen, Shibaev deserted the Raskol and joined the government-sponsored *Edinoverie* church, but later returned to the Raskol. The latter step involved considerable danger yet Shibaev risked it and suffered no penalty. For his dealings with Kelsiev, Shibaev spent two years in prison, yet retained enough vigour to open a school for Old Believer children in 1868 and to create havoc in government circles in 1883 by distributing a petition charging that the officials of the Ministry of Internal Affairs were controverting the Tsar's liberal policies toward the Raskolniks. All this serves to illustrate the soundness of Kelsiev's conclusion that Shibaev, like Pafnuty, was one of the young "progressives" within the Raskol.[19]

Contrary to the comments Kelsiev made about Shibaev

in his *Confession*, his relationship with that enterprising Old Believer merchant was a significant step forward in his drive to penetrate the inner circles of the Moscow community of the Old Believers. Kelsiev, for example, instructed Shibaev in the use of coded symbols for communicating with him in London; Shibaev was drawn into surreptitious dealings with local revolutionaries; and, although the facts are obscure, Kelsiev apparently hoped that Shibaev would be able to organize an armed group. Shortly after Kelsiev's return to London, he wrote Shibaev that the "war" was only beginning. He advised him to "weave" around himself a nest of people, including those who did not share his views. "It would be very fine," he wrote to Shibaev in July, 1862, "if you could have an armed group [*opolchenie*] ready by Christmas. I have an important proposal to make to you and your friends, and I will be returning to Russia in order to communicate with you. In the meantime, keep strengthening yourselves . . ." In another letter Kelsiev admitted that there was little prospect for winning the Priestist hierarchy to the revolutionary cause, and he advised therefore that the revolutionaries should devote more attention to Shibaev and his group of youthful "radicals." [20] In view of all this, it is evident that Kelsiev's attempt to minimize in his *Confession* Shibaev's importance was deliberate and was probably intended to minimize his own revolutionary activities. In reality, his recruitment of Shibaev to work for the revolutionary movement was the most significant achievement he made during his dangerous venture in Russia.

The other important contact that Kelsiev made with the Raskolniks on his visit to Russia was through his encounter with Paul the Prussian. Paul, whose secular name was Peter Ivanovich Lednev (1821-95), was a leading theologian of the Theodocians, a Priestless sect. In 1848 he moved to East Prussia (hence his name) where a Priestless monastery was established near Johannisburg (today Pisz, in Poland) by the wealthy Priestless centre of Preobrazhenskoe cemetery in Moscow. Paul served as the abbot of that monastery until 1867, when he left the Raskol. In the following year, along with fifteen of his disciples, he joined the Edinoverie church and became active in proselytizing on behalf of that church among his former coreligionists.

Kelsiev met Paul in St. Petersburg before going to Moscow. They were introduced by an Old Believer who was acquainted with Serno-Solovievich's brother Alexander and met in the home of a wealthy merchant Raskolnik named Ivan Vasilievich Borodin. Borodin provided accommodations for Paul, who, like Kelsiev, was in Russia illegally. In describing Paul's appearance, Kelsiev left a masterly sketch of this interesting Theodocian. "Entered a man who was tall, lean, with black hair, about forty years of age. He was dressed in a monk's attire; that is, a black cassock, a cloak (a black cape with red edging), and kamilavka—a round cap with a fur brim. This was the first time that I had seen our monastic vestment of the pre-Nikonian period . . . I looked at this man with utmost attentiveness—a man with an intelligent, perpetually-smiling face and with black sparkling eyes full of life and thought." Intellectually, Paul was at least as keen as Pafnuty, and, unlike Shibaev, was well-versed in current political affairs. It was from him, incidentally, that Kelsiev learned the true identity of Bishop Pafnuty of Kolomna. The essence of the conversation that took place between Kelsiev and Paul the Prussian concerning the possible relations between the revolutionaries and the Raskolniks has been reconstructed in Kelsiev's *Confession,* and the brevity of the passage permits us to cite it in its entirety.

"Father Paul," I said, "I want to be honest with you. You came here illegally, with a false passport, bearing someone else's name, and you are not even a Russian citizen, even though you were born in Russia. You have not told me about any of this, but, dear Father, all of this is self-evident. Thus I want to tell you that I am here in a similar situation: my name is not Jani but Kelsiev. I carry a Turkish passport. I live in London, where everything is being printed that is barred from print in Russia and where some men of good will are working for a greater freedom not only for all religions but also for the entire people. It is in this connection that I came here to acquaint myself with the followers of the old Orthodox piousness, and to discuss with them what is required, how to go about doing things, what our aims should be, and in which direction we are to head."

Then I expounded my views concerning the role the Old Believers could play in our movement with the organization they already had. Paul listened to me attentively.

"You are a sincere man," he said to me, "and you do desire good for the people. I can see this, and I understand. But I must tell you with all frankness: do not think about nor count on us. In the first place, we are not the kind of people who could meddle in the affairs of the tsars or even understand them. Our foremost task is filling our pockets, and outside of this we care nothing for the world. We think more about mammon than about the Christian faith. Secondly, you must realize that our religion does not allow us to go against the authorities . . ."

"Just a moment, Father, did you not just say that our government officials were precursors of the Antichrist? Besides, it is stated in the Scriptures that in 'the present final days the faithful will struggle against the Antichrist'."

"Yes, I have said those things and will say them again, but all of this must be properly understood. Let the spiritual be spiritual and the temporal be temporal. Render what is Caesar's unto Caesar and what is God's unto God. Yes, we quarrel with them but only regarding the faith; we do not meddle in their temporal affairs. There is no example in their lives to show that the Christians ever revolted, and the holy fathers do not teach us to do so."

"Father Paul, I, too, am not asking you to revolt."

"I understand this, my friend; you are not summoning us to an insurrection, yet you are implying that we are to resist the authorities, and this is not for us. And besides, we do not have enough brains to understand this sort of thing, to understand whether the tsar is governing rightly or wrongly."

"And do you not even want religious equality with the foreign creeds?" I asked, realizing that there was little else that one could do.

"Yes, we want it, but at the same time we are satisfied with what we have recently received. We are grateful that they do not treat us harshly," Paul answered.

"And I can also add," interposed Ivan Vasilevich [Borodin], who until then refrained from speaking, out of respect for Paul, "that it is good for us that there is the official church in Russia: this is beneficial to us."

"How is that?" I did not expect such a conclusion.

"If there were no official church, the godless ones would triumph and ruin our faith entirely. There are hordes of these Masons in our days. As long as there is the Synod, the Christian faith, although not the right one, survives. Abolish the Synod, and the godless—the godless and the Germans—and the iconoclasts who do not respect the holy fathers, would have so much freedom that they would entirely ruin the faith and eradicate the remaining piety from the face of the earth."

Kelsiev was to find that Borodin's reasoning about the possible effects of general freedom was a reflection of the attitude of many Raskolniks. In his subsequent encounters with them Kelsiev heard again and again the argument that general freedom would be worse than the existing restrictions, for it would mean giving freedom to the enemies of their faith. Such a reasoning was quite contrary to Kelsiev's assumption that because they themselves were restricted the Raskolniks were desirous of religious freedom for all.[21]

Although Borodin's words may well have hastened Kelsiev's departure from St. Petersburg, he, nonetheless, parted from Paul the Prussian on friendly terms, and the Priestless theologian invited him to visit the Theodocian monastery in Prussia. Kelsiev accepted the invitation and on his way to London spent three days with Paul at the monastery near Johannisburg. The Theodocian settlement in East Prussia consisted of eight villages, with the monastery serving as the religious centre. To Kelsiev's surprise, Paul possessed a substantial collection of books and had a printing press with Church Slavonic type. Together with his capable, self-educated assistant, Constantine Efimovich Golubov, Paul printed the religious materials needed by his followers and even published a periodical, titled *Istina* or *Truth*, in which he polemicized against his religious opponents. Kelsiev's relations with Paul proved to be more lasting than his contacts with any other member of the Raskol. Paul and Golubov contributed articles to the London revolutionary publications, and as late as 1864, when the popularity of *The Bell* was rapidly declining in Russia because of Herzen's support for the Polish uprising of the previous year, the London publications were still being transmitted to Johannisburg.

In Johannisburg, in addition to becoming further enlightened about the political potentialities of the Raskolniks, Kelsiev had his first opportunity to meet some of the "masses" of the Raskol. Describing his encounter with the Theodocian monks there, he thought them to be rather unusual. "Observing them," he wrote some years later, "one forgets that we live in the nineteenth century and that one is, even though in an out-of-the-way place, still in Prussia." According to Kelsiev, those Priestless monks observed monastic rules with primitive severity: "not only drunkenness, debauchery, and the eating of meat are debarred from inside these walls, but they do not even change their underwear until it rots on their backs." And even then, he claimed, they changed it in the darkness, with their faces turned to a corner so that no lust would ensue from gazing upon their own bodies. They did not wear trousers, in order to avoid touching their naked bodies. They did not wash and did not comb their hair, because of their contempt for the flesh. They slept on bare boards, with a log under their heads. As a result, their faces were greasy-greenish in colour; their hair was covered with a cloud of dust; and they reeked with an unusually bitter odour—an odour by which, according to Kelsiev, one could tell the presence of such a monk from ten feet away.

This group of Theodocian monks did not, of course, typify the general Raskol masses, still, they were the first group of "ordinary" Raskolniks Kelsiev had met. Their impact on the romantic revolutionary was such that for the first time since his discovery of the Raskol on the pages of the government reports his enthusiasm for its revolutionary potentiality was marred by a throb of doubt, leading him to wonder whether the kinds of Raskolniks he had discovered through readings really existed anywhere outside these reports. It was with a feeling of melancholy, provoked by his encounter with these monks that Kelsiev parted company with their superior, Paul the Prussian.[22]

Before returning to London, Kelsiev made an arrangement in Koenigsberg for transporting the London publications into Russia. Although this part of his accomplishment, together with all the other arrangement he had made during his visit to Russia, fell by the wayside soon thereafter, it is of some interest to note the relative ease with which the revolutionaries were able to smuggle their literature across the border of their homeland. According to Kelsiev, in Koenigsberg "entire streets" were occupied by offices displaying the sign *Expedition & Kommission*. These offices appeared in every respect to be legitimate establishments, yet in every one Kelsiev visited his conversation with the officials went basically as follows:

"I would like to speak with you privately . . ."
"Are you interested in sending something?"
"Yes. But in private . . ."
"Oh, be not concerned; we have no secrets here. This is our profession."
"I understand, except the goods I want to send are . . ."

"Weapons, possibly, or powder? We are used
to this. You may speak openly." "Books and news-
papers," I finally would have the courage to say,
looking from side to side. But no one would pay
any attention to me, that is how well they have become accustomed to this sort of thing.

"For what value?"

"For the first time, about one hundred talers."

"We will immediately make a contract and will
give you a guarantee: a provision that at the time
of delivery we will receive so many per cent. Our
company is well-known for the efficiency of its service . . ." [23]

Kelsiev assured his reader that there was no exaggeration in
his depiction of the situation and that the only puzzling aspect
of it was that the revolutionaries had not been using Koenigsberg as the main gateway to Russia for their illegal trans-
actions.

Kelsiev returned to London a hero to his wife and a man
worthy of admiration even from a figure as daring as Michael
Bakunin. Priding himself on the success of his daring venture
he now plunged whole-heartedly into the task of stabilizing
and expanding the contacts he had established. In order to
make the relationship between the two movements more
effective, he began to press on his London colleagues the need
for launching the much-discussed periodical which was to be
devoted exclusively to the affairs of the Raskolniks. He wrote
to a member of the Priestist hierarchy at Belo-Krynitsa, hoping
to achieve permanent contacts with the Raskolniks living on
the Danube, and he began to test the effectiveness of the communication channels he had established with the Old Believers
in Moscow. Having barely caught his breadth from the journey
he had just completed, Kelsiev began to talk about another
visit to Moscow "before Christmas." Everything at that point
seemed promising to him. The young revolutionary had just
begun to spread his wings, when his plans, projects, and accomplishments collapsed as a poorly-constructed kite collapses
in a gust of wind.

Early in May, 1862, the Russian police arrested a certain Paul Alexandrovich Vetoshnikov on his return to Russia from London. Like many of the Russians travelling in Western Europe at the time, Vetoshnikov had visited Herzen, and like many other admirers of the popular publisher of *The Bell*, he offered to take some correspondence to Russia. There was nothing unusual about this except that at the same time as Vetoshnikov was enjoying Herzen's hospitality another Russian was enjoying it too, but for a quite different reason. The other Russian was a secret agent of the Russian police. Consequently, upon his arrival in Russia, Vetoshnikov was apprehended, and his baggage yielded the incriminating correspondence. The letters he carried were from Herzen, Ogarev, Kelsiev, and Bakunin. They were addressed to N. A. Serno-Solovievich, N. S. Bakunina, M. L. Nalbandian, N. F. Petrovsky, I. I. Shibaev, N. M. Vladimirov, and O. M. Belozersky. The apprehension of Vetoshnikov proved to be the initial shock that produced a wave of arrests, which swept behind prison walls not only those to whom the letters were addressed but also most of the persons who had been in contact with Kelsiev during his secret visit to Russia. The police also used this incident as a pretext for arresting some prominent revolutionaries, including Chernyshevsky, who were in no way implicated in the Kelsiev-Vetoshnikov affair. The resulting trial was known as the "Trial of the Thirty-Two," and among those convicted were Shibaev and Nicholas Serno-Solovievich. Shibaev was confined for only two years, but Serno-Solovievich spent almost three years in the Peter-Paul fortress, was permanently banished to Siberia, and it was there that he died in 1866, at the age of thirty-two. Kelsiev was tried in absentia, was convicted, and sentenced to permanent banishment from his native country.[24]

As a result of the investigations related to the Vetoshnikov affair, the government learned the details of Kelsiev's activities during his illegal presence in Russia, and all the arrangements he had made for communicating with the Raskolniks were destroyed. The younger members of the Raskol who were implicated in these revolutionary activities were arrested and publically denounced by their coreligionists, and the government intensified its surveillance of the Raskol. In the light of these developments Kelsiev's plan for another visit to Russia became academic. "If I had only known," Herzen lamented about these events in his memoirs, "it would have been possible to have delayed Vetoshnikov until Tuesday, or even Saturday. Why did he come that morning? Why did he come at all?... and why did we write those letters?" Kelsiev's grief was even more painful. Years later, when he wrote about these events, he recalled that for several days he was like "a dead man." "All was lost, and everybody turned on us with reproaches and moral admonitions. In Russia a cry of hostility rose against us. It was stifling and unbearable. I had to escape, to escape anywhere, anywhere at all... I was unable to bear it. I had to begin anew. I fled to Turkey." These laments, as sincere and painful as they were, could not resurrect young Nicholas Serno-Solovievich who perished in Siberia or lighten the load of the others who suffered in this connection. Thus ended Kelsiev's first encounter with the Raskolniks.[25]

# CHAPTER IV

# AN ATTEMPT TO REVIVE
# THE ZEMSKY SOBOR

In his work among the Raskolniks on behalf of the revolutionary cause Vasily Kelsiev seems to have acted without a definite general plan. This lack of a clearly-defined programme may be attributed to the novelty and uniqueness of his project, for he was, after all, the first revolutionary to work directly among the religious Dissenters. On the other hand, the fluidity of his plans may also be seen as a reflection of the general instability characterizing the thought and actions of the revolutionary intelligentsia of the 1860's. For the Russian radical intelligentsia these were years of many beginnings and few accomplishments, years of trials and frustrations. Nonetheless, in the course of Kelsiev's seemingly haphazard gropings, there was one task which he and the other London revolutionaries attempted to carry out in a systematic manner. This task was the revival of the Zemsky Sobor or the Assembly of the Land.

To clarify the emergence of the idea of reviving the Zemsky Sobor—an institution which had ceased to exist by the end of the seventeenth century—it is necessary to reflect momentarily on the general concepts Kelsiev and other members of the Kolokol Group entertained concerning the socio-political reorganization of Russia. In doing so it must be understood that the juxtaposition of Kelsiev and such a prominent thinker as Herzen is not intended to signify their equality as intellectuals. In fact, in relation to Herzen, Kelsiev's position resembles that of Marmeladov in relation to Raskolnikov in Dostoevsky's

*Crime and Punishment.* Just as Marmeladov is a diminutive representation of Raskolnikov, so Kelsiev's political thinking is a microcosm of the great ferment in Russian political thought of the 1860's—a ferment in which Herzen unquestionably was the leading thinker. In focusing one's attention on this microcosm, however, one may be more appreciative of the essential meaning of the ideas expressed by more prominent men of that period than one would be by confronting the same ideas more directly. A prominent figure, after all, casts a prominent shadow; whereas a lesser one accentuates the background.

Like many of his contemporaries, Kelsiev was intensely concerned with changes in the relationship between the people and the government which were necessitated by the emancipation of the serfs in 1861. He was preoccupied with such complex problems as the position of the tsar within the Russian Empire, the federalistic character of the Empire itself, the perpetual Polish question, the unity of the Slavs, and the role that the Raskolniks might play in summoning the Zemsky Sobor.

Since most of Kelsiev's political theories were recorded by him after his break with the revolutionary movement, it is difficult to periodize them. It is possible, however, to discern a pattern which, more or less, follows the fluctuations and changes in the general political mood of his time. On the eve of the emancipation of the serfs, young Kelsiev, like Herzen, Bakunin, and Ogarev, supported the basic principle of implementing reform from above. At that time it was generally assumed that only the tsar had enough power to bring about major reforms in Russia. He believed that the people were awaiting reforms from the government and not from any popular force, because they wished to avoid the consequences of an insurrection. To insure the permanence of the reforms instituted by the government, moreover, Kelsiev hoped that the tsar would become the leader of popular forces; for Kelsiev had serious doubts as to whether the people could understand the new socialist theories of the intelligentsia. The Russian masses, he observed, had followed Kuzma Minin but not Pestel. Thus, if the tsar would become a reformer and a "people's tsar," he would prevent another Pugachev from disturbing the tranquility of the Empire.

By the term "people's tsar" Kelsiev meant a constitutional monarchy. He claimed that during his secret visit to Russia in 1862, he and Nicholas Serno-Solovievich had formulated a plan for an organization which was to serve as a sounding board for public opinion in Russia. This organization was to be instituted with the government's consent but was to be independent of government control and was to extend from the capital down to the provinces in an hierarchical order. Its primary function was to be the recording and interpreting of public opinion and communicating that opinion to the tsar. Kelsiev thought that such an organization would provide not only direct communication between the people and the monarch but ultimately bring about a constitutional monarchy in Russia. This idea was compatible with the socialistic thinking of its authors, for it is well known that Serno-Solovievich was strongly convinced that on the throne of Russia "the tsar can only be either consciously or unconsciously a socialist."

Kelsiev claimed that he had attempted to persuade Herzen to become the leader or, as he expressed it, the dictator of the proposed organization. His justification of a dictatorship was based on fear that due to conditions existing in Russia at the time, it was highly probable that an individual less magnanimous than the aristocratic publisher of *The Bell* would become dictator on his own initiative. According to Kelsiev, he passionately advocated a dictatorship, for in the context of the situation existing in Russia there was no other workable alternative. He attempted to convince his colleagues in London that unless they would assume a leading role in such an organiation, all their political influence would fall into the hands of "the first bold adventurer, more daring than sensible, who would lead the youth into the streets and expose them to slaughter by the rabble, compelling the government to treat the youth in the French manner—shooting them *en masse.*" The possibility that such a leader could appear was evident to Kelsiev, for, as he observed, "all circles feel the need for tighter organization and solidarity. A clever individual could win authority over these circles, one by one, and without antagonizing the feeling of egotism and ambition of the leaders, compel them to dance to his own tune."

Although Herzen recognized the need for arousing public opinion in Russia, he refused this offer, for he suspected that such an organization would inevitably assume a conspiratorial character, and, what is perhaps more significant, he simply did not believe that the government would allow the creation of such an organization. This plan, of course, failed to materialize, and, following the exile of Serno-Solovievich, Kelsiev abandoned it completely. In retrospect one should note that the function which this structure was to have served resembled in some respects the role played by the Petrograd Soviet in 1917 prior to the November Revolution. Like the Soviet, it was to exercise almost dictatorial authority over the government without assuming the administrative responsibilities of the state.[1]

Kelsiev's study of the Raskol led him to support the theory of *oblastnost* or regionalism pioneered at the time by Afanasy Shchapov. At first, Kelsiev thought that the Russian Empire ought to be divided into three major regions in accordance with the distribution of the Slavic population: the Great Russians, the Ukrainians, and the White Russians. Each of these people was to be given a choice of either becoming fully independent or joining with the others in a federated state. Later, however, he devised a more complex plan by which the whole of the Empire would be regrouped into a federated union along the lines of its historical and ethnic components, with each unit possessing full autonomy and the right of secession from the union. Although Kelsiev failed to elaborate on the type of political structure this federation was to assume, it is implicit in his plan that there would be no place for the traditional autocracy in the reorganized state. Since at that time Kelsiev characterized himself as being "politically a federalist and economically a socialist," it is likely that he intended this ethnic union to be either a republic or at least a constitutional monarchy.

Having arrived at the idea of ethnic federation for Russia, Kelsiev proceeded to extend his proposal to the whole of Europe. He reasoned that once the federation had been realized in Russia, the Slavs living in the Hapsburg and Ottoman Empires would follow the example of their eastern brothers and form themselves into autonomous ethnic units, thereby bringing about a disintegration of the two Empires. With the emergence of the federal system throughout Eastern Europe, the West European nations would also be compelled to allow their ethnic groups to gain autonomy. Thus freed, "natural" ethnic units of the whole of Europe would join in a federal union governed by a congress made up of representatives from each ethnic group. Kelsiev regarded the territorial encroachments of one people against another to be the chief source of European wars and believed that the proposed disengagement of ethnic groups would permanently eliminate this source of perpetual enmity. Under such conditions there would obviously be no need for national governments. Paradoxically, he concluded his proposal for this European brotherhood of the peoples on a nationalistic note. "We were overjoyed by the fact that this idea originated in Russia," he explained. "Russia will now serve as an example to Europe by adopting this new system and by spreading it to Europe—the same Europe which regards Russia to be barbaric. Our patriotic feeling was really touched." Although Bakunin had advocated, as early as 1848, the creation of a "general federation of European Republics," Kelsiev's conception of an European federation based on ethnic divisions appears to be unique in the Russian political thought of the 1860's.[2]

As we have noted, the diversity of Kelsiev's political ideas reflected the nature of the mental gropings of the intelligentsia in general and of the London Group in particular. Generally speaking, Alexander Herzen feared a violent overthrow of the tsarist government even though he was desirous of a fundamental reorganization of the existing order in Russia. This was especially true following his disappointment with the outcome of the revolutions in 1848-49. His political ideas were expressed in many of his writings, but perhaps nowhere did he state his opposition to a violent revolution so forcefully as in his commentary on Chernyshevsky's letter, which was published in *The Bell* in March, 1860, in which the latter called for the solution of Russia's ills with an axe.

Herzen explained to Chernyshevsky that the publishers of *The Bell* disagreed with him not over the ideas he held concerning the need for change but with the methods by which he wanted to implement his ideas. Herzen declared that as long as there existed any possibility at all for the solution of Russia's problems by means of reason, *The Bell* would not issue a call for the axe—"this *ultima ratio* of the oppressed." In Herzen's view the possibility of effective evolutionary social and political changes in the 1860's was more than promising, since the government was approaching the completion of the enormous task of emancipating the serfs at the very time Chernyshevsky's article was published. Thus, at that time, Herzen was extremely confident in the government's sincerity and ability to be the chief reformer. Michael Bakunin, with his yearning for a violent upheaval, held views opposite to those of Herzen. Ogarev and Kelsiev seem to have occupied the middle ground, with the former leaning closer to Herzen and the latter inclining toward Bakunin. This appraisal, however, should not be interpreted to imply a constancy in their respective ideological positions. On the contrary, Herzen's fear of violence, for example, did not prevent him from supporting the Polish insurrection of 1863, and Bakunin's passion for destruction did not always triumph over his traditional Russian sentiment for the tsar. It was in the midst of such diverse political theorizing that the idea of reviving the Zemsky Sobor came into vogue with the Russian political intelligentsia of the 1860's.[3]

The Zemsky Sobor or Assembly of the Land had functioned sporadically in the sixteenth and seventeenth centuries: it met at least four times in the sixteenth century and ten times in the seventeenth century. Although the session held in 1653 was probably the last meeting of the Sobor, it was not until the reign of Peter I that this institution definitely ceased to exist. The Sobor was not an elective body in the modern sense, for its representatives were delegated by local authorities and by influential organizations such as the church and the merchant guilds. Nonetheless, the representation was relatively wide, and at the important session of 1613 peasant representatives were among its deputies. The Sobor was usually summoned by the tsar and usually called for the purpose of assuring a

wide consensus on such matters as war or basic changes in
fiscal or legal practices. Its function was purely advisory, but
at least on one occasion, in 1613, the Sobor exercised real
power. That Sobor elected Michael Romanov to the throne
and thereby instituted the new dynasty. This function of
electing the tsars, even though it was exercised effectively
only on that one occasion, was particularly important in
making this institution a suitable object for idealization by
the advocates of political reform in the nineteenth century
who looked to Russia's past for examples of democratic practices.[4]

At the beginning of the nineteenth century the idea of
establishing a representative assembly was popular with Alexander I, who commissioned Michael Speransky to draw up a
constitution. Early in the 1820's the Decembrists were preoccupied with constitutional and republican ideas. Some of the
Decembrists used the name *zemskaia duma* in describing the
representative assembly they were planning to create. In the
1840's some of the Slavophiles, with their admiration for the
ways of pre-Petrine Russia, nostalgically looked back to the
Zemsky Sobor and considered the possibility of its revival.
With the growth of historical erudition in that century an
awareness of the constitutional implications of the Zemsky
Sobor emerged along with the general awakening of interest
in the historical past. Following the emancipation of the serfs
in 1861 both the conservative nobility and the revolutionary
intelligentsia, each for its own reasons, recognized the need
for a representative assembly. The nobles needed a stronger
voice in the government because their influence in society was
seriously undermined by the loss of their serfs; the revolutionaries, on the other hand, saw the need for an assembly
which would enable the emancipated peasantry to cope with
the state bureaucracy under whose direct jurisdiction they now
found themselves. In 1861 a clandestine revolutionary paper,
*Velikoruss*, appealed for the creation of a national assembly,
but the factor which seems to have served as the immediate
stimulus to the intelligentsia's interest in the Zemsky Sobor
was Russia's millenary, celebrated in 1862. In articles and
speeches commemorating this event some members of the

radical intelligentsia praised Russia's past by emphasizing the role of the people. They especially stressed the claim that in former years the people, acting through the Zemsky Sobor, elected the tsars. Before the millenarian year was over some of these exponents of the people's sovereignty were exiled, but the idea of reviving the Zemsky Sobor gained popularity, and demands for recreating the institution were heard in many quarters.[5]

Among the London revolutionaries the chief advocate of the revival of the Zemsky Sobor was Nicholas Ogarev. As early as 1860, Ogarev had thought of making the demand for the Zemsky Sobor the central issue in the general programme of the revolutionary movement. He advocated that representatives to this Assembly should be chosen from all districts [uezdy] of the Empire. They were to be elected by the people, voting without any class distinction. The ultimate aim of this representative body was to be nothing less than the creation of a new political order in Russia. In specific terms the Sobor, in Ogarev's view, was to strive for the realization of the following tasks: 1) immediate abolition of serfdom; 2) transference of land ownership to the village communes; 3) abolition of class distinctions and the establishment of complete equality; 4) replacement of appointed judges and local officials by elected officers; 5) unification of the districts under the elected assemblies of the provinces; and 6) unification of the provinces into a common federation governed by a duma of representatives. Ogarev insisted that such a programme could be achieved only through the Zemsky Sobor, and he warned that if the tsar should prove to be unwilling to summon the Sobor, the growing discontent would eventually lead to a revolution. Feeling that the tsar would, indeed, fail to heed his warning, Ogarev called upon the revolutionaries to begin preparing for the impending revolution in order to be able to direct it along a desired course.[6]

Other members of the Kolokol Group were also attracted by the idea of reviving the Zemsky Sobor; or, more precisely, of creating a modern representative assembly under the auspices of the old name. During the years from 1862 to 1864 this idea occupied a central position in their revo-

lutionary strivings. In fact, the possibility of a peaceful transformation of Russia through the Zemsky Sobor was sufficiently popular to win the sympathy, at least temporarily, of the
most ardent advocate of a violent revolution, Michael Bakunin. Reflecting on the political aspirations of the Russian
people, Bakunin at one point rhetorically asked whether
Russia wanted a Pugachev, a Pestel, or a Romanov, and concluded that the people wanted to retain the tsar. The tsar,
however, must agree to rule through a representative assembly,
Bakunin warned. Herzen envisaged the highly-idealized institution to be a panacea for most of Russia's ills. Being a
nobleman with a "stricken conscience," but a nobleman nonetheless, Herzen thought that the Zemsky Sobor represented a
revolutionary change which guaranteed the preservation not
only of the tsar but also of the nobility. Welcoming the new
year of 1863, Herzen described 1862 as a year of rest between
1861, when the emancipation manifesto was issued, and 1863,
when the Zemsky Sobor would be established. A year later
he justified his confidence in the popular assembly by maintaining that this was the only means whereby the government
could prevent bloodshed, for many Russians were now prepared to undertake the only alternative to the summoning of
an assembly—a bloody revolution. He admitted that the revolutionaries had no clear conception of what was to follow
the convocation of the Sobor, but he comforted himself by
saying that they would have to take the first step and then
"we shall see." [7]

The idea of relying on the Raskolniks for bringing about
the convocation of the Zemsky Sobor seems to have evolved
from Shchapov's view of the Raskol as a preserver of *zemstvo*
democracy and from Kelsiev's general preoccupation with the
Raskol. Although Kelsiev was the only member of the Kolokol
Group who devoted his time primarily to revolutionary work
among the Raskolniks, the enthusiasm he showed in his work
inspired other members of the Group to become active in
developing and propagating the idea of utilizing the Raskolniks in reviving the Zemsky Sobor. Ogarev was the chief
theorizer on the subject, but Bakunin and Herzen also expounded affirmatively on the issue. To Bakunin, as to Kelsiev,

the Raskol was a manifestation of the Russian people's persistent struggle against the autocracy. Bakunin suggested at one point that with the emergence of the Raskol, Russia was divided into two opposite elements: "the official and the people's" Russia. He argued that the continuity of the history of the people's Russia which Peter interrupted had been preserved in the Raskol. "The martyrs of the Russian people, its sanctified heroes, its sacred dreams and hopes, and its prophetic consolations are embodied in the Raskol." The Raskol, according to Bakunin, had advanced the social enlightenment of the Russian people, provided them with a secret, but nonetheless a powerful, political organization, and unified them into a force. "The Raskol will arouse the people in the name of liberty, for the salvation of Russia." Herzen's enthusiasm for the "preservers" of the people's Russia was at times nearly as ardent as Bakunin's. Expressing his support for the role the Raskolniks could play in summoning the Zemsky Sobor, Herzen idealized them as being the "most energetic" element of the Russian population. Hardened by centuries of persecution, brought up from childhood in an active struggle against the existing order the Raskolniks, he claimed, "have never backed down on anything and have instead developed, together with strict morals, an iron will. From this group the real representatives of the people's aspirations will emerge." The people's aspirations, as Herzen understood them at that time, were aimed at the summoning of the Zemsky Sobor. He claimed that in spite of the recently enacted reforms, twenty million Russians still remained outside the law. These twenty million (actually about ten) were the Raskolniks. Once they realized that the Zemsky Sobor was the means by which it would be possible to achieve equality and religious freedom, the Raskolniks, Herzen believed, would support a campaign for the establishment of an assembly.[8]

During the years when the London revolutionaries were championing the convocation of the Zemsky Sobor, their publications incessantly bombarded the Raskol population with promises of the social equality and religious freedom which that institution would allegedly bring them. Ogarev urged the Raskolniks to unite with the revolutionaries in a struggle for freedom of conscience and equality before the law. He assured them that the people's assembly would include the Raskolniks, the Orthodox, and the members of other religions, since its representatives would be elected without discrimination on the basis of religion or social class. Ogarev at the same time appealed to the nationalistic sensitivity of the Raskolniks by saying that "if the Germans and the Jews, the Tartars and the pagans are permitted to worship freely, then Russians of all denominations certainly should have a greater right to do so." He urged the Raskol population to take an open stand for religious liberty, and he stressed the basic point of his argument that only through the Zemsky Sobor could they win religious freedom. "Only when the judges and administrators are elected and the tsar is the tsar of the *zemstvo*, only then will the churches be freed, only then will the people have the freedom to arrive at the truth, only then will the kingdom of truth become possible." This, he maintained, was the chief reason why the London revolutionaries were urging the Raskolniks to summon a *sobor* of representatives from all the Old Believer denominations. Ogarev intended to convert this Old Believer religious *sobor* into an all-Russian political assembly. Russia's salvation, this non-believer insisted, rested upon the Old Believers, for they alone could establish the foundation for all freedom—the freedom of belief—without which there could be no salvation for Russian society.[9]

In the early 1860's the members of the Kolokol Group, as well as some of the revolutionaries within Russia, believed that the tsar could be most effectively induced by leaflets and manifestoes into summoning a national assembly. The London revolutionaries thought that the tsar would be particularly susceptible to an avalanche of petitions and remonstrances from the people living in the peripheral areas of the Empire, since these areas were of strategic significance, had traditionally generated civil unrest, and were the areas most heavily populated by the Raskolniks. On the basis of the latter assumption the Kolokol Group, and especially Vasily Kelsiev, began searching for ways to influence the Raskolniks to participate in such a campaign. The first important practical step in this direction was realized in London in 1862, when a special newspaper was launched, which was intended to define the role the Old Believers could play in the summoning of the Zemsky Sobor. Appropriately enough this newspaper, a supplement to *The Bell*, was called *Obshchee Veche*— a name meaning "The Common Assembly" in the language of pre-Moscovite Russia. This ancient term was especially chosen with an aim of appealing to the antiquity-minded Old Believers. Actually the word *veche* had been out of use for so long that neither the Old Believers nor many other Russians knew its meaning.

*Obshchee Veche* was founded by Ogarev and Kelsiev, and during the two years of its existence (July 1862-July 1864) twenty-nine issues of this journalistic oddity were printed. Kelsiev apparently received six thousand roubles for its establishment from Soldatenkov, the wealthy Old Believer publisher whom he met during his clandestine visit to Moscow, and a smaller sum from Shibaev. Kelsiev intended the publication to be the voice of the Raskolniks, carrying material of both a theological and a political nature. Ogarev, on the other hand, wanted *Obshchee Veche* to be aimed at the lower classes in general, for he felt that *The Bell* was directed primarily at elements possessing a relatively high level of political and intellectual sophistication. Ogarev's views prevailed, and the editorial column of the initial issue explained the aims of the newspaper by indicating that *The Bell* had been unable to devote sufficient attention to the Raskolniks and the oppressed lower clergy of the official church. *The Bell*, the editors of the *Veche* went on to say, had neglected the grievances of the peasants as expressed by the peasants themselves. The peasants' problems concerning religious issues had been bypassed in *The Bell*, and the point of view of the lower classes in general had not been sufficiently expressed on its pages. "Being aware of these shortcomings, the publishers of *The Bell*, with the collaboration of V. I. Kelsiev, decided to begin a new publication, *Obshchee Veche*, in which it will be possible to give voice to all the sufferings, grievances, religious concerns, and daily needs of the people." The publishers of *Obshchee Veche* invited contributions from Old Believers, merchants, craftsmen, peasants, servants, soldiers, and all others who wished to be heard. "Let them send their grievances," the editors assured the readers, "let them express their thoughts, needs, hopes, and wishes. The publishers will print everything possible, provided it is useful and expressed honestly, even though it may be written in a semi-literate language containing errors." Although in reality the central aim of *Obshchee Veche* was to champion the establishment of the Zemsky Sobor, the editors honoured their initial promises by printing material reflecting what Ogarev thought to be the anti-governmental mood of the lower classes in general and the Raskolniks in particular. Although the circulation of this newspaper was rather limited, some of its issues reached Raskolniks living as far apart as Nizhnii Novgorod on the Volga, Johannisburg in East Prussia, and Tulcea on the Danube.[10]

Kelsiev and Ogarev devised a specific plan whereby they hoped to implement the scheme publicized in *Obshchee Veche*. First of all, relying on their publications and on direct contacts, the revolutionaries were to strive to win the confidence and support of as many elements among the Raskol population as possible. At the same time they were to concentrate chief attention on the Priestist metropolitan see located at Belo-Krynitsa, in the province of Bukovina, then within the jurisdiction of the Austrian emperor. Once the revolutionaries had established relations with the Priestist metropolitan at Belo-Krynitsa, they would attempt to persuade him to summon a council or *sobor* of his church. Relying on the communication facilities of the Kolokol Group, the Priestists would invite to this council representatives from all branches of the Raskol and from the official Orthodox church. Once such an ecumenical gathering was assembled, discussions were to be diverted from religious to political issues, and the council was either to be led into issuing a solemn proclamation calling for the convocation of an all-Russian Zemsky Sobor or proclaim itself the Zemsky Sobor and invite secular representatives to join. It was in conjunction with this plan that in the summer of 1862 the chief attention of Kelsiev and Ogarev was directed toward Belo-Krynitsa.

To understand the presence of the Old Believers in the

Hapsburg Empire, it is necessary to recall that in their search for religious freedom, many of the adherents of the old faith fled beyond the borders of their homeland. By the middle of the nineteenth century there were three important Raskol centres outside Russia: one in the Austrian Empire, another in the Ottoman Empire, and one in East Prussia. The Raskolniks living in East Prussia were predominantly the adherents of the Priestless denomination and had little contact with other groups of the Raskol. The Raskolniks of the lower Danube region on the territory of the Ottoman Empire and those of the Austrian Empire, on the other hand, were predominantly Priestists. Because of their hierarchical organization the latter two were able to maintain close ties not only with each other but also with the Old Believers in Russia. According to the reports of the Russian government, there were in the late 1850's 4,000 Raskolniks in the Austrian Empire, living mainly in Bukovina, bordering Russia along the river Prut, and 36,000 in the Ottoman Empire. The majority of those living in the Ottoman Empire were located in northern Dobrudja, in the Danube delta; others lived in Constantinople, in other European territories of the Empire, and a few settlements were located in Asia Minor.[11]

The establishment of the Priestist hierarchy at Belo-Krynitsa in 1846 was an extremely important event in the history of the Priestists. As has been noted, at the time of the original schism in the seventeenth century only one bishop, Paul of Kolomna, remained loyal to the old non-reformed faith. He, however, was immediately incarcerated and died soon afterwards. The absence of clergymen with the rank of bishop threatened the old orthodoxy with virtual extinction, since no lower clergyman possessed the authority to ordain priests. One of the immediate results of this situation was, of course, the fragmentation of the Old Believers into the Priestist and the Priestless denominations. The Priestists who through an influx of priests from the state church succeeded in preserving clerical traditions were, nonetheless, unable to establish an hierarchy in spite of persistent attempts to do so for almost two centuries. Missions were dispatched in search of an Old Believer bishop not only to such far-away lands as Japan but also to the legendary city of Kitezh. The significance of the establishment of the hierarchy at Belo-Krynitsa in 1846, therefore, can hardly be exaggerated.

The first prelate of the Belo-Krynitsa hierarchy was Metropolitan Ambrosius, a Greek bishop whom the Priestists persuaded to accept their faith. Because of the strict anti-Raskol policies of Nicholas I, it was impossible to locate the prelacy within the boundaries of the Russian Empire. In fact, the Russian government was so perturbed by the establishment of the Old Believer hierarchy that it took drastic diplomatic measures for its suppression. The Holy Synod threatened to cut off all the financial assistance it was giving to the Patriarch of Constantinople unless he would do everything in his power to induce Ambrosius to abandon the Priestists, and the Russian Foreign Office threatened the Austrian government with reprisals unless the latter would withdraw its permission for allowing them to locate their prelacy in the Hapsburg Empire. In compliance with diplomatic pressures from the Russian government, the Austrian authorities closed the Belo-Krynitsa prelacy in the spring of 1848 and sent Metropolitan Ambrosius into exile. As a result of the revolutionary turmoil of 1848-49, however, the Old Believers were able to reopen the prelacy late in 1848, and, although Ambrosius remained in exile, the hierarchy survived, for prior to his exile he had consecrated several Russian bishops. One of these, Bishop Cyril, succeeded Ambrosius as metropolitan of the Priestists. Cyril was still officiating in that capacity in 1862, when the London revolutionaries turned their attention toward Belo-Krynitsa.[12]

In the summer of that year Kelsiev sent a letter to Belo-Krynitsa, addressed to Archdeacon Filaret Zakharovich (in the secular world Fedor Zakharovich Ulianov) who served as an administrative assistant to Metropolitan Cyril. Filaret was an efficient administrator and a self-made intellectual. Kelsiev learned of him from Bishop Pafnuty, when the latter was in London. Like Pafnuty, Filaret was one of the "progressive" activists within the Old Believer church, and, in fact, he belonged to Pafnuty's brotherhood. Although officially serving as an administrative assistant, Filaret was the real

power behind Metropolitan Cyril, for the latter's mental senil-
ity seems to have been far in advance of his physical age.
Filaret's answer to Kelsiev's letter arrived in London after
Kelsiev's departure for Constantinople. Ogarev, therefore,
was the one who attempted to nurture this newly established
link with the Old Believers by continuing to correspond with
Filaret. The texts of the letters Filaret received from London
are not available, but from his answers to these letters, and
from various references to his relationship with the revolutionaries made in other sources, it is possible to discern the
intentions of his correspondents in London. Their minimum
objective seems to have been the establishment of an additional outlet for their publications, especially for *Obshchee
Veche*, and their more important goal was the enlistment of
the prelacy for the summation of the Old Believer council,
which was to be converted into the Zemsky Sobor.

In addition to the letter, Kelsiev also sent Filaret a parcel
containing copies of the London publications. This parcel was
intercepted by the Austrian police, who confiscated its contents
and politely, but authoritatively, advised Filaret to discontinue
his extra-religious activities. The Archdeacon promised to
comply, but in his letter to London explaining this development
made it clear that he was desirous of continuing to correspond
with the revolutionaries and provided them with two alternative addresses for that purpose. The London revolutionaries
were encouraged by Filaret's willingness to deal with them
and in the autumn of 1863 dispatched an agent to the Austrian
Empire for direct contact with the influential Archdeacon.
The mysterious young emissary of the Kolokol Group identified himself to Filaret by showing him a copy of the last
letter the Archdeacon had written to Ogarev. In the course
of their conversations the young man revealed detailed knowledge of Filaret's dealings with London and reiterated the
basic message of *Obshchee Veche* concerning the alleged advantages the Old Believers would gain from close cooperation
with the revolutionaries. This secretive messenger vanished
as abruptly as he appeared, however, when Filaret warned
him of the efficiency of the local police. He left behind him
a parcel containing leaflets and blank forms. The forms were

designed to be filled out by persons making a monetary donation, and they bore an emblem showing two hands clasped
together and crowned with the words "Zemlia i Volia" or
"Land and Liberty."

This incident, although insignificant in itself, demon-
strates the extent of communications existing in 1863 between
the revolutionaries and the Old Believers. It also confirms
other evidence to support the fact that, in spite of interference
from the Austrian police, the London revolutionaries persisted
throughout 1863 in their attempts to win the support of the
Belo-Krynitsa hierarchy for the establishment of the Zemsky
Sobor.[13]

The end result of the revolutionaries' strivings for communication with the Old Believer hierarchy was not as dis-
astrous as the culmination of Kelsiev's dealings with the
Moscow Old Believers, yet in both instances their efforts
proved to be futile. They not only failed to exert lasting influence over the hierarchy but were also publicly condemned
and cursed by the Metropolitan, who appealed to his followers to avoid the revolutionaries as one avoids wild beasts.
Cyril's condemnation of the revolutionaries was issued in
February 1864 in an epistle affirming the Priestists' loyalty
to the tsar. His words to his followers left no doubt concerning the position the Belo-Krynitsa hierarchs had assumed
relative to the revolutionaries. Cyril instructed his flock to
show their good judgment and true devotion by avoiding and
fleeing from all of the tsar's enemies, whether they be "the
rebellious, seditious Poles or the insidious atheists who nestle
in London." The Prelate warned his followers that the London "atheists" were stirring up all of the European countries
with their writings and were "sowing the weedy teachings of
the thrice-cursed Voltaire—the enemy of Christ, the most
impious vessel of Satan—who has stirred up the whole universe
with his devilish teachings." He instructed them that Voltaire
had tried "to destroy belief in Christ; had tried to abolish
civil and religious laws; threatened the destruction of all ecclesiastical offices; had attempted to empty the holy altars
and destroy the holy thrones; and striven to establish total
anarchism by convincing the people that there was no God

outside the human mind." He also warned them that Voltaire's followers teach the same principles, and, therefore, "they call themselves, and they are, 'freethinkers' [vol'nodumy]." Relying on the methods earlier Raskolniks had employed in proving the allegedly satanic characteristics of Patriarch Nikon and Emperor Peter I, Metropolitan Cyril went on in this epistle to "prove" that the London "freethinkers" were the apostles of Satan, for the sum of the word vol'nodum, he claimed, was the apocalyptic, beastly figure 666. He urged the Priestist Old Believers to curse the "loathsome" freethinkers. "To all of them: to the originators of these teachings, to those who are spreading them, and to those who are accepting them—let it be pronounced by all Orthodox Christians [the Old Believers]: anathema! anathema! anathema! Avoid the thrice-cursed ones as one avoids terrible beasts and creeping serpents . . ." To Kelsiev and Ogarev these words were especially painful to read, for it was evident from the erudite contents of the epistle that it had been composed by none other than the scholarly Archdeacon Filaret Zakharovich—the main link between the revolutionaries and the Belo-Krynitsa prelacy.[14]

In considering the possible reasons for the sudden break between Belo-Krynitsa and London, two factors must be recognized as having been the most influential: an internal crisis within the Priestist denomination and the response of the Raskolniks in general to the Polish uprising of 1863. Following the creation of the hierarchy in 1846, the Priestists living in Russia had no reservations about affirming their loyalty to a metropolitan ruling from a foreign soil, for there was little possibility at that time of locating the see within Russia. Also, they were only too happy to submit to the authority of the metropolitan of Belo-Klynitsa because his very existence was a realization of their long-standing aspirations. By the 1860's, however, with the relaxation of the government's repressions against the Raskolniks and because the permanency of the hierarchy seemed to be assured, the Priestist bishops in Russia began to express separatist tendencies. When the metropolitan's policies did not coincide exactly with their wishes, they now found it possible to question the right of a "foreigner" to rule over them. These bishops had, of course, been invested by the metropolitan of Belo-Krynitsa. Nonetheless, their hesitancy in submitting themselves to his authority culminated in a serious rift which found expression in an *Encyclical* or *Okruzhnoe poslanie*, issued in Moscow, in February 1862.

The *Encyclical* was composed by a learned Priestist monk named Ksenos (in the secular world Ilarion Georgievich Kabanov). The document was signed by Bishop Anthony of Vladimir, and by three other bishops and five lesser clergymen. Anthony was aspiring to the leadership of all the Priestists in Russia, independent from Belo-Krynitsa. He employed the *Encyclical* as a means of formalizing his claim to that leadership. In the ten articles constituting the *Encyclical* the main principles set forth included a solemn affirmation of the legitimacy of the prayer for the tsar and the royal family and a recognition of the official church as orthodox, differing from the Old Believer church only in some forms and rituals. These and other principles of the *Encyclical* were contrary to the accepted practices of the Old Believer church and were considered by some to be of profound theological significance. Because of this the *Encyclical* brought about a rift within the Priestist denomination which was not healed until 1906.[15]

The turmoil evoked by the *Encyclical* seriously undermined the authority of Metropolitan Cyril of Belo-Krynitsa. His vacillation between the "Encyclicists" [*Okruzhniki*] and the "Anti-Encyclicists" [*Protivo-okruzhniki*] alienated him from both of these elements. At one point in that struggle the supporters of the *Encyclical* threatened to bring Cyril to trial. Subsequently, each side modified its respective position, but, following the outbreak of the Polish insurrection in January 1863, the conflict was again intensified. The clause legitimizing the prayer for the tsar was now strongly emphasized by the Encyclicists, because they wanted to make certain that in the face of the Polish insurrection the government would have no ground for questioning their loyalty. In their enthusiasm for demonstrating their loyalty they expelled their own Metropolitan, who in March 1863 was visiting Moscow. Their action was in part motivated by their suspicions that the

Metropolitan was implicated with the London revolutionaries. The latter, of course, supported the Polish rebellion. Curiously enough, both sides—the opponents and the defenders of the Metropolitan—attempted to voice their arguments against each other in *Obshchee Veche*. Although Ogarev refrained from publishing their arguments, he did publish an article on the subject, in which he defended the Metropolitan's position. Ogarev's support of the Metropolitan, however, did not prevent the latter from turning against the revolutionaries when he realized that by their support of the rebellious Poles, the London revolutionaries had evoked wide-spread enmity against themselves in Russia. It was in an attempt to clear himself of the charge that he was implicated with the revolutionaries, therefore, that Cyril issued the epistle anathematizing the "free thinkers" who "nestled" in London.[16]

The anathema pronounced by the Priestist Metropolitan against the revolutionaries in February 1864 terminated the expectations the latter had entertained concerning the possibility of gaining a lasting influence over the Old Believer hierarchy. The preceding description, however, is not a complete account of the revolutionaries' activities among the Raskolniks in general, for Vasily Kelsiev—the most active proselytizer of the revolutionary gospel among the religious Dissenters—had been devoting his attention during that time to the Raskolniks living in the Ottoman Empire.

Kelsiev's flight to Turkey, as he described his departure from London, began late in August of 1862, when, once again, leaving his submissive wife and child in the British capital, he undertook a mission intended to enlist the Raskolniks' support for the revolutionary cause. This time he chose the capital of the Ottoman Empire to serve as his laboratory for testing the hypotheses he had advanced concerning the Raskolniks' revolutionary potential.

Travelling by way of Paris and Marseille, he arrived in Constantinople on October 4. Through the arrangements he had made with the officials of the Polish emigrant group whose headquarters were located in the famous Hotel Lambert in Paris, Kelsiev communicated with the chief representative of that group in Constantinople, Colonel Stanislas Jordan.

The Poles had been influential in the Ottoman Empire since the early 1840's, when their leader, Prince Adam Czartoryski (1770-1861), acting on the initiative of the French government, sent his first envoy to Constantinople. Czartoryski's first ambassador in the Turkish capital was a colorful Ukrainian-born adventurer, Michael Czajkowski or Chaikovsky (1804-86) who, largely by the force of his personality, had gained wide influence for the Poles among both the French diplomatic corps and the officials of the Porte.

Kelsiev characterized Chaikovsky as a "landlord from Berdichev, a Russian by origin, a Uniate by faith, a *littérateur*, and a fantast." At the time of the Polish insurrection of 1830, Chaikovsky had organized his serfs into a military detachment and, after a skirmish with the Russian police, had joined the insurgents. Following the defeat of the Poles, he migrated to Paris and managed to win sufficient confidence from Czartoryski to be appointed as an envoy to Constantinople. Subsequently, Chaikovsky broke with his superiors at the Hotel Lambert, entered the Turkish military service, organized a cossack legion, fought in the Crimean War against Russia, accepted the Islamic faith, and assumed the name Mehemet Sadyk-pasha. Subsequent to all this, he joined the Orthodox church, returned in 1872 to his native Ukraine, wrote his memoirs, and in 1886 committed suicide. When Kelsiev arrived in Constantinople, Chaikovsky was still influential among the Old Believer cossacks living in the Ottoman Empire and with the Turkish government; Colonel Jordan, however, was now the chief representative of the Hotel Lambert Poles. The Russian revolutionaries in London maintained a liaison with the Hotel Lambert, and Colonel Jordan thus was instructed by his superiors to assist the representative of the Kolokol Group in Constantinople."

The aims of Kelsiev's mission to Constantinople have been referred to in his own and in Bakunin's writings. According to Kelsiev, by moving to the Ottoman Empire he hoped to establish new connections with and broaden the influence of the revolutionaries over the Raskolniks. He also wanted to assess the general situation in that area with the hope of creating new routes of communication for transmission of the

London publications into Russia. "All of this, together with my disappointment over the unsuccessful outcome of the trip to Russia," he claimed, "compelled me to go to Turkey and the Danubean provinces, where a great multitude of Russians live, and from where I hoped to establish contacts with Petersburg and Moscow." Writing to Herzen shortly after Kelsiev's arrival in Constantinople, Bakunin explained that there was much fruitful political work to be done in the East. He advocated more active propagandizing among the Raskolniks in that region, and he spoke of the need for the establishment of supply depots in Constantinople and Galati, from where he wanted to open commercial routes to Odessa. Bakunin also envisaged the possibility of distributing revolutionary propaganda materials to the Don and the Volga regions by way of the Caucasus. To accomplish this, Bakunin emphasized, "Kelsiev alone, in spite of all his determination, is not enough." Since there is some indication that Bakunin wrote after having received a letter from Kelsiev, it is likely that he simply reiterated the aims Kelsiev himself had formulated. At any rate, acting largely on his own initiative, but with support from London, Kelsiev attempted to carry out most of the tasks outlined in Bakunin's letter.[18]

Relying on the well-established connections with the Poles, Kelsiev did not have long to wait for an opportunity to communicate with the Russian Dissenters. Colonel Jordan introduced him to an Old Believer named Semen Ilich Vasiliev, who had been sent to Constantinople by his townsmen of Vilkovo with the difficult task of petitioning the Porte. The small settlement of Vilkovo is located on the Moldavian side of the Danubean delta. As a result of the boundary adjustments made in connection with Rumania's recently-acquired autonomy, its inhabitants lost their rights to fish in the Danube. It was about this problem that Vasiliev sought to approach the Turkish government. Vasiliev spoke neither French nor Turkish and was grateful therefore for Kelsiev's offer to assist him in presenting his case to the proper authorities. Kelsiev, of course, had no direct influence in the Porte, but, with the cooperation of the Poles, he was in a better position for accomplishing the task than the timid uneducated Vasiliev.

This arrangement was mutually satisfying, for Kelsiev saw in it an opportunity to convince the Old Believers of his own importance by performing a practical deed on their behalf. What is more, the Vilkovo fishermen had agreed to pay him for his services—a fact of no small importance to the migratory revolutionary without a permanent source of income.

In spite of Kelsiev's high enthusiasm and Vasiliev's dire need, in the end the Old Believers' plea failed to bring the desired results. Perpetual procrastination was an ingrained characteristic of the Turkish officialdom. Not only did a petitioner seldom receive an affirmative answer from the officials, but the occasions were even more rare when their answer was clearly negative. As a result of this practice, the petitioner usually abandoned the field of such a hopeless battle of his own accord, experiencing neither defeat nor victory. The Vilkovo petitioners proved to be no exception: having waited for nearly a year, they finally terminated their dealings with Kelsiev.

Simultaneously with his work on behalf of the Vilkovo Old Believers, Kelsiev was also searching for other channels through which he could spread the influence of the revolutionaries in that region. One such channel he envisaged to be in the Caucasus, a territory which was then in the process of being colonized by the Russians. Constantinople at that time was to the Caucasian refugees what Paris was to the Poles. Like the Poles in the metropolis on the banks of the Seine, the Caucasian mountaineers intrigued and conspired in the famous city of the Bosporus. The rival factions within each of the two groups were at times far more hostile to one another than to their common enemy. In view of the fact that their respective homelands were being occupied by the same enemy, however, there was a feeling of mutual sympathy and understanding between the Poles and the Caucasians. In fact, Colonel Jordan boasted to Kelsiev that there were forty thousand Polish soldiers fighting in the Caucasus against Russia. Jordan hoped that their presence there would lead to a mass desertion by Polish officers serving in the Russian army and that there might be a general uprising among the cossacks in this connection, for he regarded the latter to be historically loyal to Poland.

With Jordan's assistance, Kelsiev became acquainted with several influential Caucasian tribesmen in Constantinople. From them he learned that the Old Believer cossacks, who had been brought to the Caucasus as colonizers, were generally more sympathetic to the conquered indigenous population than to their own government which exiled them there. The information Kelsiev gleaned from these contacts led him to consider the possibility of creating an independent federation of Caucasian tribesmen and Russian cossacks. He discussed his idea with some of the chieftains, and they, according to Kelsiev, were favourably impressed with his plans. With the aid of the Poles, he began to send *The Bell* and *Obshchee Veche* to the Caucasus, hoping to establish a permanent route for their distribution into the Kuban and the Don regions. With the Russian suppression of the Polish insurgents in 1863, however, Colonel Jordan's anti-Russian feelings negatively affected his relationship with Kelsiev. One of Jordan's acts in this connection was to remind the Caucasian chieftains that Kelsiev, after all, was a Russian and hence their enemy. A word from the influential Colonel sufficed for alienating Kelsiev from his newly-found Caucasian friends. Realizing the impossibility of dealing with the Caucasians against Jordan's wishes, Kelsiev was compelled to abandon his "Caucasian project" without having derived from it any lasting benefits.[19]

Another scheme engendered by Kelsiev during his adventure in Constantinople was a plan for the establishment of an Old Believer bishopric under the direct control of the London revolutionaries. Although in terms of its fruitfulness this scheme was another wink in the dark, it is worth mentioning for the purpose of adding to one's appreciation of the diversity of Kelsiev's revolutionary gropings.

Of all the members of the Kolokol Group, Kelsiev was the most realistic in appraising the significance of the rivalry generated by the *Okruzhnoe poslanie* of 1862. Long before the Belo-Krynitsa Metropolitan had cursed the London "Voltaireans," Kelsiev perceived that there was little possibility for the revolutionaries to win Metropolitan Cyril to their cause. He also was able to surmise that because of the separatist tendencies within the Priestist hierarchy, Cyril was no longer the powerful personage he had once been. Thus as early as July 1863, Kelsiev warned his companions in London that Belo-Krynitsa was already "a part of history," meaning that the authority of the Metropolitan was a thing of the past. Consequently, Kelsiev began to search for other means by which to gain influence over the Old Believer hierarchy, and this search led him to write a letter to a bishop of the official Russian church, inviting him to join the Old Believers.

At the time of Kelsiev's activities in Constantinople, the chief Russian ecclesiastical representative in Jerusalem was Bishop Cyril of Melitopol (not to be confused with the Priestist Old Believer Metropolitan Cyril of Belo-Krynitsa). In 1863 Bishop Cyril was summoned by the Holy Synod to return to Russia. Desirous of spending Easter in the Holy Land, Cyril delayed his departure. Upon learning of these developments, Kelsiev surmised that the Bishop was on the verge of defecting from the Orthodox church. The resourceful revolutionary hastily dispatched a letter to the Holy Land, inviting Cyril to become the bishop of the Old Believers living in Asia Minor. They were a group of cossack migrants who had refused to recognize the Belo-Krynitsa hierarchy because its founder was a Greek. Kelsiev assured the Bishop of Melitopol that he, because he was a Russian, would readily win the loyalty and the obedience of the Old Believers, and because the Bishop was also a young intellectual, he would be likely to attract other intellectuals into the Raskol. The religiously-political revolutionary attempted to cajole the Bishop by eulogizing the Raskol's allegedly democratic attributes. He wrote to Cyril about the uniqueness of the Raskolniks' way of life, which, in his view, contained the seeds of "a unique new civilization." What was needed, Kelsiev syllogized, were the kinds of leaders who would be capable of developing this new civilization. "It was on the basis of such an assumption," he explained, "that Herzen's group, which I represent here, is trying to do everything possible to establish close relations with the Old Believers . . ." The Synod and other official institutions, Kelsiev went on to explain, would be against the Bishop, but "all those who believe in liberty, equality, and the brotherhood of man" would be on his side. He assured Cyril that *The Bell* and the whole emigrant press would be at his service and that he would be supported by all of the revolutionary organizations in Russia.

From the tone of his letter one can readily perceive that Kelsiev envisaged for Cyril a role much more important than that of being bishop over a few Old Believer villages in Asia Minor. Without stating this precisely, he apparently contemplated the possibility of replacing one Cyril with another at the helm of the Priestist hierarchy. The versatile revolutionary was fully aware that the new Cyril would be indebted to the Kolokol Group for his position. In spite of the potential potency of its contents, however, Kelsiev's letter evoked no reply from Bishop Cyril of Melitopol. For a time Kelsiev thought of going to Jerusalem, but unable to meet the expenses of such a journey, he was compelled to relegate the entire fanciful scheme to his growing index of failures.[20]

Kelsiev's most important undertaking in Constantinople involved an influential lay leader of a group of Old Believer cossacks. This man, Osip Semenovich Goncharov, sometimes called Ganchar (1796-1880), was an Ataman of the Nekrasovtsy—the Old Believer cossacks living in the Turkish province of Dobrudja. Dobrudja is located between the Danube and the Black Sea, extending from the mouth of the Danube in the the north to just north of the city of Varna in the south. Presently it is divided between Rumania and Bulgaria. Goncharov was closely associated with Sadyk-pasha or Chaikovsky. He was sufficiently prominent to merit a personal interview with a French foreign minister and sufficiently subtle to maintain secret connections with agents of the Russian government. Both Goncharov and Chaikovsky had been instrumental in founding the Old Believer prelacy at Belo-Krynitsa, and there existed between the two a symbiotic necessity for the maintenance of their respective influence over the Dobrudja cossacks. Goncharov needed Chaikovsky's influence with the Porte, and Chaikovsky needed Goncharov's influence with the cossacks. When Kelsiev met Goncharov in 1862, the latter was engaged in commercial pursuits, in the course of which he travelled in both Russia and Western Europe.

Upon learning of Goncharov's forthcoming business trip to Marseille, Kelsiev persuaded him to visit Herzen and Ogarev in London. Having won Goncharov's consent, the jubilant revolutionary hastened to send a letter to London simplifying the complexity of Goncharov's character and, at the same time, magnifying his importance in order to impress Herzen and Ogarev with the effectiveness of his own diplomatic skill. Kelsiev explained to his comrades that Goncharov was a simple fellow, "a sack which carries whatever one places in it." At the same time, he wanted to impress upon them that Goncharov was an influential figure among the Dobrudja Old Believers. Those Old Believers, according to Kelsiev, regarded Goncharov as a "kind of Mazzini, an expert in political affairs," and they hardly took a step without his advice.

Goncharov fulfilled his commitment to Kelsiev and spent six days in London (August 14-19, 1863). Herzen was amused and somewhat bewildered by his unusual visitor from the East. In his famous memoirs, the publisher of *The Bell* drew a colorful sketch of his initial encounter with the Old Believer Ataman.

> We were then living in Teddington. Without knowing the language, it was not easy to reach us, and therefore I went to the railroad station in London to meet him. Out of a passenger car stepped a well-to-do Russian peasant. He was dressed in a grey caftan, had a Russian beard, was rather lean but strong, muscular, tall, and tanned. He carried a bundle made of a colorful kerchief.
>
> "Are you Osip Semenovich?" I asked.
>
> "I, dear Father, I." He gave me his hand.
>
> He opened his caftan, and I saw on his undercoat a large star, obviously Turkish, for they do not give stars to peasants in Russia.

Goncharov stayed with the Herzens, and he insisted on eating only bread (which he had brought with him) and drinking only water. Only on Sunday did he allow himself to indulge in a small serving of boiled fish, a glass of milk, and a small glass of sherry. In spite of Herzen's repeated objections, Goncharov continued to address the aristocratic London revolutionary with the honourific title "Your Excellency." "Just in case," he explained, that his host might be an important person. Herzen did not agree with Kelsiev's appraisal of the old Ataman. He found him to be neither simple nor easily manipulated. According to Herzen, Goncharov was a man with a characteristically Russian mind, armed with Eastern cunning, the circumspection of a hunter, and the hesitancy of a man who from early childhood had been accustomed to lawlessness and close proximity to powerful enemies. Herzen thought that Goncharov had come to London not because of the power of Kelsiev's persuasion but because he wanted to find out more about the connections the London revolutionaries maintained with the Raskolniks and to learn about the extent of their influence in general. He wanted to determine whether the Raskolniks would profit by their relationship with London, because, according to Herzen, "he would side with Poland, Turkey, or whatever group he would find the most advantageous to his Nekrasovtsy."

Herzen's explanation of the reasons for Goncharov's visit to London appears plausible, and it was substantiated by Natalie Ogarev who was with Herzen at the time. Natalie noted that the Old Believer did not discuss the purpose of his trip, not even with Herzen. She explained, however, that Herzen nevertheless understood that "the Turks were beginning to exert pressure on the Nekrasovtsy," and the latter wanted to have the support of the London revolutionaries, since they could not rely on the Russian government which they, allegedly, distrusted and feared. Goncharov, therefore, was trying to determine "whether Herzen's party had any real power." Having heard a great deal about the Kolokol Group from other Old Believers, the Polish emigrants, and from Kelsiev, Goncharov came to London probably to ascertain the extent of their influence. A number of specific concerns made it important for him to learn more about the revolutionaries. He was, for example, suspicious of their motives yet anxious to deal with them in order to elevate his own standing among the Old Believers, for the wider were his contacts, the weightier was his authority. Above all, for nearly a decade he had been trying to gain freedom for two Old Believer bishops exiled by the Russian government during the Crimean War. In connection with the latter point he probably reasoned that by writing about the subject in *The Bell* Herzen might be able to influence the Russian government in favour of the prisoners. Although this was most unlikely, one should also consider the possibility that, since he was implicated with agents of the Russian government, Goncharov could conceivably have travelled to London on their behalf.

The London revolutionaries spared no efforts in explaining to Goncharov the need for a close cooperation between them and the Old Believers. He was well-briefed on the subject by Kelsiev; when he was in Marseille, he received a letter from Ogarev dealing with the subject; and he listened most attentively to the revolutionaries' explanations of the matter in London. Yet, the only definite commitment that Goncharov made in London was his promise to take the initiative in submitting a petition to the tsar on behalf of the Poles and the Old Believers. Outside of this matter he apparently made few promises. In fact, Herzen observed that each time Goncharov was asked to make a definite commitment on some issue, they received from him either a plea of ignorance or a splash of verbal borsch such as, "We, of course, cannot understand, being little and ignorant people. And they, of course—just look at them—well, they are noblemen, properly so, only so nonchalant in their manners. They tell you, for example, 'Well Ganchar, don't worry, we'll cope with it; we will do it for you. Do you understand? . . . Everything will be to your satisfaction.' Yes, it is true, they are generous people, but think of it, *when will they* cope with it? . . . with such Palestine." Although this is an illustration of Goncharov's comments on the negotiations he had conducted with the Polish officials in Paris, he apparently employed the same technique in his discussions with Herzen.[21]

Following his return to Constantinople, Goncharov, together with Bishop Arkady of Slava (an Old Believer settlement and a monastery near Tulcea) submitted a petition to the tsar on behalf of the Dobrudja Old Believers. Goncharov mentioned this fact in a conversation with Kelsiev but did not elaborate on the contents of the petition. A short time later, Chaikovsky, who, by virtue of his influence in the Porte, still considered himself to be the senior Ataman of the Dobrudja cossacks, allegedly told Kelsiev that the Turkish officials were greatly disturbed about the petition the Old Believers had submitted to the tsar. The Turkish government became aware of the address when its text was printed in the French language newspaper *Courier d'Orient*, published in Constantinople. Chaikovsky himself was seriously disturbed by the event, because the officials held him responsible for the actions of the Old Believer cossacks. The text carried in *Courier d'Orient* called upon the tsar to intercede on behalf of the Dobrudja cossacks and allow them to migrate to Russia. Chaikovsky supposedly told Kelsiev that the Turks would carry out severe reprisals against the cossacks for this. When Kelsiev transmitted this warning to Goncharov and Bishop Arkady, the latter fled across the Danube to the city of Izmail. Goncharov, too, genuinely feared for his own as well as the safety of his coreligionists.[22]

Kelsiev credited himself with averting the impending consequences. He allegedly persuaded Chaikovsky to minimize the importance of the affair and the latter was able to convince the Turkish authorities of the cossacks' innocence. Furthermore, to insure the permanence of this pacification, Chaikovsky arranged for the appointment of Kelsiev as an interpreter and an administrative assistant to the Turkish governor of Dobrudja. Cordial relations were restored, and Bishop Arkady returned to his monastery without suffering any reprisals. No action was taken against the Old Believers, and our account of this affair would have terminated at this point were it not that this incident contributed to the final break of the relations between the Old Believers and the revolutionaries.

Goncharov held Kelsiev responsible for the publication of the controversial address and notified Herzen of the developments surrounding this issue. In his letter to Herzen, Goncharov explained that Kelsiev was unhappy with the Old

Believers because they had failed to establish a printing press for him. He implied that Kelsiev had created this incident in order to obtain a position for himself. The aged Ataman especially resented the fact that Chaikovsky had compelled him not only to write a letter of recommendation on Kelsiev's behalf but even forced him to pay Kelsiev's fare to Tulcea where the latter was to work in his new position. Goncharov's allegation that Kelsiev was unhappy with the Old Believers because they had failed to establish a printing press for him was a valid one. Kelsiev had spent a great deal of time trying to set up printing facilities in Turkey, but, after months of negotiations with the Old Believers, he was dismayed to learn that in September 1863 Bishop Arkady had made an agreement with an Ukrainian printer for the establishment of a printing press in Dobrudja independent of the London revolutionaries. To Kelsiev this was still another failure in his revolutionary career, and he blamed it on Goncharov and Arkady.

The focal point of Kelsiev's activities in Constantinople was, undoubtedly, his search for ways to summon an Old Believer church council which was to be expanded into the Zemsky Sobor. In this regard he expected a great deal from Goncharov's visit to London, and he was disappointed when he realized that Herzen and Ogarev had failed to effect any appreciable change in the political notions held by the staunch Old Believer Ataman. It is possible, therefore, that following Goncharov's return from London, Kelsiev decided to change his revolutionary tactics. Shortly after Goncharov's return from London, Kelsiev's brother Ivan (who had arrived in Constantinople in July and of whom more will be said in the chapter that follows) wrote a letter to Herzen explaining the reasons for his planned departure from Constantinople to Dobrudja by saying that the revolutionaries should concentrate their attention chiefly on the masses instead of the leaders of the Raskol. The leaders, Ivan maintained, were too dogmatic to be influenced by new ideas. He reasoned that since the leaders have the masses behind them, the revolutionaries must temporarily deal with the former, but only for the purpose of gaining time to turn the masses against

their leaders. Shortly after he had written this letter, Ivan
moved to Dobrudja to work among the Raskol population
there. Ivan's ideas concerning these tactics had undoubtedly
developed in conversations with his elder brother. In fact, two
and a half months after Ivan's departure to Dobrudja, Vasily
himself moved there. None of this, however, could serve as a
direct evidence of Kelsiev's complicity in the publication of
the Old Believers' petition to the tsar.[23]

Chaikovsky, too, was involved in the controversy generated by the petition. Being a romantic adventurer at heart,
Chaikovsky aspired to become another Bohdan Khmelnitsky
and dreamed of the day when he would re-establish the famed
Zaporozhie Sich. Since the Nekrasovtsy were the only cossacks
over whom he could exercise his fictitious hetmanship, he was
jealous of anyone who infringed upon his authority over them.
It is quite possible, therefore, that Chaikovsky saw Goncharov
as a rival in this respect. Even though in the past Goncharov's
submissiveness to Chaikovsky was ostensibly beyond reproach,
the Old Believer Ataman did enjoy a considerable degree of
personal influence over the cossacks, and, what is more, he was
beginning to develop independent connections with the Porte.
Conceivably, therefore, Chaikovsky may have used the address
to the tsar as a means of discrediting the cossack chieftain in
the eyes of the Turkish authorities. The appointment of Kelsiev as an interpreter to the governor of Dobrudja, moreover,
could be seen as an attempt by Chaikovsky to undermine Goncharov's standing with the governor and the Dobrudja
cossacks. Here again, however, one finds an abundance of
circumstantial evidence but no definite proof of responsibility
for the incident.

In considering the central figure in this controversy—
Osip Semenovich Goncharov—it must be noted that in the
petition which he claimed he had sent to the tsar (a copy of
which he forwarded to Herzen) Goncharov did not make a
request for moving the Dobrudja cossacks to Russia. Yet, the
Ataman who possessed "the circumspection of a hunter" may
well have petitioned the tsar on this issue. This is possible in
view of the fact that only two years earlier he conducted
negotiations with the Russian government on this very issue.

The grievances and problems which had precipitated the earlier negotiations still existed in 1863,[24] and the fact that Goncharov spent the final years of his long and eventful life in Russia may also be of some relevance to the case in point. It is possible, therefore, that Goncharov may have written the address which was published in the French-language newspaper, yet it is inconceivable that he would have wanted this address printed in any newspaper. In view of the lack of sufficient information, however, it is simply not possible to clarify the latter point in more precise terms.

Although the controversy over the address helped to precipitate the break between the Raskol leaders and the revolutionaries, it must not be overlooked that this relationship was in jeopardy even before the eruption of that controversy. Goncharov clearly was not "a sack which carries whatever one places in it." He had his own reasons for making his trip to London, and the adamancy of his will did not melt, as Kelsiev had expected it would, under the torch of the revolutionary eulogies he heard there. He was willing to cooperate with the revolutionaries only to the extent that it was beneficial to his own interests and those of the Dobrudja cossacks. Finally, causes external to the immediate issues involved in the controversy between Goncharov and Kelsiev, especially the repercussions of the Polish uprising, also had a negative effect upon their relationship.

By late summer of 1863, Kelsiev was becoming aware of the signs foreboding a decline in the prestige of the Russian revolutionaries in the East. Their popularity with the Polish emigrants was undermined because they were of the same nationality as those who crushed the Polish insurgents, and their relations with the Raskolniks were strained because of their support for the same insurgents. In the months following the Polish insurrection the Old Believers living within the Russian Empire seem to have been especially anxious to affirm their allegience to the tsar, and, like many other groups of the society, they sent loyalty addresses to him. The Old Believer cossacks in Dobrudja had wide contacts with their coreligionists across the border, and, following the latter's example, wished to affirm their own loyalty to the tsar.

Goncharov's controversial petition, therefore, could simply have been such a loyalty address. Along with the Metropolitan's *Epistle*, which anathematized the London revolutionaries, this address seems to have been part of a concerted effort by leaders of the Old Believers to disassociate themselves from the revolutionaries. In the end, the breach between the Old Believer leaders and the revolutionaries convinced the latter of the futility of their efforts in respect to the convocation of the Zemsky Sobor. Following the publication of Cyril's *Epistle* in the spring of 1864, the London revolutionaries continued for a time to print their outcries for the summoning of the Zemsky Sobor, but, with the cessation of the publication of *Obshchee Veche* in July of that year, their outcries tapered off to hardly audible whimpers.

# CHAPTER V

# GOING TO THE PEOPLE OF DOBRUDJA

Although the phenomenon known in Russian history as *khozhdenie v narod* or the "Going to the People" movement has generally been associated with the decade of the 1870's, the basic elements which inspired this movement were articulated in London in the preceding decade. What is more, several young men connected with the Kolokol Group ventured to "go to the people" in the 1860's. Among these was Vasily Kelsiev. The people among whom he went were the Russian Raskolniks living in Dobrudja.

The publishers of *The Bell* first expressed the idea of "going to the people" in commentaries related to the student unrest which, in 1861, led to temporary closure of the University of St. Petersburg. Writing in his anti-tsarist publication about the events taking place in St. Petersburg, Herzen challenged the students of that University to spread across the country and begin working for the revolutionary cause among the people. "Listen," he directed them, "from every corner of our vast fatherland—from the Don and the Urals, from the Volga and the Dnieper—the groans are growing, the murmur is rising. It is the gathering roar of an ocean wave—a wave pregnant with storms, a wave which, following a dreadfully oppressive calm, is beginning to seethe. Go to the people! To the people!—that is your destination, banished men of learning . . ." Several months later Ogarev reiterated Herzen's message and developed further the idea of "going to the people." He appealed to the faculty and students of the

University of St. Petersburg to spread their knowledge among the people. "Let them close the universities!" he defiantly cried out. He advised the students and the professors to scatter into the provinces and become teachers of the masses. "We need wandering teachers," he told them. "The apostles of science, like the apostles of religion, cannot remain seated behind the locked doors of their houses of prayer. Their mission is to propagate their learning everywhere. Until now we have not had teachers for the people, but the government is creating them—unwittingly, accidentally, senselessly. Make use of this opportunity." Ogarev directed the restless St. Petersburg academics to scatter themselves throughout the Empire and begin establishing public libraries, schools, museums, and hospitals. Speaking specifically to members of the faculty, he urged that they establish academic chairs throughout the country: in municipal halls, in the public buildings of the provinces, in private dwellings, and, indeed, in the market places. "Forward, young generation!" he commanded. "Leave your stuffy auditoriums, scholastics, and enter the openness of free understanding and social action. Abandon your dead letters and create living thought. Go out as warriors in the name of common truth and the freedom of the common people." The general mood of Ogarev's appeal was at least as fervent as that characterizing the participants in the "Going to the People" movement of the 1870's.[1]

As was the case with the idea of reviving the Zemsky Sobor, the concept of "going to the people" was mainly expounded by Herzen and Ogarev, but Vasily Kelsiev was the one who attempted to apply that concept in practice.

Because his efforts seldom culminated in success, it is not an easy task to discern the basic aims behind Kelsiev's revolutionary undertakings. This is true of his work among the Old Believers in Dobrudja. The overall aim of the London revolutionaries relative to the Raskol was to establish close relations between the revolutionaries and the Raskolniks. There was no single plan outlining the way this was to be accomplished. Various activities in this connection were undertaken, and of these Kelsiev's work among the Old Believers and the publication of *Obshchee Veche* were the most significant. The general purpose for establishing these relations remains extremely vague and can be identified only as an attempt to win the support of the Raskolniks for the revolutionary cause. The interpretation of this cause, as has been stated earlier, varied from one revolutionary to another and from one period of time to another. While it is true that many of the radical intellectuals in the 1860's spoke of a revolution, they also spoke of the Zemsky Sobor and a people's tsar. Four decades were to elapse before the Russian revolutionaries were provided with a definitive answer to the incendiary question "What is to be done?" The revolutionaries of the 1860's were only asking the question, and this was to a large extent Kelsiev's predicament. He wanted to "revolutionize" the Raskolniks, but he was not exactly certain what this process involved. There does not seem to be any other way to describe his aims, therefore, except through a careful analysis of his general ideas and through a description of his specific acts.

The masses whom Kelsiev chose to "revolutionize" were the Old Believer cossacks who called themselves Nekrasovtsy or the Nekrasovites. Kelsiev had learned from the government reports in London that these Old Believers were the descendants of the Don cossacks who had revolted against Peter the Great under the general leadership of Kondraty Bulavin. They called themselves Nekrasovtsy in honour of their Ataman, Ignat Nekrasov. In 1708, to avoid surrendering to the armies of Peter the Great, Nekrasov led his detachment of some two thousand cossacks and their families across the Turkish border into Kuban, a region north of the Caucasus. The main contingent of these cossacks was later resettled on the lower Danube in the province of Dobrudja.

As has been indicated in the preceding chapter, Dobrudja is presently divided between Rumania and Bulgaria. It is located between the Danube and the Black Sea, extending from the Danube delta to just north of Varna and covering an area somewhat larger than that of Massachusetts. The entire province remained under the Ottoman rule from its occupation by the Turks in the fifteenth century until its partition between Rumania and Bulgaria by the Treaty of Berlin in 1878.

The Nekrasovtsy established themselves in the vicinity of the city of Tulcea, in the northern part of the province. In return for a pledge to fight against Russia, they received special privileges from the Porte, including exemption from taxation and the right to practice their old Orthodoxy in complete freedom. Subsequently, some members of their group moved to Asia Minor, but the majority remained in Dobrudja, where their number increased because of the influx of other Old Believer refugees from the Russian Empire. By the middle of the nineteenth century, eight thousand of the forty thousand Raskolniks living in the Danube region were Nekrasovtsy.

Tulcea, a city with a population of about fifteen thousand, was at that time the provincial capital. Its population was a conglomerate of many diverse languages and cultures. In its streets it was not unusual to hear a Moldavian speaking to a Bulgarian in broken Greek and a Ukrainian swearing at his Russian neighbour in Polish. These alien surroundings took their toll from the collective identity of the Nekrasovtsy; although they succeeded in maintaining thei rreligion, their native language, and the cultural mores of their ancestors, by the 1860's they had lost many of cossack attributes. In spite of the fact that the Nekrasovtsy organized a military detachment at the time of the Crimean War, the descendants of the fiery combatants were far more proficient in fishing than in fighting when Kelsiev began his revolutionary activities among them. In fact, in the year following his arrival on Dobrudja, the Nekrasovtsy, at their own request, were relieved of the obligation of fighting against Russia, forfeiting, of course, the privileges they enjoyed in conjunction with this obligation. They lived in five villages (Slava, Zhurilovka, Sarychiol, Syry-Kioi, and Kamen) in the vicinity of Tulcea and maintained themselves mainly by fishing, trading, and farming. In religion they were Priestist Old Believers, and, with the exception of those few who migrated to Asia Minor, they recognized the authority of the Belo-Krynitsa hierarchy.

Kelsiev had begun to exert some influence over the Old Believer masses in Dobrudja even before his break with Goncharov. With the aid of the Polish emigrants he began sending the London periodicals and various revolutionary proclamations to Dobrudja soon following his arrival in Constantinople. One of these proclamations was his own. It was lithographed in Constantinople in February 1863, and some three hundred copies of it were distributed in Dobrudja. Its text was also printed in *Obshchee Veche*, assuring thereby its distribution among the Raskolniks in Russia. Instead of a title, Kelsiev's proclamation bore the Russian Orthodox cross, and its opening sentence began with these words: "The day of reckoning is coming." "Any day now," Kelsiev assured the Dobrudja Old Believers, "our Christ-loving warriors will march on Moscow to summon the people's representatives to the Zemsky Sobor. The evildoers will be driven out beyond our borders, to the Germans." He entreated the Dobrudja cossacks to begin organizing and arming themselves. "The present parasitic state rule," he told them, "a foreign rule, is coming to an end." The new age, Kelsiev claimed, was to be the age of the people's government, a Holy Russian government, and he stressed the *holiness* of the new revolutionary order which was to be created. From the general tone of this proclamation it is evident that he was attempting to deal directly with the Old Believer masses.[2]

The first revolutionary to encounter the Dobrudja cossack masses, however, was not Vasily Kelsiev but his younger brother Ivan (1841-64), whose arrival in Constantinople was mentioned in the preceding chapter. While it has not been possible to determine a great deal concerning Ivan's earlier life, it is possible to gain considerable insight into his mental attributes and the intensity of his commitment to the revolutionary cause.

Ivan arrived in Constantinople in July 1863. At that time he was only twenty-two years of age, yet he had already experienced exile and imprisonment for political activities. His arrest resulted from the leading role he assumed among students during the political unrest at the University of Moscow in October 1861. In the spring of the following year he was exiled to Verkhoturie, a provincial city west of the Ural Mountains in what is today the district of Šverdlov. Several months later, however, he was moved to the Peter and Paul fortress and soon thereafter to a temporary prison in Moscow. In Moscow he was sentenced to be confined in a fortress for four months, but before this sentence was carried out he escaped from the prison and fled abroad. In both his escape from prison and his flight from Russia, Ivan was aided by the Land and Liberty society, of which he was a member. He planned to go to London, but having learned of his brother's presence in Constantinople, decided to share Vasily's burdens there.[3]

Unlike his elder brother, who had failed to develop a systematized political philosophy, Ivan Kelsiev, in spite of his youth, was committed to a clearly defined set of beliefs. He proclaimed himself to be a socialist, and he believed in the Hegelian principle of subordinating the individual to the state. In a letter confiscated by the police when he was in exile at Verkhoturie, Ivan expressed his political philosophy in a concise and forceful manner. The letter was written to Countess Elizabeth Vasilievna Salias, a prominent Moscow socialite of liberal leanings whose son was one of Ivan's close acquaintances. Ivan informed her that he had renounced the beliefs and convictions held by her and her class and that he had moved over to the side of the "radicals." He explained to the Countess that, having thought a great deal about political problems, he now accepted socialism and republicanism. "To me," he argued, "as an idealist and a Hegelian, the autonomy of the individual, which is the basis of the culture you desire, is an unbearable concept." Human society, in his view, was an organic whole, and the individual was only a part of that whole, only a facet of it. From this assumption he deduced that no legal right, no tradition should be such as to justify the domination of the whole by any of its parts.

Ivan's view of human society as an organic whole led him to believe that the autonomy of the individual would be detrimental to the well-being of society. It would be in the interest of the whole, however, to provide for the well-being of its parts, since the organic whole recognizes itself in each individual. Because of this, Ivan thought, a socialist society need not be afraid of despotism, since the latter condition is impossible under the order in which the conscience of the individual is subordinated to a consciousness of the whole. Despotism can exist only when one part tries to absorb "the best juices of the organism." Ivan challenged the Countess to look at the reality surrounding her for proof of his views. Myriads, he pointed out, work for a few, yet those myriads— "the builders of Crystal Palaces"—live in hovels. "Where is justice?" he demanded. How can one find justice in such "unnatural conditions?" As was the case with many other Russian radical intellectuals, Ivan Kelsiev felt responsible for the Hegelian unfolding of history. Having placed himself in this melioristic position, there was no way for him to compromise with a socio-political order which allowed the "builders of Crystal Palaces" to live in hovels. The aim of his life, Ivan declared, was to promote universal moral perfectibility [*nravstvennoe sovershenstvo*]. "I have already become accustomed to looking at this aim," he explained, "as the one to which all other, private, aims must be subordinated. This for me is the universal criterion of mankind. Everything that does not coincide with it I reject, even if it be life itself."

Ivan's political ideas reflected the various developments which were influential in his day. His letter to Countess Salias was written when the evidence and implications embodied in Darwin's *Origin of Species* were stirring the minds of educated Russians no less than they were exciting the intellectuals of Western Europe. Ivan's organic theory of human society and his assumptions concerning moral perfectibility were a mixture of ideas he had evolved from his reflection on the Darwinian notion of evolution in the biological world and the Hegelian proposition concerning a progressive unfolding of history. Ivan was convinced that progress was an inherent characteristic of the natural world, and man had no choice but to align himself with this progressive development, because to oppose it was to fight against the general process of nature.[4]

Because of his keen intellect and his moral sensitivity, the burden of the disparity which existed between the morality he desired and the realities of the social and political world fell on Ivan's shoulders at an early age. It offended him, stirred his emotions, and intensified his latent idealism. Ivan subordinated all other interests to his urge to change the world. For him, the only alternative to a total belief in progress was reconciliation with injustice and a surrender to hypocrisy. Ivan Kelsiev was a youth with a noble spirit; he chose to believe in progress and moral perfectibility.

In spite of his membership in the Land and Liberty revolutionary organization, Ivan Kelsiev was not quite certain that the betterment of the world must necessarily be achieved through violent revolution. In answering the questions put to him in 1862 by the investigating commission, Ivan contended that he was not one of those radicals who advocated a fundamental change in society through a violent revolution. On the contrary, he was a radical in the sense that he advocated a fundamental transformation of society. He had dedicated himself, he averred, to perfecting society through education of the people and the propagation of high moral principles. In another letter to Countess Salias, written when he was abroad and therefore at a time when he was free to express genuine opinions, he made it clear that he was not at all convinced of the need for a violent upheaval in Russia. Also, in spite of his belief in the necessity of subordinating the individual to society, he himself was far from being a mere automated sloganist. On the contrary, he was sufficiently individualistic to violate one of the cardinal principles of the revolutionary ethic—the expediency of eulogizing the people— by calling the Russian people "Tartars and wild hordes." He even thought that the Russians had the kind of government they deserved, for government, he reasoned, is the product of society. In view of this condition the Russian intelligentsia, he thought, should work not so much for a change of government as for a transformation of society.

Theoretically, then, Ivan was committed to the development of a society which morally, culturally, and intellectually would be superior to the one in which he lived. It was only natural, therefore, that within the society of his time he would tend to find more of these "superior" characteristics among the elite groups than among those whom he called the rabble or *chern*. "My mission," he wrote to London from Dobrudja, "is the destruction of the rabble; my ideal is an aristocratic republic in which everyone is an aristocrat and from which the rabble is entirely absent; my concept of equality is the equality of people who are intellectually fully developed and are ennobled by a rational cultured relationship with one another . . ." Since he regarded his fellow intellectuals to be champions of the idea of moral perfectibility, he urged them to assume leadership of the masses; and, because of the circumstances in which he found himself in Dobrudja, he made it his personal mission to assume leadership over the Raskol masses living there.[5]

Ivan's decision to approach the Dobrudja Old Believers was made before his brother's break with Ataman Goncharov. In a letter explaining his decision Ivan spoke of the "first half of the war" as the period in which the revolutionaries would work with the leaders, and the "second half" as the period in which they would have to turn the masses against their leaders. Because of the influence the Raskol leaders maintained over its masses, it was essential for the revolutionaries, according to Ivan, to begin their work with the leaders. At the same time, however, the revolutionaries' real aim should be the development of influence among the masses. Ivan thought that sooner or later the leaders of the Raskol would react against the revolutionaries, and therefore it was essential that the latter should have sufficient independent influence over the masses to counteract that reaction. By going to Dobrudja, Ivan aimed not only to expedite the "first half of the war" but also to begin working on the second stage. Another consideration in Ivan's move to Dobrudja was the fact that Tulcea, being close to the Russian border, was more suitably located than Constantinople for him to reestablish contact with Land and Liberty in Russia. Upon arriving in Tulcea early in September 1863, his immediate aim was to follow up his brother's work related to the establishment of a printing press, while his general goal was still the summoning of the Zemsky Sobor. Since Bishop Arkady of Slava was the most influential Old Believer of that region who had had dealings with the revolutionaries, Ivan's first task was to arrange for a meeting with him.[6]

The Priestist Old Believers of Dobrudja were divided into two bishoprics, with one bishop residing in Tulcea and another in Slava. Arkady of Slava was the more influential of the two, and his activities extended far beyond the religious domain. Arkady (in the secular world Andrei Rodionovich Shaposhnikov) became bishop of Slava in 1854, and in that capacity he virtually ruled over the Dobrudja Old Believers until his death in 1868. Chaikovsky referred to him as "a bearded fox," for, according to Vasily Kelsiev, the Bishop had a beard "a half-yard long," with each hair being so distinct that one was reluctant to believe that his beard was not artificial. The "foxy" attributes were Arkady's keen intelligence, unusual craftiness, and his ability to speak softly but act decisively. He, for example, was successful in establishing and maintaining order among the traditionally quarrelsome cossacks and went so far as to prohibit the drinking of tea among them, yet he did not find it inappropriate to make a profit by investing money donated for the construction of a church. Furthermore, like his friend Goncharov, he was sufficiently broadminded to communicate with the revolutionaries but adequately cautious in preserving his own position to report his contacts with them to the tsarist consular officials.

Shortly after Ivan's arrival in Dobrudja, he spent a whole day with Bishop Arkady in the latter's monastery at Slava. Slava, or, as the Turks called it, Kyzyl-Hissar [The Red Castle], was a beautiful village situated at the foot of a steep hill some fifteen miles from Tulcea. The monastery was located in a forested area, with each monk living in a small individual hut and practicing a trade, such as making shoes or pottery. According to Vasily Kelsiev, the monks knew how to read and write and were less dogmatic and superstitious than their lay Old Believer neighbours. Writing to London about his visit to the monastery, Ivan boasted that he had been able to expound on his revolutionary aims to the Bishop and others for a whole day "without any interruptions." The Old Believers, he claimed, listened as no one had listened to him before. They not only memorized to the smallest detail everything he said but also agreed with him on everything. Although the Old Believers were apparently reluctant to make any specific promises relative to the Zemsky Sobor, Bishop Arkady did reaffirm his willingness to solicit funds in order to finance the establishment of a printing press. Ivan viewed this meeting as a promising beginning in his revolutionary venture among the Old Believer cossack masses.[7]

Ataman Goncharov was one of the influential Old Believers present at the marathon political seminar conducted by the young Hegelian in the Old Believer monastery. The cunning cossack chieftain may well have memorized most of the things the vociferous young revolutionary uttered there, but if he appeared to have agreed with everything Ivan said, then his skill in operating under a double standard of morality was at least as high as that of the young revolutionary. Ivan, after all, was trying to win the leaders for the first stage of "the war" so that the revolutionaries would be able to liquidate them in the second stage, and Goncharov had sent a loyalty address to the tsar only a few weeks before his alleged agreement with Ivan's anti-tsarist views. In comparison to Arkady and Goncharov, then, it appears that Ivan Kelsiev was their junior in more than just age.

In spite of the claim of being highly successful at Slava, on his return to Tulcea Ivan found himself alone among strangers. In the same letter in which he boasted to Ogarev about his meeting with Arkady, Ivan described the unbearable conditions in which he had to live in Tulcea. He possessed no material means for survival, yet for several months was unable to find employment. He wrote to London that he was "grounded in shallow waters" and was using all his strength to bring himself "afloat again." For several months he received no word from his brother and possessed "not a penny" in his pocket. The only reason he had a place to live was because he was taking advantage of the hospitality which had been extended to him. "A most unusual thing has happened to me," he confessed, "something which I am ashamed to admit, but must tell you. I am utterly at a loss. I have lost all of my ability to propagandize among the Raskolniks. I am unable to continue my relations with them, to invent or to undertake any-

thing new, or to complete that which I have started." He went
on to say that his personal misfortune absorbed him to such
an extent that not one single political idea came to his mind
and that he was unable to lift his hands to perform any worth-
while task. Had he been merely poor, Ivan explained, he would
not have abandoned the political work, but to live for two
and a half months at the expense of a person who is a complete stranger to him and to his cause was morally almost
impossible to bear. To search for work from morning tonight
for two and a half months and then not find it; "to beg for
work, as one begs for alms, from people whom one despises
yet has neither the right nor the ability to scorn; to know
finally that even the kind of work I might be able to find here,
after these prolonged efforts, will be degrading and poorly
rewarding, and, worst of all, will have no relation to my real
mission—all of this, think what you may, is beyond my power
to endure . . ." To comfort himself and his fellow-revolutionaries in London, Ivan sorrowfully added that if he could only
have his own hovel to live in and his own bread to eat, he
would resume his revolutionary work, "for there is so much
to be done here."

His hopes for betterment of his predicament were soon
realized. A month after he had written to London, Ivan succeeded in securing a teaching position. "I am being resur-
rected again, my dear friend," he wrote to Ogarev in December
1863. "After a long struggle I have finally persuaded the local
Ukrainians to open a school, and now, as a teacher, I have
my own hovel." Although this was a significant improvement
over his earlier situation, the new conditions were far from
ideal. Ivan complained that his teaching was seriously ham-
pered by the demands the parents of his charges imposed upon
him. He was not allowed, for example, to use any book other
than an old psalter as a text; and, moreover, the parents ob-
jected to having their children taught "too much." They
merely wanted their children to learn to read and write "a
little." They considered it harmful to teach "these knaves
everything," because they thought that children who learn
too much stop respecting their parents. Both Ivan and later
Vasily Kelsiev noted in their writings that these Ukrainians

were especially hostile toward the teaching of geography to their children. "We are not Mericans [Americans]," Vasily quoted them as saying, "we live off the land. Why should you teach our children to know about the deep? If they learn about the sea, they will no longer be willing to plow the land. To the devil with your gography [sic]; we are Orthodox and not Mericans." Ivan never did have more than ten pupils in his school, and some of these did not attend regularly, since the parents considered their education to be less important than their work at home.

The harshness of Ivan's existence even after this improvement is well illustrated by the fact that his letter, quoted in the preceding paragraph, was not mailed for four months because he lacked the money to pay for the postage. In March of 1864 he informed his comrades in London that he had resigned from his pedagogical duties with the Ukrainians and moved to a more lucrative teaching position with an American Methodist mission. Even then, however, he still complained about the enormous hardships he had endured during his earlier months in Tulcea. He complained that he had worked like a slave from morning to night and at night was tormented with nightmares because of exhaustion. Yet, for his work, he received literally only bread. With a sorrowful tone he informed his more affluent friends in London that it was cold and damp in Dobrudja, that he had no books, no underwear, no paper, and that all around him was "ignorance of the worst kind—ignorance, superstition, and coarseness." The latter conditions were especially difficult for him to bear, because they tended to undermine the very essence of his spiritual vitality—his belief in man's capacity to attain a state of moral perfection. In desperation he was beginning to suspect that "there is not the slightest hope or possibility of improving the society that surrounds me . . ." [8]

As one reads the correspondence of these revolutionaries, one cannot but sense a striking similarity in tone between their letters and the fictitious epistles of Dostoevsky's *Poor Folk*, published two decades earlier. The mood of their letters induces one to sense that there is something of Makar Devushkin, something of Varvara Dobroselova in the lives of these heroically ascetic socio-political alchemists.

With his move to the new teaching position in the winter of 1864, Ivan's lot improved significantly. The American Methodist Mission, which worked with the Russian Molokan sect in Tulcea, proved to be more generous in remuneration than his previous employers. Moreover, the Molokans were rather liberal in respect to the curriculum he was to follow. And more important, he now was no longer alone, for his brother Vasily and the latter's family joined him in December. Vasily's arrival in Tulcea was a happy event for both brothers, for they were deeply devoted to each other.

Vasily's wife, Varvara Timofeevna and their daughter Maria, endearingly nicknamed Malusha, had come from London to Constantinople in August. Varvara's presence in Tulcea brought comfort to both brothers, for their "hovel" now assumed the semblance of a home. For the "lean, lymphatic" and tubercular Varvara Timofeevna, however, the burden of physical existence did not lighten with her move from the foggy shores of the alien Thames to the swampy lowlands of the inhospitable Danube, for at the time of her arrival in the East her husband's meagre political fortunes were rapidly declining. The devastating effect of the Polish uprising had already begun to undermine the prestige of the entire Kolokol Group. Describing his life in Constantinople in the last months preceding his move to Dobrudja, Vasily complained to his associates in London in much the same terms as Ivan was doing in his letters from Tulcea. Vasily wrote his aristocratic colleagues that he was lost, crushed, insulted, and weak in spirit. Alcohol, Vasily informed them unashamedly, was his main source of comfort now. He told them that he could clearly see that he was reaching a dead end and that he was a stranger not only to the West but to Russia itself. He thought that his native land was now lost to him and that it was no longer possible for him to go on living, as he had done in London, with the hope that someday he would be able to return to Russia. Europe and Westerners in general, he claimed, "from a Frenchman to a Greek or a Bulgarian," became unbearable to him. "I simply hate a man in a frock coat," Kelsiev said. "I cannot endure the sight of *homo à la franca*. Following the betrayal of Poland by the West and the betrayal of *The Bell* by Russia, my last beliefs, my last hopes have collapsed. Formerly I had many illusions—now I am pure. I have freed myself from ancient Adam and have paid the price of a broken heart. I had to find myself a corner to live in, a piece of bread to eat." To use his own words, Vasily Kelsiev had arrived in Constantinople "like a prince" and left it "like a pauper."[9]

When Kelsiev first came to Constantinople, the fact that he was a member of the Kolokol Group "opened all doors" for him; whereas in Tulcea, when it became known that the influence of the Kolokol Group was waning, many Raskolniks deliberately avoided the revolutionaries. The "doors" that were opened to Kelsiev in the capital were mainly those of the Polish emigrants and of the Greek and Italian merchants sympathetic to the liberal cause which Herzen represented. Some of them fed and sheltered Kelsiev and at times even advanced small sums of money to him. In Dobrudja, on the other hand, he faced an entirely different situation. For one thing, the masses with whom Kelsiev chose to work scarcely had enough to meet their own needs, and secondly, the Dobrudja Old Believers reflected the general mood of hostility toward the revolutionaries caused by the latter's support of the Polish insurrection. The Poles, as has been noted, had also become hostile toward Kelsiev, only their hostility was motivated by the fact that he was from the country which crushed the insurgents.

Thus, the man who left Constantinople "like a pauper" arrived in Tulcea without any household necessities and without underwear. In Tulcea the Kelsievs were greeted by "a ringing frost," for they came there late in December. Shortly after their arrival, Varvara Timofeevna fell ill and had a miscarriage. Vasily himself had to serve as midwife. Later, living in utter poverty, they were "nearly overpowered" with lice. "It was repugnant," Vasily wrote to London. "The four of us—I, my wife, my brother, and Malusha—used to lie there, almost on a bare floor, our teeth chattering from the cold; and yet, having grieved over our misfortunes, we still managed

to sing the *Marseillaise* and *Ça ira*. This was the way our
new life began and our revolutionary consulate in Turkey was
established." Having poured out his grief, Vasily, like his
younger brother, went on to add a hopeful note. "We have
established ourselves," he remarked with compulsive joviality,
"and already have a samovar, and we no longer snuff the
candles with our fingers. We have beds, too. In other words,
we live in *a gentlemanlike manner* and can take another person [another revolutionary] tomorrow if necessary."[10]

At the time of his arrival in Dobrudja Ivan was still preoccupied with plans for the summoning of the Zemsky Sobor.
Following Vasily's break with Goncharov, however, this aim
was all but abandoned by the two brothers. With Vasily's
move to Dobrudja, therefore, the Kelsiev brothers were still
guided by a general theory of revolutionizing the Raskolniks,
but they acted largely on the basis of the demands and op-
portunities arising in their day-to-day existence. The only
political task which they systematically planned at that time
was the organization of what they called a revolutionary
phalanx. The phalanx was to be established in Dobrudja as a
permanent community or *obshchina* of revolutionaries, subordinate to the London revolutionary centre. The general aim
of this task force was to include the following: 1) to "civilize"
the local youth by training them as propagandists, 2) to dis-
seminate propaganda within Russia by all possible means, and
3) to serve as a refuge to all those who would be compelled
to leave Russia for political reasons. The phalanx was to work
in close cooperation with Land and Liberty.

At the practical level Ivan considered his teaching to be
the first step in "civilizing," that is, revolutionizing, the Raskolniks' children. Vasily, serving as an interpreter and adviser
to the governor of Dobrudja on behalf of the Nekrasovtsy
cossacks, hoped to use his influence for the general advancement of the revolutionary mission, especially in respect to the
organizing of the phalanx. The two revolutionaries thought
that in the future the phalanx should develop and control
educational institutions for the entire Raskol population of
Dobrudja. They planned to found a secondary school or
gymnasium and establish printing facilities for the purpose of

printing their own educational materials and a revolutionary newspaper. They also hoped to create an orphanage for the numerous homeless children of the region. These children, the Kelsievs reasoned, were excellent prospective converts for the revolutionary cause. In fact, in a letter written in February 1864, Vasily even boasted to his London colleagues that he was contemplating the purchase of some children for that purpose from a widowed father. In order to appreciate the real meaning of such seemingly innocent acts, it must be remembered that these were religiously political men, and, no matter how innocently apolitical some of their acts may appear, the motives behind them, or at least their justification for them, were almost invariably related to their political commitments.[11]

Ivan and Vasily Kelsiev were active in distributing printed propagandistic materials both in Dobrudja and across the border into Russia. Ivan wrote to several influential Old Believers within Russia and to the central committee of Land and Liberty. One of the difficulties that the two brothers encountered, however, was the shortage of published materials from London. That shortage was due to the disruption of communications brought about by the abortive Polish insurrection. In their letters to London they constantly implored Herzen and Ogarev to send them more copies of *The Bell* and *Obshchee Veche*, but to no avail. Channels which had been available to them before the Polish uprising simply were no longer operative. Ivan's letters to Russia also brought no response. The sensitive youth was utterly frightened by the prospect of being permanently isolated from Russia. Must he, Ivan rhetorically argued in his letters—a person whose only passion for life was his political cause—remain separated from that cause? "This cannot be," he wrote. "It frightens me even to think of it. I will run away from Tulcea a thousand times before I reconcile myself to the thought that all the connections between me and the new emerging world are severed. This simply cannot be! This connection—my love for that world—nothing can break." Vasily, too, was concerned about and increasingly more depressed by the isolation in which they struggled in Dobrudja. Repeatedly, he begged Herzen and Ogarev for more news and publications. Without books, he wrote, not only were the Tulcea revolutionaries perishing of boredom, but their political work was being jeopardized. In spite of these demands and pleas from Tulcea, London publications seldom reached Dobrudja after 1863.

In retrospect, the difficulties in communication between the Tulcea and the London revolutionaries appear to have been mutually beneficial, for in 1864 the optimism of the revolutionaries in London was not much higher than the optimism of those in Dobrudja. Like the all-pervasive London fog, a painfully oppressive melancholy or *khandra* seems to have imbibed the very souls of the once spiritually vibrant publishers of *The Bell*. Even before the defeat of the Polish insurgents became apparent, Herzen seems to have had a premonition of the calamitous effects it forebode.

> Rare are the moments [he wrote in his diary in February 1863] when it comes to my mind to write something down in this book—another pain, another misfortune, another worry... If it were not *zu deutsch* to do so, this book could be called *the book of groans*.
>
> The Polish insurrection, the fate of the Russian officers, all around me sickness, discord, ignorance, parting. The familiar phrase again comes to my mind: "What endless chances are given to man to suffer and what minute ones to enjoy!" What is more, happiness and harmony fly away, hardly cutting into, hardly touching the present; but sorrow, sickness, the expectation of misfortune, misfortune itself—all this lingers and lingers, cutting deeper like a coarse wooden plow [*sokha*] upturning the graveyards.

Herzen's New Year's eve entry in his diary greets the approaching year of 1864 with a feeling of outright horror. "Never since 1851 have I stood on the threshold of a new year with such horror. There is no hope for anything bright either in my political or private life." Thus, inadvertently, the Tulcea revolutionaries were fortunate in hearing so infrequently from London, for one sorrow seldom extinguishes another.[12]

In spite of the serious hardships in their personal lives, the Kelsiev brothers managed to nurture at least a grain of optimism for the success of their plans so long as they confined these plans to theorizing. Confronted with the actual conditions existing in Dobrudja, however, their confidence in the efficacy of their ideas tended at times all but to abandon them. The Nekrasovtsy, on whose whim, after all, the final outcome of the Kelsiev brothers' plans actually rested, did little to dispel the doubts of the young revolutionaries. As the months passed, Ivan could hardly cope with the swarming thoughts which challenged his convictions concerning the feasibility of man's attaining a state of moral perfection. While pursuing his goal of winning the Raskol masses to the revolutionary cause, Ivan at times reasoned quite contrary to his basic convictions. The peasants, he wrote to his friends from Dobrudja, attract the revolutionaries by their sufferings, but this does not mean that those who live in misery are necessarily more noble than those who do not suffer. "Give the peasant the freedom to express his own individuality, unfasten the chains that hold him, and you will see the kind of fat burgomaster he would become. Watch, and you will see the kind of belly he would grow, and how his fat fists would glide over the backs of his fellow peasants." The Dobrudja Old Believers, according to Ivan, were so slavish that they would never dare to challenge the authority of their superiors. This characteristic, he thought, was deeply ingrained in them. Being a slave to the priest, an Old Believer, according to Ivan, was an intolerable despot in his own home. Among the Dobrudja Old Believer cossacks the wife never dared to sit at the table with her husband, and the children must remain standing until their parents told them to sit down. The father seldom spoke to his family; and when he did, he spoke authoritatively and in short outbursts. "They all fall to their knees before their superiors: the layman before the priest, the priest before the monk, the monk before the bishop, the wife before her husband, the children before their parents. . . . No wonder that drunkenness and lewdness on one side and mental dullness and superstition on the other are carried to such extremes among them." [13]

Vasily, too, was appalled by the extreme traditionalism of the Dobrudja Old Believers. He discovered that they were even fearful of the reforms Alexander II was implementing in Russia. The tsar was giving too much freedom to the peasants, they thought, and this would only encourage disrespect for the authorities. Words such as "uprising" and "revolution" were despised by the Dobrudja Old Believers, and they considered it absurd to try to change the world. When Kelsiev attempted to discuss political problems with them, they would simply shrug their shoulders and say: "We are unimportant people and there is nothing we can do about these matters. Go and talk to the rich merchants: if they will agree with you, we too will be on your side." In their individual contacts with the revolutionaries the Old Believers usually listened politely, said little, and did nothing to implement the proposals they had heard.

On the basis of his observations of the ways of the Dobrudja Old Believers, Vasily at times generalized about the character of the entire Russian Raskol and even about the character of the early Slavs. The Dobrudja Raskolniks, he thought, were factional, distrustful, and quarrelsome. Such a view was a drastic departure from the conclusions he formulated about the Raskolniks on the basis of the reports he had read in London. He even thought that the factionalism which characterized the Dobrudja Raskolniks was analogous to conditions which had allegedly existed among the Slavs in Riurik's day. Among the Dobrudja Raskolniks, according to Kelsiev, every clan hated every other family. Suspicion and distrust, he claimed, were so prevalent among them that the presence of an outsider served to ease somewhat the psychological tension under which they lived. Long after he had abandoned Dobrudja, Vasily wrote that it became fully clear to him "why the Slavs had sent envoys to the Varangians with their humble request: 'Judge and rule over us, for our land is great and rich, but there is no order in it'."

Much to Vasily's consternation and dismay, he also

learned that the Dobrudja Old Believers did not respect honest, munificient officials such as he regarded himself to be. In his capacity as interpreter to the governor of Dobrudja, Kelsiev at times performed administrative tasks involving the Old Believers. (Russian and French languages were used in communications between the governor and the Russian-speaking Old Believers. Kelsiev spoke no Turkish, and the governor, while being fluent in French, spoke no Russian.) When his clients, mainly from among the Nekrasovtsy, came to realize that he neither expected them to undergo the customary bureaucratic delays nor to bribe him, they lost respect for him. In fact, they became suspicious of his motives, stopped paying him for his services, and, to his surprise, some even began to call him a Mason. Although they probably had no conception of the real meaning of the term "Mason," they nonetheless used it as a strongly derogatory label and applied it to "freethinkers" such as the Kelsiev brothers. These, then, were the Raskol masses of Dobrudja as they appeared to Vasily Kelsiev and his younger brother Ivan. These descendants of the warriors who had defied the authority of one of Russia's greatest and most cruel tsars, Peter the Great, certainly lacked the kind of dynamism Kelsiev expected them to possess.[14]

Struggling against overwhelming odds, lamenting the harshness of their fate, doubting at times the basic soundness of their revolutionary philosophy—in the tradition of the legendary Ilia of Murom or in the tradition of the heroic Archpriest Avvakum or, possibly, simply in the manner of the slavish Volga bargemen—the two idealistic Russian revolutionaries still persisted in their Promethean task of enlightening the seemingly nescient world.

Of all the specific undertakings the Kelsievs attempted in Dobrudja, their project of establishing a revolutionary community or phalanx was undoubtedly the most significant. The idea for organizing a revolutionary centre within the Ottoman Empire was mentioned as early as November 1862 in Bakunin's letter to Herzen. Bakunin, in fact, thought that this was to be Kelsiev's chief task in the East. Herzen, too, was interested in developing a more effective communication system between London and Russia, and within the total context of the Kolokol Group's revolutionary activities Kelsiev's presence in the Ottoman Empire could be viewed as an attempt to establish a communication centre in that area. There were, for example, beginnings of such centres in northern Germany, in Dresden, and in Italy, and in 1863 Bakunin attempted to create a network in Sweden. With Ivan's arrival in Constantinople, the possibility of establishing a phalanx became a definite goal. Ivan was affiliated with Land and Liberty, and it is possible that at the time of his flight from Russia, which was arranged by that organization, he was instructed to establish a revolutionary cell abroad. In any case, Ivan made it his duty to organize such a cell, and even prior to his departure from Constantinople he spoke of the need for additional revolutionary personnel in the East.[15]

The ambitious project was in part realized, but before the Tulcea phalanx had succeeded in recruiting any new members, it tragically lost one of its two founders. A noble youth, an idealistic adamant believer in progress, a champion of the ideal of moral perfectibility, Ivan won no victories. He died at twenty-three. "One emigrant is no longer with us," Vasily wrote to London without really believing it himself. "Last week I buried my brother. He died on Tuesday, June 21, 1864, at sunrise."

Ivan Kelsiev died of typhus. Apparently, most of the newcomers to the lowlands of the Danube delta contracted this disease. Vasily himself nearly died of it just before Ivan fell ill. Describing Ivan's death, Vasily tells how he and Varvara Timofeevna took turns watching over the bedridden Ivan throughout the long nights. The night prior to the fatal one Ivan felt stronger, and Vasily thought that this was a sign of recovery. The following night, however, Vasily found Ivan in agony, and then his agony began to subside and his eyes rolled upward in their sockets.

> There was nothing left to do but blood-letting. I sent for the barber, but then myself cut his vein with a penknife. No blood came from it. When the barber arrived, it was too late, and I did not allow him to disturb my dying brother, whose hands were already

cold. The convulsions ceased, and we heard the death rattle. It grew weaker and weaker and finally ceased. I closed the eyes of the deceased . . .

The funeral was held the following day, yet by the evening of June 21, the body odour was already foul. A small group of close acquaintances gathered . . . Archpriest Khariton and Priest Ilia came and dragged in with them the crosses and the gonfalons. On the high hill, from which one can see the Danube, Bessarabia, and the cupolas of the churches of Izmail, we buried our first emigrant in an alien land.

I had become so accustomed to have near me one who was not only a brother but also a friend that now I feel being completely alone with my family. You did not know him, but he was a holy man: a great intellect, energetic, a pious heart—yet, at twenty-three he had to drop down and begin to rot!

He was a poet. I greatly regret that I did not induce him to write down his verses. He knew a bacchanalian song, filled with frightful melancholy. Oh, how he used to sing that song, without really having a good voice. And what a feeling of melancholy he experienced in Tulcea, and how much he wanted to break away from here and go to you, as if sensing that he would not survive in this barbarian land.

When Vasily buried his brother, he buried with him much of what remained of his own revolutionary vigour. "Blessed are the believers," he lamented in the same letter to London. "You believe that Russia will soon awaken from the plague. I will not argue with you, but in me there is no such belief— I have lost Russia. I see only Prussia and *Staatsphilosophie* . . . Russia, Prussia—*alles mir gleich.* I am a stranger to all, and everything is strange to me." [16]

A short time before Ivan's death, Vasily had lost his position as an interpreter. He charged Chaikovsky, Goncharov, and the Russian ambassador to Constantinople (N. P. Ignatiev) with having influenced, independently of one another, the Turkish government against him. Chaikovsky and Goncharov, Kelsiev thought, were motivated in their action by the fear that their own influence over the Nekrasovtsy might be undermined, and Ignatiev was simply interested in checking the spread of anti-tsarist revolutionary activities in that region. In order to provide for himself and his family Vasily accepted the teaching position held by his late brother, but this solved only some of his problems. Whatever influence he had had over the Nekrasovtsy was now seriously undermined, and grief over his brother's death all but consumed him. He saw little meaning in his revolutionary pursuits and at times felt that there was little meaning in life itself. "We are floating in an endless ocean of space and time on a poorly-constructed raft," he wrote a month after his brother's death. "The waves are snatching us off the raft one by one; the raft itself will collapse. What good is all our knowledge, our suffering, our principles? . . . All of this is a senseless play with blood and tears—humorous and repugnant at the same time—and, what is more, it is all in vain."

As a sidelight, it is of some interest to note that a greater Russian, Leo Tolstoy, several decades later, expressed his feelings on the human predicament in a strikingly similar way. "In the very middle of the stream," the creator of *War and Peace* brooded, "amid the crowd of boats and vessels floating down, I had altogether lost the course and thrown down the oars . . . I was carried far, so far that I heard the roar of the rapids in which I was bound to perish, and I could see the boats that had been broken up in the rapids. I saw before me the destruction toward which I was hurrying, which I dreaded, but I could see no salvation and knew not what I was to do!" [17]

The overwhelming tragedy of Ivan's death, no news from London, and alienation from the Old Believer cossacks—these were the conditions Vasily Kelsiev was facing when in July 1864 a volunteer for the revolutionary phalanx arrived in Tulcea. His name was Michael Semenovich Vasiliev. He had served as a lieutenant in the Russian army, but during the Polish uprising of the previous year he had deserted and fled to Western Europe. Living in Paris, Vasiliev had been recruited for the Tulcea phalanx by the Kolokol Group. Although Kelsiev left only a caricatural description of Vasiliev, emphasizing his excessive boastfulness, his arrival in Tulcea did help Kelsiev regain some confidence in himself. Once again Kelsiev began to think of establishing a gymnasium for the Tulcea Old Believer youth and of building up the organization envisioned for his revolutionary phalanx.

To Kelsiev's delight, only a month following Vasiliev's arrival two more volunteers came to Tulcea and offered to work on behalf of the revolutionary cause. One of these was a Russian-born Pole, named Slivovski, who in the previous year had served in the Caucasus as a member of the Polish legion organized by Colonel Jordan. Slivovski's presence served not only to encourage Kelsiev in renewing his revolutionary work but also to relieve the latter's intellectual boredom. "He was far from being a fool," Kelsiev wrote about Slivovski. "He was well-educated and unpretentious. It made me happy to see him settling down with me and beginning to offer music lessons—now, I at least had someone to talk to intelligently." The other volunteer who joined Kelsiev at approximately the same time as Slivovski was Peter Ivanovich Krasnopevtsev. He was a Russian, a former captain in artillery, who was involved in the revolutionary activities of the Land and Liberty society. He served in Poland, and with the outbreak of the Polish revolt deserted the Russian army and fought against his compatriots. When the defeat of the Poles became apparent, Krasnopevtsev fled into Austrian territory, was briefly detained there, then made his way to Paris. Being aware of Kelsiev's work in the Ottoman Empire from his earlier contacts with the Kolokol Group and unable to find any useful activity in the French capital, he moved to Tulcea. Kelsiev found him to be a person "with whom one could exchange an intelligent word and one who was able to comment critically" on the questions which tormented Kelsiev.

Having thus found himself with three other individuals eager to work for the same cause, Kelsiev decided to implement his idea of founding a school. In November 1864 he travelled to the Moldavian city of Galati, where he was able to recruit four émigré-students to serve as teachers in his school. Two of these were Ukrainians and the other two were Czechs. The Ukrainian named Stankevich was a former student of the University of Kiev and the Czech named Schwarz was a graduate of the University of Prague. The other two, the Ukrainian named Levitsky and the Czech named Dausha were former students of a military school and a polytechnic school respectively. All of them had actively supported the Polish insurgents' cause and emigrated in connection with their work on behalf of that cause.

The arrival of the four new volunteers boosted the number of men under Kelsiev's command to seven. Had such a detachment been available before Ivan's death, the phalanx might indeed have become an active organization. Now, however, conditions had to be nearly ideal for this group to remain together, for Ivan's death had simply sapped Vasily of the revolutionary fervour which characterized the early years of his political career. While it is true that he did regain some of his confidence with Vasiliev's arrival, he was no longer an incensed crusader with the capacity for total commitment to the cause. The conditions under which the revolutionaries had to work in Dobrudja had also taken a turn for the worse. In November, 1864 a new governor had been appointed to administer Dobrudja. He proved to be an innovator, and, contrary to the long tradition of official negligence within the Ottoman Empire, he was determined to enforce the law. Since the revolutionaries were not only acting illegally in their political work but their very presence in the country was illegal, what little influence Kelsiev had had over the Old Believer population was practically nullified. Kelsiev's wife was ill with tuberculosis; he himself was still suffering from the effects of typhus; and several of his companions fell ill with the latter disease. Discouraged by these conditions, the refugee students whom Kelsiev had brought from Galati drifted away. Then, one night, Krasnopevtsev fulfilled his life-long ambition to commit suicide. He hanged himself on the vane of a windmill. Krasnopevtsev's death convinced the remaining members of the revolutionary community of the hopelessness of their situation, and the phalanx dissolved before it could become a formal organization.[18]

In April, 1865, two months after the death of Peter Krasnopevtsev, Vasily Kelsiev, with his suffering wife Varvara Timofeevna, their five-year old daughter Malusha, and their Tulcea-born son Vania, moved from Dobrudja across the Danube to the Moldavian city of Galati. Behind them, on a hill overlooking the solemnly-moving waters of the Danube, they left the grave of Ivan Kelsiev. They also left behind them the bearded Old Believer Nekrasovtsy, whose adamantine loyalty to their traditions and whose intransigent confidence in their religious faith had made them inaccessible to the ideals for which Ivan Kelsiev had paid the ultimate price.

Kelsiev's departure from Dobrudja marked the end of his revolutionary activities among the Raskolniks. Invariably, these activities met with failure. Yet, in assessing the total situation in which he worked, it is possible to recognize a number of conditions attesting to the credulity of the assumptions underlying his undertakings. The popularity of *The Bell* and the general influence of its publishers, for example, were a significant attribute which ought to have added to the effectiveness of any project Kelsiev decided to carry out. Kelsiev's own commitment and his willingness to face dangers and depravations were factors conducive to the success of his revolutionary aspirations. The support he received from his wife was by no means a minor asset to his revolutionary career. Like Avvakum's consort, Varvara Timofeevna proved herself willing to sacrifice everything for her husband's cause. His brother Ivan was admirably suited to Kelsiev's mission, for he was passionately dedicated to the task of changing society through education and moral rejuvenation. The mission of "going to the people," therefore, could hardly have been performed by better suited revolutionaries than the Kelsiev brothers.

Kelsiev's revolutionary experiment among the Raskolniks was conducted during a decade when many Russians were inflamed with a new burst of energy and enthusiasm for creating a better society. There were others, such as Shchapov for example, who had expounded on the revolutionary or "democratic" attributes of the Raskolniks. There were, moreover, some apparent similarities between the Russian religious and political dissenters. The Raskolniks stood in opposition to a government which was Western in orientation and at times in its actual composition. The revolutionaries advocated a replacement of the "German" or foreign rule of the Russian monarchy by a government which, in their view, would be representative of the Russian people. The representation of the Russian people, as advocated by the Kolokol Group at the time of Kelsiev's work among the Raskolniks, was to be manifested in the form of the Zemsky Sobor, which was envisaged to be the representative body of the peasant communes. Since the commune, according to Herzen, was most fully preserved within the Raskol population, the Raskolniks would seem to have possessed the greatest interest of all Russians for supporting the idea of establishing the Zemsky Sobor.

Many of the Raskolniks resisted the government, fearing neither exile, bodily mutilations, nor death. Although this was especially true of the earlier times, the uprising at Bezdna in 1861 testifies to the fact that even in the 1860's the adherents of the old faith were still capable of facing death in the heroic manner of Avvakum. The revolutionaries of the second half of the nineteenth century were also characterized by an unreserved commitment to their respective cause. In their resistance to the government they, too, were willing to face hardships of exile, public humiliation, and death. Thus in the extent of their commitment, which in both instances involved resistance to the same existing order, there seems to have been a strong similarity between the two dissenting elements. In retrospect it might be pertinent to note that no less a revolutionary than Lenin, in his time, seriously considered the possibility of enlisting the Raskolniks' participation in the revolutionary work of his party.[19] Yet, the fact remains that Kelsiev failed consistently and completely.

Why?

Although the full meaning of the answer to this question must be discerned from the events described in this and the preceding chapters, it might be useful to consider more specifically several outstanding situations which seem to have contributed to Kelsiev's failures.

The Polish uprising of 1863 was undoubtedly one of such important elements which seriously undermined his work among the Old Believers. As a certain visitor to London, named Martianov, expressed it, Herzen "buried *The Bell*" when he committed himself to the Polish cause. With the decline of *The Bell* the political fortunes of the Kolokol Group suffered a marked and rapid decline. The weakening of their influence in general led to the weakening of their popularity among the Raskolniks.

Still, the revolutionaries' failure to join forces with Bishop Pafnuty of Kolomna, for instance, cannot be related to the Polish uprising, for that breach preceded the Kolokol Group's commitment to the Polish cause. There were, then, other factors which contributed to the negation of Kelsiev's efforts in his work among the Raskolniks.

Although the similarities between the revolutionaries and the Raskolniks were extensive, in many respects these similarities were decidedly superficial. The Old Believers' resistance to the government, for example, was in its essence quite dissimilar to the rational, calculated, and wholly political designs pursued by the revolutionaries. Whereas revolutionaries sought a fundamental reorganization of the existing socio-political order, the Old Believers' concerns were of a more specific nature. The latter simply sought freedom for their faith. If the persecution of the adherents of the old faith were to be stopped and if the tsar were to return to the religion of his ancestors, the chief "political" goals of the Old Believers would have been realized. Whether the Old Believer tsar would rule through a zemsky sobor or through a ministerial system was immaterial to them, for they were essentially a non-political element.

Some of the incompatibilities between the revolutionaries and the Raskolniks stemmed from the fact that the former were atheists and the latter devout believers. The early Raskolniks regarded the Nikonian or Orthodox church to be under the influence of Satan. By the 1860's, however, the majority of the Raskolniks were reconciled to the existence of the official church—reconciled to the extent that they no longer regarded it to be an instrument of Satan but merely a church which was in error. With the "godless ones," however, there was no possibility for reconciliation. It was quite paradoxical, therefore, for the non-religious revolutionaries to speak to the devout Old Believers, for example, about religious freedom.

Although both the revolutionaries and the Raskolniks were anti-Western, there were significant differences in the nature of their anti-Westernism. The anti-Westernism of the revolutionaries resembled the anti-Westernism of the Romanov tsars: it was a tendency toward Westernization against the West. The Raskol, on the other hand, originated in part as a reaction to such "anti-Westernism." Although it is true that by the 1860's the intensity of the Raskolniks' xenophobia had abated considerably, such a feeling was still potent nonetheless. Whereas in the 1660's, that is, at the time of the Raskol's origin, the Raskolniks viewed the foreign influences in Russia to be manifestations of the work of Satan, in the 1860's they were willing, to use a modern term, to co-exist with the West. Co-existence, however, did not signify a willingness to adopt Western ways. The Raskolniks position relative to the West, therefore, conflicted with the position of the revolutionaries, including Kelsiev, for, by their attempt to graft Western socialistic theories on the Russian Zemsky Sobor and on the village commune the revolutionaries sought to ferment the Russian kvass with Western yeast. The Old Believers who dealt with Kelsiev did not overlook these differences, and their position on this issue was clearly expressed in Metropolitan Cyril's *Epistle* condemning the London revolutionaries.

Thus, there were some similarities and some common interests between the revolutionaries and the Raskolniks, and there were some external conditions which seemed conducive to cooperation between these two elements, yet, these positive conditions must have been outweighed by their negative counterparts, for the result was the series of disheartening failures accompanying nearly all Kelsiev's political actions involving the Raskolniks.

# CHAPTER VI

# ACROSS THE PRUT LIES MOTHER RUSSIA

Kelsiev's migration from Dobrudja to Moldavia was intended to be the beginning of a longer journey: he planned to abandon the Danubean lands altogether and move to Paris. Lacking the necessary financial resources, however, he was compelled to find temporary employment in the Moldavian city of Galati.

Selectivity is seldom a beggar's prerogative, and this is especially true of a beggar with a family. Kelsiev became a rock crusher. He found employment with a construction company building a road from Galati to Bucharest. For crushing rock the workers were paid a sum equivalent to two and a half silver roubles per cubic meter. Serbian stonemasons, according to Kelsiev, were able to crush a cubic meter a day per man. The Polish emigrants—among whom there were former soldiers, officers, students, office workers, and land-lords—could, after some experience, crush one half of a cubic meter each. Kelsiev, however, proved to be much less adroit at that craft than all the others. "Not a cloud was in the sky," he described a typical working day. "The sun was beating down, and the dust was hanging in the air. In large drops the sweat fell to the stone and evaporated almost instantaneously. The palms of my hands were bleeding, but I was unable to do more than a quarter of a cubic meter . . ." Fortunately for him the management took pity on the exhausted Russian revolutionary and gave him a position physically less demanding. Instead of crushing rock, he counted the number of loads of

171

rock and sand delivered to the construction site and in some cases supervised the actual loading. This task was not an easy one, for he still had to work under the hot sun from morning till night, but in contrast to the hardships he endured as a rock crusher the new position was at least bearable.

As humiliating as all of this must have been for the proud self-appointed liberator of the masses, Kelsiev had to stoop before his family's needs and attempt to condition himself to this new way of life. Misfortunes, however, seldom haunt one with a solitary dirge: they often descend upon their victim as a landslide falls upon a mountain stream. So it was with Kelsiev. Shortly following the Kelsievs' arrival in Galati, their infant son, Vania, died. Quite naturally, his death disturbed the precarious balance of Varvara Timofeevna's health. She, after all, was suffering in an advanced stage of tuberculosis, and the separation from her husband and the risks entailed in his revolutionary career had kept her for years living in a state of a perpetual anxiety. Seven of her twenty-five years had been spent in exile. She had lost her first child, then had a miscarriage, and now her only son succumbed to the miseries they all were experiencing. In spirit she was still undefeated, but her body was no longer capable of standing up to the misfortunes of their lives. Following her son's death, therefore, her condition became so serious that she was placed in a hospital, and the only bright star left to fan the flickering flames of the Kelsiev family was five-year old Malusha.

Malusha was a charming, intelligent, and healthy child. Her lively eyes sparkled with such a bright smile that no matter how dark were the clouds enveloping their lives, in her presence the family seldom was totally bereft of joy.

One gray autumn morning, as he was counting the loads of sand on the road, Kelsiev was overwhelmed by the message of death in his family. Without a full understanding of the words of the Moldavian worker who brought the shattering news and hardly feeling the jagged stones under his bare feet, Vasily ran to the hospital expecting to find the corpse of his long-ailing wife. To his utter bewilderment he learned on his arrival that it was his daughter Malusha who was no longer living. She had died of cholera. "There was now nothing in my heart but madness and damnation," Kelsiev was able to record later. "The firm health, the intelligence, good character, and beauty of my child had accustomed me even to have dreams about the future. I had wanted to devote my life to her upbringing. I had counted on her like one would count on the permanence of a mountain. She was the only friend I had any hope of being able to rely upon in the future. She was to be my Antigone. And now, everything was shattered in one night." [1]

Not many nights were to pass before everything indeed was shattered, for the tragedy of Malusha's death was too much for Varvara Timofeevna. On October 15, 1865 she followed her children into the grave. "All is finished," Kelsiev cried out in a lengthy and passionate letter to Herzen.

*Finit est.*

The curtain fell on the Sunday before last at twelve o'clock at noon. The drama was endured to the end with full consciousness. No tears, no reproaches against fate, no prayers. She was a titan by nature; there was nothing childish about her.

"Do not cry! Do not cry!" she kept telling me, putting her hand on my head as I stood on my knees sobbing. You know what it means for a man to weep.

"Do not cry! Tell me, what am I dying of? What is my sickness? Remember, you promised to warn me, you promised when we were bride and groom . . ."

"You have terrible consumption, galloping consumption. Your lungs have decayed; you have nothing with which to breathe. Another hour or an hour and a half and you will suffocate. There now, I have kept my word, the word I gave when we were a boy and a girl."

"Do not cry, do not cry! It is all right; I will die in your arms."

I was choking with madness . . .

"Are you still conscious? You have always valued your consciousness so much. Our whole life has been a life of thought."

She nodded.

"I want to die in full consciousness . . ."

Her hands and feet were already cold. Her forehead began to cool. A repulsive, sticky, cold sweat appeared on her face, on her neck and chest.

"My child, my child, have you not lost your consciousness?"

She continued to nod; her thoughts were still clear . . .

The coughing began again.

"Rub my back; rub it like you did during delivery . . ."

When the coughing subsided, she motioned with her arms toward the blanket lying at her feet. I understood. I folded the blanket and placed it beneath her shoulders. She always liked to sit that way. I asked the watchwoman for a pillow, but she did not understand me, for I speak terrible Moldavian, and instead of a pillow she brought some curtains. I was grateful for the curtains, for now the other patients could not see us. We had privacy. She waved her arm again. I sat down beside her and stretched out my arm, and she, cold and sweaty, reclined on my shoulder. Another half hour went by.

"My child, are you still conscious?"

"Do not cry."

Suddenly she leaned back, her eyes fixed on the window, her breathing tightened. You know how the dying have a rattle in their throat and how their last breath stops.

Suddenly her head fell to her right shoulder. Her eyes were as bright as always. Her face was as tender as usual, and there was on it the usual expression of résigné. Has everything really ended? I touched her head—her mouth opened.

I don't know how much longer I sat there, but there was no mistake. I walked out from behind the curtain.

"*A murit!* [Died]," I told the nurse. She clasped her hands and ran for the intern. The intern, a Pole, a good friend of mine, became excited: "I will call the watchman right away to move her to the mortuary . . ."

"Leave her—I'll do it myself," and I took the corpse in my arms, moved and undressed it.

On Monday morning they made an autopsy. Both lungs were decomposed almost one-third of the way from the top. I myself put her into the coffin and accompanied her to the cemetery. There we found that someone else had been put into her grave. We had to dig another grave. The gravediggers were drunk. Finally, they managed to dig a new grave. I lifted the coffin, tried to place it in the grave, but the grave was too short. I pulled the coffin out, and they dug some more. I tried it again, but the grave was still too small. It was already evening. There were stars in the sky. The evening star was shining, and the Danube was glittering below. For the fourth time I lowered her into the grave, and still the grave was too small. I climbed onto the top of the coffin, danced on it a kind of a cannibal dance, and the coffin finally slid down into the grave.

I walked to the city—an orphan, alone in this world, without sorrow, without joy, not comprehending anything, not sympathizing with anything, a stranger to everything, a stranger to myself. And thus I remain. There is only one thing missing for my complete alienation from this world, and that is emasculation. I don't know yet whether I should comply in this respect with the advice and the prayers of my Castrate friends. Apparently my engagement with life has ended—I am a free bird; I am a man whose song has been sung; I have emigrated from the human race."[2]

This time Kelsiev was indeed alone. He continued to write to the Kolokol Group, which by that time had moved to Geneva, but received no replies from them, for their correspondence to him was channelled to the Russian consulate in Bucharest by the man whose address Kelsiev was using. He returned to his work on the road, but the Russian consul compelled Kelsiev's employers to deprive the homeless revolutionary even of that meager livelihood. The winter of 1865-66, therefore, was probably the most dreadful period in Kelsiev's trying existence. Without permanent employment and without a place to live in, he attempted to subdue with alcohol the pains induced by his misfortunes. He wandered about for weeks at a time without washing, and he slept wherever he could find a place: "on a bench in a tavern, on a bare floor in a friend's house, on a billiard table in an inn." He found solace only in his dreams, for he often dreamt that he was talking and playing with his wife and children. He rejected the real world and recorded his spite—his "black thoughts"—in writing.

His uneasy thoughts ranged from deep gloom to outright hallucinations. Apparently he drank so consistently that there was real possibility of his becoming an alcoholic. According to his own mercilessly candid description, following prolonged indulgences in alcohol he began to see grotesque faces and other weird images appearing before him. One such image, which repeatedly appeared to him, was that of a pretty child whose face was engulfed before his very eyes by a rapidly expanding sore. He witnessed a peasant and an old woman rising up into the air before him and soaring over his bed. At another time, as he walked in the street, a flying giant accompanied him. Whatever significance a specialist in the field of human psychology may attribute to these visions, their occurrence testifies to the seriousness of Kelsiev's condition during that terrible winter.[3]

Although winter comes and lingers, binding one's limbs and repressing one's spirits, it also culminates in spring. Unwashed and ragged, Kelsiev was tramping through the streets of Galati when he began to notice that the trees were beginning to bud and "strings of birds were being pulled northward."

He looked and looked at the birds, he listened to their voices, and began to yearn "to go away somewhere." A wish to fly, however, has made no man into an eagle. Kelsiev lacked funds to move from Galati. Fortunately, however, he had made the acquaintance of a Serbian captain operating a steamship on the Danube. With that captain's assistance the homeless Russian wanderer once again sought a new home. He was still thinking of going to Paris, but the Danube is not the Seine. He disembarked within the borders of the Hapsburg Empire and made his way to its capital. He remained in Vienna from April to October 1866. Although his devotion to the revolutionary cause remained dormant, he was successful during those months in revitalizing some interest in living.

He earned his livelihood in Vienna by writing articles for *Russkii vestnik* and other Russian journals, for which he apparently received substantial remuneration. This was evident in the fact that soon following his arrival in Vienna, he was not only able to attend lectures on Zend, Sanskrit, and Old Slavonic at the University but also to maintain himself in a state of respectability sufficiently high to become a member of an important club (*Slavanska Beseda*) composed of Slavic intellectuals. Although he continued to communicate with the Kolokol Group, the summer in Vienna proved to be the final phase of his association with the revolutionary movement. The prime element purging him of the lingering effects of the political malady with which he had been afflicted since childhood was the loyalty shown to Russia and to the tsar by the Slavs he met in the Hapsburg Empire. According to Kelsiev's account, the men he met at the Slavic Club in Vienna looked toward Russia as their only hope for liberation from Germanic domination, and they regarded the Russian language and the Russian political system as essential for the creation of pan-Slavic unity. These intellectuals, Kelsiev claimed, felt that the Poles, who sought independence from Russia, were disloyal to the Slavic world. In fact, Kelsiev went as far as to say that these Pan-Slavists were so intensely pro-Russian that had they discovered his true identity, they would have unhesitatingly turned him over to the Russian authorities.[4]

The accuracy of the preceding assertions is difficult to judge, for Kelsiev's *Confession*, in which they were expressed, was a plea for a pardon addressed to the tsar. It may be significant to note that Kelsiev made no reference to the Pan-Slavists' loyalty to Russia in the letters he wrote to Herzen at the time of his association with them. On the other hand, one should not readily dismiss his allegations, for this was a time of political agitation among the Pan-Slavists in preparation for the important congress held the following year in Moscow. It is also a well known fact that some of the Hapsburg Slavs, especially the Czechs, were seeking Russian aid for their own liberation. In any case, it was during his stay in Vienna that Kelsiev's reawakened Slavic and nationalistic pride finally extinguished the last sparks of the rebelliousness which eight years earlier had led him to renounce his native land and had exposed him to so many calamitous misfortunes.

At the time of his departure from Galati, Kelsiev was still thinking of joining the Kolokol Group and possibly of settling down permanently in the West. In Vienna, however, he abandoned his plan and in June 1866 terminated his correspondence with his fellow-revolutionaries. Instead of moving westward to Geneva to join his former comrades, he went eastward (in October) to explore Galicia—a Slavic territory acquired by Austria at the end of the eighteenth century as a result of the partitioning of Poland. In his writings, Kelsiev dramatized his final break with the revolutionary movement just as he dramatized his other sudden "conversions." One such dramatic account involves a romanticized episode which occurred at the tomb of the Polish national hero, Thaddeus Kosciuszko, in Cracow.

Travelling through the famed city of Cracow, Kelsiev visited the Gothic Stanislaw Cathedral on the Wawel, which was the coronation and burial place of the Polish kings. Cracow is a city famous for many things, especially for its Jagellonian university, which was established in the fourteenth century, and as the home of a student from that university named Nicolaus Copernicus. The Wawel is a hill overlooking the Vistula River—a hill with which an imaginative legend is associated. According to that legend, once upon a time a serpent lived in a cave under the Wawel. This serpent fed on people, and for many years many people fell victim to the monstrous cave-dweller. Then, one day a man named Krakus filled a ram with burning sulphur and fed it to the serpent. Having devoured the ram, the serpent became extremely thirsty and drank so much water from the Vistula that he burst. In gratitude for this deed, the people made Krakus their king and called their city Krakow. The power of this legend, in combination with Kelsiev's inherently romantic mood, served to enchant the Russian dreamer during his visit to the Stanislaw Cathedral on the Wawel.

During his visit to the Cathedral, Kelsiev was approached by an attendant who offered to show him an especially venerated tomb. Carrying a lighted candle, the attendant led him into a vault below the main floor, and the repenting Russian revolutionary came to a tomb on which, in large letters, was inscribed the name of the famous Polish revolutionary hero—*Kosciuszko*. Reflecting the dim candlelight, that name momentarily transfixed the sensitive Russian intellectual. His knees began to tremble and his heart palpitated as he lowered himself to the dias and, sobbing like a woman, whispered in a prayerful way:

> Kosciuszko, Kosciuszko! What if you too were mistaken, like I have been? What if you risked your life and the lives of others in vain? What if you too believed in the possibility of the impossible? I shall be obligated to go against your compatriots if on this journey I become convinced that they are wrong and the ideals for which they are spilling the best of their blood are unattainable! You were an honest man; you will understand me and will bless me in my pursuit of an honest cause . . .

Apparently, by some ineffable means, the dead Polish hero did give his blessing to our quiescence-seeking Russian antihero, for, as Kelsiev was leaving the Cathedral, he felt as if a heavy stone had fallen from his conscience, and a satisfying feeling of relief engulfed his entire being. The "stone" he

relinquished on the legend-inspiring Wawel was the feeling
of guilt he experienced for his break with the revolutionary
movement. Now, his painful suspicion that the revolutionary
cause was a belief in the "possibility of the impossible" seemed
to him to be confirmed.[5]

In Galicia, Kelsiev planned to visit various other historical sites and to do some ethnic studies of the local peasantry,
who preserved some of the cultural elements of the primitive
Slavs. Ethnology had been of special interest to him throughout his life, and he also needed material for the articles he
had promised to write for several publishers in Russia. Shortly
after his departure from Cracow, however, Kelsiev was arrested on suspicion of being a Russian spy and on November 7
was deported to Moldavia. Thus, once again he found himself
in the land where in the previous year he was rendered "an
orphan" and a pauper.

Kelsiev established himself in the city of Jassy, a cultural
and commercial centre in northeastern Moldavia, situated some
ten miles from the present-day Russian-Rumanian border on
the Prut. The mental anguish he experienced during this winter
was nearly as trying as the misfortunes he had suffered during
the previous winter in Galati. Having liberated himself from
the "liberation movement," he was a sheep without a herd,
a professional believer without a belief. He continued to write
articles for publication in Russian periodicals, but this activity
failed to dull the anxiety which fed upon the uncertainty of
his predicament. No matter how diligent he attempted to be
in his writing, the work went poorly, "the pen was falling
out" of his hands, and his thoughts and words could hardly
be "pasted together." Heavy thoughts settled in his mind and
weighed down his ability to reason to such an extent that at
times he was unable to write at all. The substance of his
heavy thoughts was a single problem: should he—a former
revolutionary and a political criminal—return to his native
land?

Many schemes passed through his mind; many fears
pierced his body. Five years previously the State Senate in
Russia had declared him an "unconvicted" political criminal.
What fate would befall him upon his return? Should he sur-

reptitiously go to Russia and at an opportune moment throw himself down at the tsar's feet? The customary and possibly the most reasonable way would be to bargain with the government for his freedom. But this was "not the Russian way," he thought. Compromise is not a Russian trait, he kept telling himself. For a Russian it is either "everything or nothing." In the end he rejected all plans offering anything less than a total, dramatic solution to his grave, ambiguous predicament.

He lived on in the Moldavian city of Jassy through the winter of 1866-67, rejecting what he had recently believed in and seeking to believe in what he had earlier rejected. Early in May he visited the Russian consul in Jassy and declared his intention to return to Russia. The consul was surprised, congratulated the repentant revolutionary, and advised him to submit a formal request in writing. Kelsiev agreed and made a promise to do so but then spent three days immobilized by fear of his impending fate and in the end failed to muster sufficient courage to fulfill his promise. His anxiety apparently was so devastating that he was weakened both spiritually and physically. Finally, on Saturday, May 20, 1867, the adventurous warrior, having spent nearly a decade challenging the ways of his country, was brought in a horse cart by a Castrate friend to the small border outpost of Skuliany, where he boarded a ferry and crossed the Prut to his native Russia.

Consistent with most of his other undertakings this one was not entirely free of difficulties. He crossed the Prut to the Russian side, but the officer in charge was absent, and, since Kelsiev lacked a visa, the soldiers wanted to take him back to the Moldavian shore. After some deliberations, he wrote a note to the officer. The soldiers agreed to deliver the note, but they nonetheless delivered Kelsiev to the other shore. This was quite contrary to Kelsiev's expectations, for he had thought that the Russians would place him in chains the minute he stepped down from the ferry. After a brief delay the soldiers returned, and this time he was taken to his own shore never again to leave it. In spite of the confusion which tended to dull the intended bravado of his voluntary return, the contents of Kelsiev's note to the Russian officer at Skuliany testify to the unmistakenly Byronic spirit of its author. "Unconvict-

ed political criminal Vasily Ivanovich Kelsiev," he curtly had
written to the officer, "is surrendering himself into the hands
of the government and begs you to take the necessary measures
for his arrest." Vaska Buslaev triumphed even in defeat![6]

Let us allow Vasily Kelsiev a moment of respite following his arduous crossing of the Prut and turn our attention
to the remainder of the Kolokol Group. A year before Kelsiev's crossing of the Prut the other London revolutionaries
crossed the English Channel and permanently moved to Geneva. As was the case with Kelsiev's desperate act, the crossing
of the Channel by the editors of *The Bell* proved to be a forced
withdrawal heralding the inevitability of final defeat. *Obshchee Veche* had gone out of circulation in the summer of
the previous year, for it had lost its contributors and its readers. A similar fate was threatening to befall the once popular
*Bell*. All this was brought about largely by the fact that the
Russian public interpreted Herzen's support of the Polish uprising of 1863 not as a part of his political opposition to the
tsarist government but rather as a betrayal of his fatherland.
It was in the hope of finding support from Russian emigrants
on the continent that Herzen and Ogarev decided to move to
Geneva. Their hope proved groundless, for the popularity of
*The Bell* continued to decline. Finally, in 1867, on the day of
its tenth anniversary, the famous *Bell* carried its own obituary
in the form of an editorial announcement that its publication
would be suspended temporarily. The editors hoped that by
stopping the publication of this, once powerful, political organ,
a public outcry would be evoked for its revival. Four months
later, however, Herzen observed that not a single voice was
pleading for the revival of *The Bell*, not a single voice was
lamenting its death. The temporary suspension became a permanent one. The famed editor of *The Bell* did not survive
his unique creation by many years: on January 21, 1870, Alexander Herzen's remarkable life ended, and with it the last
semblance of the informal organization which we have chosen
to call the Kolokol Group dissolved.[7]

Following his dramatic crossing of the Prut, Kelsiev was
placed under arrest and spent the first night of his home-
coming in the home of an official in a settlement near Skuliany.

The following day he was moved to a prison in the city of Kishinev and immediately proceeded to expedite his own transference into the hands of the political police of the Third Section. For that purpose he wrote a lengthy letter to the head of the Third Section, Count Alexander Andreevich Shuvalov. In his letter to Shuvalov, Kelsiev left to posterity a passionate, Rousseauistically confessional account of the reasons for his return to Russia.

Dear Count:

Be so magnanimous as to forgive me for daring to appeal directly to you.

Throughout my life I have acted according to my convictions. With conviction I joined the Russian emigrants in London at the end of 1859; with conviction I left them in the middle of 1863 [sic]; and on May 19 of this year, 1867 [actually on May 20], once again acting with conviction, I voluntarily surrendered into the hands of the government at the custom-house of Skuliany.

During the three and a half years of my political activities, the ideas of my London comrades were for me almost the last word in human thought. I was proud that such ideas were being spread in Russia, which I have never stopped loving passionately. I believed that from Russia the light, shedding goodness, truth and love, would spread throughout the entire human race. "You just wait," I used to say to the foreigners, "we Russians will show you how to apply socialism in practice. You will be coming to us to learn and to look for truth!" This was when I was twenty-four to twenty-eight years of age. My knowledge of Russia was then limited to St. Petersburg and its suburbs. I knew the people only through books. I could distinguish the real from the impossible only on the basis of my own reasoning. Politically I was a federalist and economically a socialist. But a bloody revolution has always been abhorrent to me—this is evident from my letters which were confiscated in the summer of 1862 from the unfortunate Vetoshnikov.

I believed passionately and sincerely in the attainment and righteousness of our cause. But then the Polish uprising occurred. Everyone around me, it seemed, was shouting and harping that this uprising should receive a favourable response from our side, and that it would serve as the cornerstone in the creation of a federated Russia in accordance with her historical characteristics. I had little confidence in the success of the Poles, but being a follower, I had to support their side, even though with a feeling of guilt. I reasoned that since rivers of blood had already begun to flow, they should not flow in vain. Soon afterwards I became completely disillusioned—and what a painful process it was . . .

Both our and the Polish causes failed for the same reason: they both were impracticable. We failed to recognize that it was not permissible for one class to sacrifice the interests of all other classes; we were forgetting that the people have their own beliefs in accordance with which they want to conduct their affairs. Because of our excessive consistency, we were abruptly interrupted. The Poles, too, failed for nearly the same reasons: they, too, lacked an understanding of both the material with which they had to work and the means at their disposal. The peasantry failed to develop a desire for [an independent] Poland, and France failed to provide the Poles with assistance.

Filled with spite and remorse, convinced that all the long years of work and deprivations had failed, and would continue to fail, to lead to anything constructive; that everything I believed in and rendered service to was nothing more than a student's dream, a noble phrase without content, I asked myself the question: what is to be done? The notion of returning to the West was repugnant to me; besides, there was nothing for me to do there.

It was impossible for me to return to Russia (although even then I was thinking of it), because I had a family to support. I had no right to risk their lives. I went to Tulcea in Dobrudja where I settled down, for there, at least I was among Russians. There it was possible for me to be useful and to study the Sectarians and other simple people.

A year and a half in Tulcea, where I served as a representative of all Russian emigrants, led me to gain an understanding of many things of which I had been hardly aware before. Our sects do not possess any characteristics of a revolutionary nature. Our Sectarians are loyal to the tips of their fingernails, even though at times they do regard the tsar as the Antichrist and other officials as the angels of Satan. Our simple folk will not revolt against the authority of the tsar. Even the Russian refugees who fled to Turkey either because of their religion or from penal servitude, even they, deep in their hearts, are loyal subjects of the tsar. It was lonely to live among them, for not one of them is even slightly educated. I left them because of this, but they did infect me with their anguish for the motherland.

In Galati during the summer of 1865, I experienced a frightful misfortune: my wife and two children died, after I had already buried my brother in Tulcea. I spent the winter in total despair, renouncing everything in a world in which nothing is permanent. My soul, however, continued to yearn for a solution, for a man cannot endure a negative existence for long.

I was still interested in learning. I went to Vienna where I studied Slavic dialects, Zend, Sanscrit, and Slavic myths (which I have been studying for nearly seven years) and where I became acquainted with various representatives of the Slavic peoples who recently attended the ethnographic exhibition [opened in Moscow in April, 1867].

When they heard the tales of my adventures, the tales about the God-forsaken places to which my curiosity had led me but to which no other decent man would ever go, they begged me to write about these lands. Be so kind, dear Count, as to glance even briefly through my articles in *Russkii Vestnik* ("A Russian Village in Asia Minor" and "The Slovak villages Near Pressburg"), in *Golos* of last year and of this year ("A Travel Through Galicia," "The Polish Emigrants," and "Observations in Jassy"), and various other short articles about the Slavs, about Vienna, etc. All of these articles are signed with the pseudonym V. P. Ivanov-Zheludkov. Prior to my surrendering at Skuliany no one even suspected that a well-known political criminal was hiding under that name. Be so kind, Count, as to glance through these articles and you will see the impression which I carried away from my acquaintance with the Slavs and especially with the Galician Russians. The result of this was a winter spent in anguish and meditation in Jassy, and finally, my unconditional surrender into the hands of the government during the preceding week.

From a youth attracted by the populist movement which appeared in Russia in 1855 at the time of the Sebastopol misfortunes, from a youth who became a revolutionary agitator and organizer, I was transformed into a passionately devoted subject, an ardent patriot prepared to do anything for the tsar and the fatherland. Because of this, I found it dishonest—my conscience would not allow me— to remain abroad any longer. The present reign is so great, it has so distinguished itself with grandeur and splendour that Russia's whole present-day history appears to be a kind of continuous ovation, a holiday, a festival. Even the unfortunate and tragic events [Karakozov's attempt on Alexander II's life in April 1866] occurring in Russia seem to be sent deliberately by Providence in order to bring forth a

new rejoicing from the bosom of our titanic people.
I've followed the past and present events and was
unable to remain in an alien land any longer. I am
now in prison, but I have no regrets or any feeling
of remorse because of my act [his return]. My future
is gloomy and menacing, but one thought comforts
me—the realization that, in spite of everything, I
am at home. And it is better to suffer at home than
to be happy but alone among foreigners.

What fate is awaiting me, Count? I have caused
no harm either to Russia or to the government . . .
I *wanted* to harm and actually attempted to do harm,
but all my attempts were futile: my theories were
inapplicable in practice, and all I did was mill the
wind. No harm has been caused by me to the state:
I am guilty only of intentions and efforts. Describing
these efforts would be pointless, would require several
months, and would prove to be neither beneficial
nor interesting. But if the government will allow me,
I would be willing to publish an account of various
episodes in my adventure as an agitator, which
would serve as a lesson to those young men who are
trying to saddle the wrong horse. Presently, Count,
I would request one thing: I am most desirous to
meet and talk with you. I have much to report to the
higher authorities. Summon me to appear before you
in St. Petersburg.

Nine years of living abroad in the company of
revolutionaries, emigrants, sectarians, vagabonds,
etc., and the common people of the neighbouring
tribes have made it possible for me to learn a great
deal about attitudes which are known neither to
our government nor to the press. The government's
information comes either from official reports or
from testimonies obtained through legal investigations. Neither of these sources, as I have learned
through experience, should be trusted. The official
reports are based largely on hearsay, because an
official is seldom in a position to be directly ac-

quainted with the illiterate masses, and the testimonies obtained in legal investigations represent
merely a daguerreotyped copy of the confused state-
ments of the accused. My situation was different:
all doors were open to me and all tongues spoke
freely in my presence, for everywhere I went I was
one of the people. Summon me to appear before
you in St. Petersburg. I have a great deal to tell you,
but certain things one should not write on paper.
On the basis of my accounts you will become convinced that I am a sincere man and that I will testify
before the government just as sincerely as I have
surrendered myself to it. Everything that you hear
from me you may report to the Emperor, for whose
mercy I do not even dare to ask. Whatever his verdict
might be, I will accept it with the humble submissiveness that befits a truly loyal subject.

> Count, do not disregard the man
> who completely entrusts him-
> self to you,
>
> Vasily Ivanovich Kelsiev.[8]

Kelsiev returned to Russia because he lost confidence in
the success of the revolutionary cause. He returned out of his
personal despair resulting from the loss of his family. And,
we must venture to suggest, he returned because he was a
Vaska Buslaev, a Byron, although without a *Childe Harold,*
a representative of the nineteenth-century Russian intelligentsia. His return conforms to a well-established category of
"conversions" experienced by such great writers as Gogol and
Tolstoy. Upon hearing the news of his return, Herzen rhetorically asked: "What is this: despair, knavery, or simply madness?" The eloquent dean of Russia's political emigrants probably knew the answer, for he himself, as another famous
Russian emigrant, Berdiaev, observed, returned to his native
land even if only in spirit. The trait of hating one's own
country because of his love for it was not peculiar to Kelsiev.
The well-known Russian intellectual, Vladimir Pecherin, for

example, hated his native country far more intensely than did
Kelsiev—and all of this was because of his equally intense
love for it. One could also be puzzled by the experience of
Kelsiev's more famous contemporary in that respect—Dostoevsky. For the author of *Brothers Karamazov*, after all, was
inspired to love the autocracy by its command for his own
execution. And in the present century, following the Revolution, hundreds of intellectually prominent Russians spent
their lives withering away either as external or internal emigrants consumed by a passion of love and hate for their
enigmatic fatherland. In the light of such inexplicable con-
tradictions it seems fruitless to seek a more exhaustive explanation for Kelsiev's return in purely rational terms.[9]

Count Shuvalov did not require a personal plea from
Kelsiev to hasten the latter's transference to the capital: the
very day Kelsiev composed his lengthy letter to him, the
authorities in Kishinev received orders to conduct their
prisoner to the capital without delay. The Kishinev officials
promptly complied with the orders, and after a week's journey
in a horse-driven carriage, Kelsiev was safely delivered to a
prison in the city of his childhood.

Ten days later, on June 13, a special commission began
a formal investigation of his case. Kelsiev, in the meantime,
proceeded to write his confession to the Tsar. Contrary to the
assumptions generally held concerning the alleged supineness
and inefficiency of the tsarist bureaucracy, Kelsiev's case was
handled most expeditiously. His *Confession* was completed
by July 12 and was immediately sent to the Tsar. Having
studied it, Alexander II granted Kelsiev a pardon with the
restoration of all his rights as a citizen. On September 11, less
than four months following his return, Vasily Kelsiev was
freed from prison.

He was pardoned primarily on the basis of his *Confession*, yet in that forceful outburst of passion he neither denounced his former associates nor displayed an excessive
degree of obsequiousness toward the Tsar. Both those who
rejoiced at Kelsiev's return because of the political implications of his act and those who regarded it as a betrayal expected a wave of arrests to follow his testimony. Kelsiev,

however, confessed and was freed without implicating anyone. Although this was largely due to the fact that most of those who worked with him against the government and were named in his *Confession* had already been punished in connection with the Vetoshnikov affair in 1862, the fact remains that in the *Confession* Kelsiev reiterated his respect for Herzen and Ogarev and at least in part blamed the government for the revolutionary unrest in Russia.

His *Confession* is far from being an expression of self-pity by a frightened man. It is an address to a monarch by a professed patriot who admitted his heresy of disloyalty but at the same time entreated his sovereign to eliminate the conditions which, he thought, served to induce such disloyalty in that sovereign's subjects. Kelsiev attributed a major part of the responsibility for the revolutionary unrest in Russia to the excessive government censorship and the general restrictions on the freedom of the individual imposed by the government. He criticized the inadequacy of educational facilities in Russia. He advised the government to provide an institution through which the people could openly exert influence upon the government. He urged the tsar to break the barrier which was allegedly separating the government from the people and to utilize the native talents of all members of society in improving living conditions in Russia. The future of Russia, he declared, depended on the government's understanding of the people. On the other hand, he also claimed that the doctrinaire revolutionaries, with their abstract theories, were even further removed from the people than was the government.

In his criticism of the governmental institutions Kelsiev specifically isolated the Russian consular service. He claimed that the Slavs in the Ottoman Empire invariably felt that to go to a Russian consul was like going before a judge and that "it was easier to deal with the Turks than with the Russian consuls." The Russian consular representatives, he complained, lived in isolation from the local people and neither accepted invitations to attend social events nor themselves ever entertained. According to Kelsiev, such reproaches against the Russian representatives could be heard not only in the Ottoman

Empire but also in Austria, England, or "anywhere else."
What is more, the complaints emanated not only from some
displaced and oppressed nationalities but also from Russians.
"Whereas an American, Italian, or a Prussian, who for some
reason finds himself abroad, may confidently go to his respective consulate knowing that he will always receive both
assistance and encouragement, a Russian is received by our
consulate with arrogance and even rudeness. The consular
officials will not take an extra step on his behalf, especially if
he is in trouble and is not well-known."

Kelsiev pointed out that of all the envoys representing
Russia among the European states and Ottoman Empire, only
one, Count Nicholas P. Ignatiev, serving in Constantinople,
was ethnically Russian. All the others, he claimed, were
German, and he advised the tsar to start Russifying the Russian foreign service. He suggested that Russian should become
the language of diplomacy and that persons entering the
foreign service should be thoroughly familiar with Slavic
history and the other Slavic languages. He went on to propose
a rather modern scheme which called for the creation of a
society of Russian travellers. This society was to be secretly
sponsored by the government but appear to be acting independently of it. Its members "would surround the whole of
Europe with their friends," creating thereby an efficient network of Russian agents throughout the continent. Thus, Kelsiev was advising the tsar to strengthen the government by
the very same methods he, Kelsiev, had only recently been
using in trying to undermine that same government.[10]

Although he did not denounce the revolutionaries as
individuals, Kelsiev did reject the revolutionary movement.
In the case of the Raskolniks, on the other hand, he defended
both individuals and the movement. In defending them he
stressed the intensity of their alleged patriotism. The Raskolniks, he stated many times in his *Confession*, were unjustly
restricted by the government. They constituted no political
threat to the government, he argued, and only a dreamer such
as he had been would entertain the notion that they were a
potential revolutionary force. The Russian masses in general
and the Raskolniks in particular, he claimed, were so tradi-

tion-bound that many of them still adhered to the notion of
Moscow's being the Third Rome. To substantiate his argument,
Kelsiev cited a verse from Russian folklore which allegedly
was still popular with the masses.

> The Holy Russian land is the mother of all lands.
> It is the mother of all the lands because
> It believes in a faith which is truly Christian,
> Which is Christian and Orthodox.
> The Holy Russian tsar is the tsar of all tsars.
> He is the tsar of all tsars because
> He builds cathedral churches,
> Cathedral churches which are sacred.
> And all tsars, kings, and mirzas will bow down
>     before him;
> All tsardoms will come under his authority.

He insisted that the Russian people believed in this, and that
they regarded themselves to be superior to all other people
on earth. The real reason for the emergence of the Raskol, he
explained, is found in the fact that "Nikon and Peter, in pul-
ling out the darnel, pulled out the wheat as well and thereby
offended the people's pride."

As for the Raskolniks living in Dobrudja, Kelsiev thought
that both their loyalty to the tsar and the harsh conditions of
that region made Dobrudja a suitable place for purging young
idealists, such as he had been, of their revolutionary illusions.
By bringing him face to face with reality, Dobrudja changed
him, he claimed, and he advised the government that it would
change anyone else who would be sent there for a year or two.
The radical youth, he suggested, should be exiled to Dobrudja. "You should send there the young men who join the
'organizations' and the 'hells'. In Dobrudja there is complete
freedom, such freedom as does not likely exist even in the
United States. Let these young men preach their revolutionary
propaganda in Dobrudja; let them make their revolutions
and establish their communes. Dobrudja will cure them of
their *febris revolutionaris.*" He proposed that the government
should rely on him for bringing back to Russia the Raskolniks

who were living abroad. Significantly enough, the Tsar heeded his advice on this point and ordered the Ministry of Internal Affairs to undertake a study of the feasibility of his proposal. Although, like most of Kelsiev's projects, this scheme, too, failed to materialize, it did serve to convince the Tsar of Kelsiev's potential usefulness to the state, and it influenced the monarch in his decision to pardon the former revolutionary.[11]

The drama of his return, combined with the sensation evoked by the Tsar's unexpected pardon, momentarily made Kelsiev a *cause célèbre* in the Russian capital. Even when he was still abroad, his stature as a revolutionary had been significantly enhanced in the eyes of the residents of St. Petersburg and Moscow by the anti-revolutionary articles of Michael Katkov, the well-known publicist and editor of the influential journal, *Russkii Vestnik*. Katkov depicted Kelsiev as the leader of an allegedly powerful band of revolutionaries—the Tulcea phalanx—which, according to Katkov, was responsible, among other things, for the fires which had been causing extensive damage in southern Russia and in the two capital cities. Kelsiev's importance was thus significantly exaggerated in the press, and even such intellectuals as Dostoevsky seem to have been prone to ascribe to him an importance far in excess of his true stature. Following his release, Kelsiev was invited to lecture before the Geographic Society; his articles were in great demand by influential journals; and he became the centre of attraction at social gatherings in the literary salons. Prominent personages among the literary intelligentsia, such as Alexis K. Tolstoy (the creator of the famous fictitious aphorist Kuzma Prutkov) and Prince Vladimir F. Odoevsky (a noted social philosopher and Hoffmannesque writer) served as his hosts. The real extent of his popularity may be gleaned most effectively from the fact that shortly following his release from prison, an adventurous literary-minded woman named Zinaida Alekseevna Verderevskaia became his consort, apparently with the prime motive of partaking in the adulation he was receiving from the literary circles.[12]

Finding himself in the midst of literary personages, Kelsiev attempted to live up to the expectations of their guild: he began to apply his literary talents as he had never applied

them before. The years that he had lived following his return
to Russia, therefore, proved to be the most fruitful period in
his literary career, which as a whole, one must admit, was far
from fruitful.

Throughout most of his life Kelsiev imagined himself
to be a writer. Yet, even during his most productive period
he failed to counteract the centrifugal forces of the literary
world which kept him on a distant periphery from its centre.
During his studies at the University of St. Petersburg he had
been, somewhat obliquely, exposed to the literary world,
through an acquaintance with an upcoming poet of radical
bent, Nicholas Dobroliubov, and with Dostoevsky's brother
Michael. In July 1862 he apparently met Dostoevsky himself,
when the latter visited Herzen in London. In any event, Dostoevsky was very much interested in Kelsiev's career. In a
letter written to a friend in 1867 the great novelist expressed
approval of Kelsiev's return to Russia and exclaimed, "That
is the right way, that is truth and reason!" It is also possible
that Kelsiev served as a prototype for Dostoevsky's Shatov
in *The Possessed*—a novel dealing with the revolutionary
movement. There are many similarities between the revolutionary of Dostoevsky's novel and Vasily Kelsiev. Both Kelsiev
and Shatov learned to love Russia only after they had gone
abroad, both voluntarily returned from abroad, and both expressed the idea that the separation of the revolutionaries from
the people was the chief source of atheism and nihilism among
the revolutionary intellectuals. According to Dostoevsky, when
Shatov was abroad, he abandoned his revolutionary convictions and went to the other extreme. "He was one of those
idealistic Russians who, struck by some compelling idea, become incurably possessed by it. They are quite incapable of
mastering it, but believe in it so passionately that their whole
life passes, as it were, broken under the weight of a heavy
stone which has half crushed them." For many years Kelsiev,
too, was "half crushed" by a weighty ideological boulder.[13]

Kelsiev's productive literary career began in London,
and, like his revolutionary career, it began in failure. The first
article he attempted to publish was rejected by his own friends,
the publishers of *The Bell*, and it was rejected on the basis

of its literary merits. Thereafter he made numerous attempts at creative writing, but prior to his return to Russia they remained mere attempts. Upon his discovery of the government reports on the Raskol, for example, Kelsiev thought of writing the Raskol's history, but in the end merely edited the documents. In London he also undertook at one point the curious task of translating the Old Testament from Hebrew into modern Russian. His literal translation of it was so vulgar that even the atheistic Herzen thought that it would be a sacrilege to print it. Following his secret mission to Russia in 1862, Kelsiev set out to write a Russian grammar for English-speaking people, but, as Herzen expressed it, the secret journey to Russia "ruined his last *Sitzfleisch*," and he went to Constantinople without completing the project. From Dobrudja he wrote once to Herzen of a plan for publishing a collection of Tartar songs in English, but he never wrote about the subject again.[14]

In spite of the meagerness of his literary output prior to his return to Russia, Kelsiev never ceased thinking of himself as an important writer. The significance of the role literature played in his life can perhaps best be seen in that in the process of emancipating himself from his political religiosity, he sought refuge in the world of literature and ultimately traded one fictitious world for another. A commentary on his own literary talents, written at the time of bereavement for his brother Ivan, is interesting both as a reflection of Kelsiev's psychological state at the time and as an illustration of the image he entertained of himself as a writer.

The form of my narration is somewhat mystical [he wrote to one of his acquaintances in Russia]: I am telling unbelievable anecdotes about the discovery of the elixir of life, about magic, gnomes, creatures of the planet Mars, etc., but in these allegories I am posing questions concerning the real and good. Mix together Poe, Gulliver [sic], Herzen, and Chernyshevsky, add the humour of Cervantes and the bile of Dante, and you will have some understanding of the style and content of my writings. As their creator,

> I can only say that there is a great deal of originality
> in my works, and were there no one else occupying
> Chernyshevsky's place, then I would, without any
> embarrassment, assume that position in the broken
> chain of Russian thinkers . . .

The editor of Kelsiev's *Confession* remarked in reference to
this passage that "this sounds altogether *à la* Khlestakov," al-
luding, of course, to the famous braggart of Gogol's *Inspector
General*. One should not, however, be excessively harsh with
Kelsiev on this score, for great men of literature, too, have
been noted for their egocentrism. Pushkin, after all, "erected
himself a monument not made by human hand" [*pamiatnik
sebe vozdvig nerukotvornyi*], and Shakespeare surely claimed
prerogatives reserved to the gods with his confidence that "So
long as men can breathe, or eyes can see; So long lives this,
and this gives life to thee." Regardless of the verdict one may
pronounce on Kelsiev for his egocentric indulgence, the truth
is that, unlike the boastful claims made by the literary giants
mentioned above, his were empty, for the gnomes and dwel-
lers of Mars whom he aspired to create failed to partake in
the elixir of literary life.[15]

During his residence in Vienna and Jassy, Kelsiev published a number of travel accounts in Russian periodicals. To
the Russian reader of the 1860's these accounts were undoubtedly of considerable interest, for they dealt with people who
were little known to Russians. None of these articles, however, could be considered a creative literary work, and it probably would be accurate to suggest that his first and possibly
the only literary work was his *Confession*. In addition to
being a valuable historical document, Kelsiev's *Confession,
like* Avvakum's *Life*, is a powerful work of literature, resembling in style and form Tolstoy's *Confession* (written in
1880-82). The passages in Kelsiev's *Confession* range from
catalogued enumerations of names to forceful dramatizations
of the emotional conflicts experienced by the author. Both
in his letters and in the *Confession*, Kelsiev demonstrated a
commendable ability to describe pathos and formulate mini-
ature character sketches. In the latter respect he attains at

times the level reached by a true master of the craft, his political associate, Alexander Herzen.

A person whom Kelsiev disliked, Peter Martianov, for example, emerges from under Kelsiev's pen as a man possessing "a strong mind and character, proud, ambitious, even vengeful, but lacking in formal education. For his intellectual development he was indebted exclusively to himself: he educated himself by reading Russian books. He did not know any foreign languages, but he learned from everything he read. Unfortunately, there was in him, as in all *parvenus*, who rise up in the world on their own resources, a hidden feeling of enmity..." A revolutionary named Arthur Beny, according to Kelsiev, "was born in Poland, lived in England, practiced medicine in Paris, and became a Russian publicist and agitator in St. Petersburg..." Nicholas Serno-Solovievich was "a very enthusiastic man, very intelligent, energetic, always ready to do anything that is honest and noble, and a man who loved Russia." His brother Alexander, on the other hand, "was a sick man, nervous, gloomy, no less talented but less firm in character: he did not possess Nicholas's kind of indomitable courage to speak the truth to another's face and stand by his convictions." Ivan Shibaev, the young Raskolnik with whom Kelsiev communicated in Moscow, was a man "of diminutive mind and rather weak character. He was an enthusiast, a dreamer, always ready to become involved in something, and blazing out like burning straw at every new and honest thought, especially in every difficult and unusual undertaking." Finally, noting once again, Paul the Prussian— the benign, ubiquitous abbot of the Theodocians—is captured by Kelsiev with unquestionable artistic mastery. "Entered a man who was tall, lean, with black hair, about forty years of age. He was dressed in a monk's attire; that is, a black cassock, a cloak (a black cape with red edging), and kamilavka— a round cap with a fur brim. This was the first time that I had seen our monastic vestment of the pre-Nikonian period... I looked at this man with utmost attentiveness—a man with an intelligent, perpetually-smiling face and with black sparkling eyes full of life and thought. We began to talk." [16]

The existence of Kelsiev's *Confession* became a well-known fact even before its author was freed from prison, yet it was not released for publication until after the Revolution of 1917. The Tsar's pardon of Kelsiev on the basis of the information contained in the *Confession* served to stimulate wide interest and many speculations among intellectuals about its contents. Thus, when Kelsiev published his memoirs, *Perezhitoe i peredumannoe* [*My Life and Thought*] in 1868, which was based on his *Confession*, he momentarily reigned supreme over the politically-oriented literary intelligentsia—but only momentarily.

When Herzen first learned about the publication of *Perezhitoe i peredumannoe*, he nearly shouted in excitement. "Kelsiev's book, please... a half a kingdom for Kelsiev's book," he begged his friend Ogarev in a letter. At that point Herzen was most anxious to write a polemical review of the book. Six weeks later, however, he wrote to Ogarev in quite a different tone: "I have finished reading Kelsiev. I resolutely decline to write the review and would not advise you to do it." The marked fluctuation in Herzen's mood evoked by Kelsiev's book appears to parallel the response to it by the literary intelligentsia in general: a tension built up by the drama of Kelsiev's return and his unexpected pardon; a desire to defend or denounce the political renegade, depending on one's own political alignment; then a sigh of disappointment on both sides of the political dividing line. Instead of a lion, a mouse had been born. Several political radicals reviewed the book nonetheless, ignoring whatever literary merits it possessed and quartering its author on political grounds.[17]

The title of Kelsiev's memoirs was apparently modeled on Herzen's *Byloe i dumy*, but qualitatively there is little ground for comparing the two works. In *Perezhitoe i peredumannoe* Kelsiev presented essentially the same material as in the *Confession*, omitting, however, most of his political theorizing and his criticisms of the government. *Perezhitoe i peredumannoe* is useful for studying Kelsiev's life in general and especially his childhood. As a work of literature, however, it is amateurish. It lacks unity, is permeated with an artificial lyrical sentimentality, and in stylistic vigour is but an emasculated shadow of his *Confession*.

The hostility levelled against Kelsiev by the reviewers of *Perezhitoe i peredumannoe* failed to extinguish his determination to claim a place among writers. In 1869 he published a work called *Galichina i Moldaviia [Galicia and Moldavia]*. This is an ethnographic account of his travels in Eastern Europe. It, too, was severely criticized. In subsequent years he published three short historical novels: *Moskva i Tver'* (1871), *Pri Petre* (1872), and *Na vse ruki master* (1871-72). In spite of his life-long interest in ethnology and history, his historical novels met the worst possible fate: they received no criticism. He was compelled to reciprocate the ominous public silence in kind, and Kelsiev the writer met the fate of Kelsiev the revolutionary—only this time there was no Prut to cross, no tsar to supplicate or challenge, and his confession had already been written.

In generalizing on his role as a writer one may dismiss Kelsiev as having been a literary dreamer void of talent; on the other hand, one may ponder the possibility of Kelsiev the writer falling victim to Kelsiev the revolutionary. Although it may be argued that a writer's active concern with the affairs of his society may serve to stimulate his artistic expressiveness, it is probably also true that an intense involvement in such affairs serves to impede his literary creativity. A writer institutionalized is a writer sterilized. This would seem to be especially true in the case of compulsory institutionalization. The essence of this problem has been picturesquely captured in a quatrain by an eighteenth-century Russian poet:

> They caught a sweet-voiced bird,
> And tightly clutched the wildwood thing,
> Instead of a song squeaks are heard—
> But they keep at it:: "Sing, bird, sing!" [18]

Social and political involvement tended to absorb the literary talents of many Russian intellectuals in the nineteenth century. The famous literary critic, Vissarion Belinsky, attributed Gogol's decline, for example, to the latter's devotion to religion. One may also wonder if Belinsky himself would not have been a greater critic and writer had he been less involved with the affairs of contemporary society. The talents of young poets such as Dobroliubov and Lermontov appear to have been dented by their reactions to their respective socio-political problems. A classic example of the undermining of literature through extreme involvement in social affairs is the tragedy of Tolstoy. Although Tolstoy did produce several works of art after his "conversion," his obsession with the problem of reforming society tended to purge him of his former creative vigour. Thus, it is not entirely unjustifiable to ponder the possibility that Kelsiev's maximalist devotion to social and political problems served to undermine whatever literary talents he possessed. In order to be fair to Kelsiev and other Russian writers as human beings, however, one should appreciate the difficulties which they faced. For them to have been preoccupied solely with aesthetics while living under the conditions existing in Russia would have been tantamount to a poet's singing praise to the firmness and beauty of the human body in a leper colony. And yet, one may wonder whether Pushkin's Tatiana was not more essential than Chernyshevsky's Rakhmetov even for a hungry Russia.

Kelsiev's failure to achieve recognition in the world of literature was consistent with the tenor of his entire life. His popularity with the social and literary circles of St. Petersburg was ephemeral. The government did act upon the proposals he made in his *Confession* concerning the resettlement of the Danubean Raskolniks in the Caucasus, but, in studying the problem the Ministry of Internal Affairs did not call on him for assistance. A report was made on the subject indicating that there were no suitable tracts of land available in the Caucasus for resettling the Raskolniks without dispersing their communities, and in May 1869, the project was cancelled altogether. To Kelsiev this was another failure, and he felt himself a slave unwanted by his master.[19]

An entry of May 3 (o. s.) of that year in the diary of Alexander V. Nikitenko—a member of the social circle in which Kelsiev was momentarily lionized—reveals that at that time the repentant revolutionary had already entered the final phase of his tragic existence.

An evening with Kelsiev. His wife held a musicale. She herself played the piano and played it magnificently. There were two other musicians: two young men, one of whom played the violincello and the other the violin. They, too, played well. Kelsiev himself is leaving for America, in search of a new way of life. He intends to lecture there about Russia. His situation here is becoming outright impossible. He is permitted to live in Russia but has been denied the possibility of finding work and supporting himself. This is simply absurd. Either they should have not allowed him to enter Russia or they should have provided him with some lawful means of existence. He wanted to publish a newspaper, but they did not permit that. In this particular case one might suppose that there might be good reasons for that decision, but there were various vacant positions which he could have filled fruitfully both for himself and for the profession, but all of these were denied to him.

The newspaper he planned to publish was to be called *Vostok* or *The East*, and it was to serve as an aid in promoting Russia's national interest in China and possibly in India. The government considered the project, but, because of Kelsiev's revolutionary past, refused to grant permission for its realization. The frustrations arising out of these failures led him to intensify his literary activities, but these activities, as has been noted, yielded neither fame nor a livelihood.[20]

The final failure of our suffering warrior lacked the dramatic intensity which characterized many of his other misfortunes. With the admission of his failure in literature he lowered his arms in resignation and was rapidly engulfed in the dreadful process of withering away. On October 15, 1871 (o. s.), a year before Kelsiev's death, Nikitenko deposited in his diary another grain of malice formulated through the dialectical collision between his obvious resentment of Vasily Kelsiev and his equally obvious admiration for Kelsiev's new consort.

Mrs. Kelsiev was here. This poor woman has spent
the best part of her life in adventures—adventures
which usually befall a woman richly endowed with
beauty and talent but deprived of a sensible upbringing and discipline. From the age of seven she lived
in Italy, where, among other things, she acquired an
excellent training in music but failed to acquire any
good sense. Twice she was married under doubtful
circumstances, and finally in St. Petersburg she fell
in love with Kelsiev, who had just returned from
abroad with the permission of the Emperor. Since
everything unusual appealed to her, she was undoubtedly attracted by the unusual fate of this political
adventurer, who is, to be sure, not entirely devoid of
talent, but who is in the highest degree frivolous
and whimsical, as are many of our young political
liberals with red coloration. She united with Kelsiev expecting to find in him a nearly great man.
Instead, she found a man who was totally incapable
of any constructive task and, what is more, a man
devoted to drinking.

For two years she managed to endure him, and
finally, as she has said, she was compelled to leave
him to his pitiful fate. She apparently wants to
rejoin a social group in which intelligence and talent
are valued. She wants to be active in literature . . .[21]

Information about Kelsiev's second wife is extremely scarce,
and little can be added to Nikitenko's remarks about her.
Apparently, she could rightfully boast of talent, beauty, and
prominence in salon society. Born Zinaida Alekseevna Verderevskaia (1834), she was best known by the name of her
first husband, Agrenev. Nikitenko's diary indicates that by
November 1868 she was already married to Kelsiev and that
their marriage dissolved sometime before October 15, 1871
(o. s.) There is a curious note by the editor of Nikitenko's
diary which suggests that the two literators lived together
without a legal marriage. During her association with Kelsiev,
Zinaida published several articles in journals, including

*Otechestvennye zapiski,* but her literary talent was apparently inferior to the other attributes she employed in acquiring popularity. Following Kelsiev's death, which was probably hastened by their separation, the perpetual adventuress fulfilled the plan which she and her late husband had entertained: she emigrated to America.

Thus, following his release from prison, Kelsiev's claims on life were, one by one, frustrated. His reading public abandoned him; the government pardoned but did not forgive him; the literary intellectuals became bored by and began to avoid him; and the revolutionaries simply despised him. Under these circumstances the sorrowful idealist turned to a remedy which for centuries had absorbed the bitterness and sorrows of many a Russian: he turned to alcohol. His choice of escape from the world hastened his talented wife's contemplated desertion of him. On October 4, 1872 (o. s.), at the age of thirty-seven, the romantic dreamer, who had struggled so passionately and at times valiantly with the world, abandoned it forever. He died an alcoholic and a pauper. The immediate cause of death was heart failure. He died in the arms of his old teacher, a certain A. E. Razin. An acquaintance recorded the final event with a sorrowful sigh of relief: "When I heard about this, I unwittingly felt glad for him. His life was difficult during its final years. It was a difficult, fruitless, needless, broken, and an unsuccessful life." [22]

Kelsiev lived at a time when the Newton-Kepler explanations of the mechanics of the universe, the glorification of man by the eighteenth-century rationalists, the implications of Darwin's writings concerning man's worldliness, and the deification of man as an historical personality by Hegel—all of these weighty ideas—descended upon the Russian intellectuals with dramatic suddenness. This suddenness was due to the rapid appearance of the intelligentsia from the ranks of the hitherto unenlightened Russian masses. Blinded by these revelations of a new world, many a Russian intellectual expressed his surprise by announcing a hastily-arrived-at conclusion that there is no God. Having shouted thus, these intellectuals became frightened by such a thunderous message emanating from such diminutive creatures as they now sensed themselves to be. On this level of reasoning, much of Kelsiev's revolutionary fervour can be seen as having been a search for personal security by a man claiming total jurisdiction over his own destiny. His insecurity stimulated an intense activism and instilled in him a feeling of religiosity toward his revolutionary commitments. Having become thus activated, Kelsiev had little choice but to follow the course predetermined by his commitment. To break away from that course was to betray not only his cause but also his inner self and meet the fate he, indeed, met following his return to Russia.

On the other hand, the throbbing and tragic humanness of Kelsiev's life begs the historian for an empathic response. In prison in 1867, Kelsiev addressed the historians of the future with the following plea:

> The time will come—perhaps a hundred or a hundred and fifty years from now—when my *Confession* will come up from the archives and appear before the judgment of historians. Perhaps they will find that I have erred, that I failed to understand the events of our time, but they will not fail to recognize that I sincerely desired the well-being of Russia, and that, while confined behind bars within the walls of prison cell No. 4, I thought less about myself than about the programmes which I think our government should follow for the good of our great nation . . . My conscience is clear, my duty has been fulfilled; and the generations, which I will not see, will remember me as an *honest man.*[23]

One hundred years have now passed. Kelsiev's *Confession* did "come up" from the archives, and at least one historian—duty fulfilled, conscience clear—considers him a dreamer who deserves to be remembered as an *honest man.*

# NOTES

## NOTES TO CHAPTER I

[1] When applied to the socio-political developments in Russia the term "1860's" is generally used to denote the fifteen-year period from the ascension of Alexander II in 1855 to 1870. This usage will be adhered to in the present work.

[2] Nikolai V. Shelgunov, *Vospominaniia* (Moscow, 1923), pp. 162-63.

[3] Whereas in 1859, according to a Soviet source, there were only 91 peasant disturbances in the Russian Empire, in 1860 the acts of open violence increased in number to 126, and in the very year of the emancipation the number of violent outbreaks reached an unprecedented high of 1,259. (Militsa V. Nechkina, ed., *Revoliutsionnaia situatsiia v Rossii v 1859-1861 gg.* [Moscow: Izdatel'stvo Akademii Nauk SSSR, 1960], p. 128).

[4] The term "intelligentsia" will be used here to denote collectively all of the Russian intellectuals. The terms "revolutionary intelligentsia," "radical intelligentsia," or "revolutionary movement" will be used, synonymously, to designate that element of the Russian intelligentsia which actively supported a radical socio-political reorganization of Russia. In Soviet terminology this same element is referred to as the "liberation movement."

[5] Founded in 1799, the Russian-American Company maintained a monopoly over the commercial colonization of Alaska and other North American territories claimed by Russia. Subsequently it also became active in populating and developing the south-eastern maritime province of Siberia and the Island of Sakhalin. In spite of the subsidies the Company received from the government, it failed to compete effectively with the Hudson's Bay Company in the fur trade. In 1868, following the sale of Alaska to the United States in the previous year, the Russian-American Company was dissolved.

[6] Vasilii I. Kel'siev, "Ispoved'," *Literaturnoe nasledstvo*, vols. XLI-XLII (1941), pp. 272-73. Hereafter cited as Kelsiev, *Ispoved'*.

[7] *Ibid.*, p. 271.

[8] Vasilii I. Kel'siev, *Perezhitoe i peredumannoe* (St. Petersburg, 1868), pp. 253-54.

[9] *Ibid.*, pp. 253-58, 260-61.

[10] Vasilii I. Kel'siev, "Pol'skie agenty v Tsaregrade," *Russkii vestnik*, LXXXIV (November, 1869), 167.

[11] Kelsiev, *Perezhitoe i peredumannoe*, pp. 248-49, 265; Kelsiev, *Ispoved'*, p. 270.

[12] Kelsiev, *Ispoved'*, p. 286.

[13] Kelsiev, *Perezhitoe i peredumannoe*, p. 295.

[14] Nikolai A. Berdiaev, et al, *Vekhi* (Moscow, 1909), pp. 180, 42, 2-3, 192-93.

[15] *Ibid.*, p. 80.

[16] Aleksandr I. Hertsen, *Sobranie sochinenii* (Moscow, 1954-64), vol. XI, pp. 330, 332.

[17] Shelgunov, *Vospominaniia*, pp. 146-47, 152-53.

[18] Kelsiev, *Perezhitoe i peredumannoe*, p. 303.

[19] *Ibid.*, pp. 248, 309; Kelsiev, *Ispoved'*, p. 269.

[20] Kelsiev, *Perezhitoe i peredumannoe*, pp. 393-94.

[21] Nikolai A. Dobroliubov, *Polnoe sobranie sochinenii* (Moscow: Gosudarstvennoe izdatel'stvo "Khudozhestvennaia literatura," 1939), vol. VI, p. 459.

[22] Herzen, *Sobranie sochinenii*, vol. XI, pp. 330, 336.

[23] Aleksandr I. Gertsen, *Byloe i dumy* (Minsk, 1957), vol. II, p. 517.

[24] Vasilii I. Kel'siev, "Emigrant Abikht," *Russkii vestnik*, LXXIX (January, 1869), 241-43.

[25] Herzen, *Byloe i dumy*, vol. II, p. 518.

[26] Herzen, *Sobranie sochinenii*, vol. XXVII, p. 719; Natal'ia A. Tuchkova-Ogareva, *Vospominaniia* (Moscow, 1959), pp. 196-97. The novel is *Histoire du veritable Gribouille*, with the Russian title *Pokhozhdeniia Gribulia* (London, 1860).

[27] An extensive list of the names of the individuals who contributed to *The Bell* has been compiled by Mitrofan M. Klevenskii in "Gertsen—izdatel' i ego sotrudniki," *Literaturnoe nasledstvo*, vols. XLI-XLII, pp. 572-620.

[28] For archival materials on Ogarev see *Literaturnoe nasledstvo*, vol. XI. pp. 459-702; and vol. LXIII, pp. 855-879.

## NOTES TO CHAPTER II

[1] Vasilii I. Kel'siev, "Ispoved'," *Literaturnoe nasledstvo*, vols. XLI-XLII (1941), p. 285.

[2] Aleksandr I. Gertsen, *Sobranie sochinenii* (Moscow, 1954-64), vol. XI, p. 334.

[3] The reports were published under the title *Sbornik pravitel'stvennykh svedenii o raskol'nikakh* (London: Truebner and Company, 1860-62). Hereafter cited as Kelsiev, *Sbornik*.

[4] Sergei M. Solov'ev, *Istoria Rossii s drevneishikh vremen* (Moscow, 1960-66), vol. I, p. 59.

[5] Nikolai F. Kapterev, *Patriarkh Nikon i ego protivniki v dele ispravleniia tserkovnykh obriadov* (Moscow, 1887), p. 27; and his *Kharakter otnoshenii Rossii k pravoslavnomu Vostoku v XVI i XVII stoletiiakh* (Sergiev Posad, 1914), pp. 426-27.

[6] Sukhanov's writings are found in Sergei Belokurov, *Arsenii Sukhanov* (Moscow, 1891-94); Vasilii O. Kliuchevskii, "Zapadnoe vliianie v Rossii XVII v.," *Voprosy filosofii i psikhologii*, VIII (January, 1897), 137-155; (May, 1897), 533-558; and (September, 1897), 760-800.

[7] As far as I know, no systematic study has been made of the ethnic composition of the Raskol. In view of the fact that the Raskol originated in Moscow and that its strongpoints were initially located in the areas populated

predominantly by Great Russians, in the seventeenth century the Raskólniks were almost exclusively of Great Russian stock. A possible exception to this may be found in the case of the Old Believer cossacks of the Don region, where the cossack population included a strong admixture of the Ukrainian element.

[8] Kel'siev, *Sbornik*, vol. I, pp. 219-21.

[9] Avvakum's experiences in Siberia are described in his *Zhitie protopopa Avvakuma im samim napisannoe i drugie ego sochineniia* (Moscow, 1960), and in his "O zhestokosti voevody Pashkova," *Russkaia istoricheskaia biblioteka*, XXXIX (1927), 701-04.

In referring to Nikon, Avvakum often used epithets such as "a son of a whore," "an accursed dog," and "a black satan." Nikon's brutality toward his opponents is vividly depicted in Avvakum's "Kniga besed," *ibid.*, pp. 246-49.

[10] Avvakum, *Zhitie*, pp. 72-73 86. In translating the passages cited here I closely followed the English text appearing in George P. Fedotov's *A Treasury of Russian Spirituality* (Belmont, MA., 1975).

[11] Avvakum, *Zhitie*, p. 87.

[12] *Ibid.*, pp. 95, 105, 106.

[13] Protopop Avvakum, "Chelobitnaia tsariu Alekseiu Mikhailovichu," *ibid.*, pp. 159, 206.

[14] "Akty otnosiashchiesia k istorii Solovetskago bunta," *Chteniia v Imperatorskom obshchestve istorii i drevnostei rossiiskikh pri Moskovskom universitete* (October-December, 1883), part 4, p. 87; Kel'siev, *Sbornik*, vol. I, p. 177.

[15] Nikolai I. Kostomarov, "Istoriia raskola u raskol'nikov," *Vestnik Evropy*, VI (April, 1871), 469-85.

[16] Of the twenty thousand Raskolniks committing suicide by fire from the beginning of the schism up to the last decade of the seventeenth century, more than sixteen thousand immolated themselves in the years following the enactment of Sophia's decree of 1685. (Paul Miliukov, *Outlines of Russian Culture* (New York, 1960), vol. I, p. 59.

[17] Although on his return Peter found the rebels under control, he nonetheless took matters into his own hands and instituted a reign of terror unparalleled in Russian annals since the massacres of the boyars during the reign of Ivan the Terrible. "Tortures were followed by waves of mass executions, gallows and execution blocks being erected in Red Square, around the convent where Sophia was incarcerated, in Preobrazhenskoe. On September 30, 201 men went to their death; on October 11, 144; on October 12, 205; on October 19, 106; on October 20, 2." (Michael T. Florinsky, *Russia: A History and an Interpretation* [New York: The Macmillan Company, 1953], vol. I, pp. 324-25.)

[18] According to the official who dealt with this problem in the government reports, the original parchment with which the government had tampered was written in 1157. After the forgery had been proven, the parchment was placed in a container, secured with the imperial seal, and hidden in the Synodal library. Even Karamzin, an official historiographer of the Russian state, one hundred years later, was unable to gain access to it. In 1857, the parchment was still being held under the imperial seal and had been assigned the catalogue number 518. (Kel'siev, *Sbornik*, vol. I, pp. 180-81.)

[19] Kel'siev, *Sbornik*, vol. I, pp. 36-40; Afanasii P. Shchapov, *Sochineniia* (St. Petersburg, 1906-08), vol. I, p. 176.

[20] Kel'siev, *Sbornik*, vol. I, pp. 185-87; Vladimir D. Bonch-Bruevich, *Izbrannye sochineniia* (Moscow, 1959), vol. I, p. 304.

[21] Kel'siev, *Sbornik*, vol. I, pp. 183-84; vol. II, pp. 176-77; and vol. IV, p. 295.

[22] *Ibid.*, vol. II, pp. 146-47; Miliukov, *Outlines of Russian Culture*, vol. I, pp. 116-17.

[23] Kel'siev, *Sbornik*, vol. IV, p. 70.

[24] *Ibid.*, vol. IV, pp. 252-53.

[25] *Ibid.*, vol. II, pp. viii, 9, 44-45, 48-50; vol. IV, p. 288.

[26] Kel'siev, *Sbornik*, vol. I, p. xxviii; vol. II, pp. xiv, 136-39; Miliukov, *Outlines of Russian Culture*, vol. I, p. 116.

[27] Kel'siev, *Sbornik*, vol. I, p. 174; vol. II, pp. 21, 79-82, 87-89; 135-36, vol. IV, pp. 22-23.

[28] *Ibid.*, vol. I, p. xxviii; vol. III, pp. 15-20; Vasilii V. Rozanov, *Apokalipsicheskaia sekta* (*Khlysty i skoptsy*), (St. Petersburg, 1914), p. 117; Pavel I. Mel'nikov, *Polnoe sobranie sochinenii* (St. Petersburg, 1897-1901), vol. XIV, p. 208.

[29] Kel'siev, *Sbornik*, vol. II, pp. 116-18; vol. III, pp. 63-67, 150-54, 209, 236.

The *oskoplenie* or castration was of two types: partial castration or the "minor seal" and full castration or the "royal seal." The minor seal involved the removal of the testes from males and the nipples of breasts from females. The royal seal consisted of the removal of both the testes and the penis from males and both the breasts and the vulva from females. There were a number of methods employed: in some cases it was self-castration; in others it was a private castration performed by another; and in still others it was a ceremonial ritual. In ceremonial castrations hot irons were used, and the amputated organs were thrown into the fire in which the irons had been heated. The flesh from the virgins' breasts was in some cases eaten as sacramental food. Castration was referred to as baptism by fire, and the members of the sect called themselves the white doves. (*Ibid.*, vol. II, p. 121; vol. III, pp. 124-29.)

[30] Iosif I. Kablits (pseud. Iuzov), "Politicheskie vozzreniia staroveriia," *Russkaia mysl'*, V (May, 1882), 181-218. The quotation is from p. 197.

# NOTES TO CHAPTER III

[1] Bishop Makarii, *Istoriia russkago raskola izvestnago pod imenem staroobriadstva* (St. Petersburg, 1854); Ministerstvo vnutrennikh del, *Sobranie postanovlenii po chasti raskola* (St. Petersburg, 1875), pp. 537-42; [Afanasii P. Shchapov], "O prichinakh proiskhozhdeniia i rasprostraneniia raskola, izvestnago pod imenem staroobriadstva, vo vtoroi polovine XVII i v pervoi polovine XVIII stoletiia," *Pravoslavnyi sobesednik*, IV (1857), 629-89, 857-91; Pavel I. Mel'nikov, *Polnoe sobranie sochinenii* (St. Petersburg, 1897-1901), vol. I, p. 117.

[2] Vasilii I. Kel'siev, *Sbornik pravitel'stvennykh svedenii o raskol'nikakh* (London, 1860-62), vol. II, p. xvii; Aleksandr I. Gertsen, *Polnoe sobranie sochinenii i pisem pod redaktsiei M. K. Lemke* (St. Petersburg, 1919-25), vol. III, pp. 402-03 and vol. IX, pp. 180-81; *Izbrannye filosofskie proizvedeniia*

(Moscow, 1946), vol. I, p. 333 and vol. II, pp. 140-43, 146; *O razvitii revo-liutsionnykh idei v Rossii* (Moscow, 1958), pp. 51, 76, 106; *Sobranie sochi-nenii* (Moscow, 1954-64), vol. VII, pp. 259-63; August von Haxthausen, *The Russian Empire* (London, 1856).

³ Kel'siev, *Sbornik*, vol. I, pp. iii-iv, xxviii-xxx.

⁴ Vasilii I. Kel'siev, *Perezhitoe i peredumannoe* (St. Petersburg, 1868), p. 302.

⁵ Vasilii I. Kel'siev, "Ispoved'," *Literaturnoe nasledstvo*, vols. XLI-XLII (1941), pp. 298-299.

⁶ *Ibid.*, pp. 300-306.

⁷ *Ibid.*, pp. 301, 462; G. [Nikolai I. Subbotin], "Raskol kak orudie vrazh-debnykh Rossii partii," *Russkii vestnik*, LXVIII (April 1867), 724-26.

⁸ *Ibid.*, pp. 714-15; Kel'siev, *Ispoved'*, p. 304.

⁹ *Ibid.*, p. 305; Subbotin, "Raskol kak orudie," pp. 725-26.

¹⁰ *Ibid.*, pp. 702-06.

Edinoverie or the Uniate church was officially recognized in 1800. Its position relative to the Orthodox church was somewhat similar to the position of the Uniate church in Poland relative to the Roman Catholic church. The Edinoverie members used pre-Nikonian books and practiced old rituals but recognized the administrative authority of the Orthodox church. The govern-ment had hoped that Edinoverie would serve as the stepping stone for the mass return of Raskolniks to the Orthodox faith. The government reports show that in reality Edinoverie served as a channel for members of the Orthodox faith to join the Raskol. (See for example, Kel'siev, *Sbornik*, vol. II, p. 22.)

¹¹ Aleksandr I. Gertsen, "12 aprelia 1861 (Apraksinskiia ubiistva)," *Kolokol*, No. 101 (June 15, 1861), 848-49.

¹² Subbotin, "Raskol kak orudie," pp. 708 13.

¹³ Kel'siev, *Ispoved'*, p. 307.

¹⁴ *Ibid.*, pp. 307-308, 340-41.

¹⁵ Herzen, *Polnoe sobranie sochinenii*, vol. X, pp. 302-03; Kel'siev, *Ispoved'*, p. 312.

¹⁶ "V. I. Kel'siev to N. A. Serno-Solovievich," London, July 7, 1862, cited in Mikhail K. Lemke, *Ocherki osvoboditel'nogo dvizheniia "shestidesiatykh godov"* (St. Petersburg, 1908), pp. 37-38; "Arthur Beni to V. I. Kelsiev," St. Petersburg, February 7 (19), 1862, cited in *Literaturnoe nasledstvo*, vol. LXII, p. 26.

¹⁷ There are still many unsolved problems concerning the history of the Land and Liberty society. Apparently, the society emerged toward the end of 1861, and by the middle of 1862 had acquired its name and the form of its organization was well defined. The principal inspirers of this secret revolu-tionary organization were Herzen, Ogarev, and Chernyshevsky; among its active organizers were Nicholas Serno-Solovievich, A. A. Sleptsov, and N. N. Obruchev. *Zemlia i Volia* was headed by a central committee located in St. Petersburg. The Kolokol Group in London served as its foreign centre, and a Russian officer, A. A. Potebnia, created a branch of the society among the Russian officers serving in Poland. The latter group participated in the Polish uprising of 1863. As a result of their participation in that uprising the popularity of the society declined, and the society disappeared by the end of 1864.

Among the more valuable sources on this subject are the memoirs of A. A. Sleptsov published in vol. XVI of Herzen's *Polnoe sobranie sochinenii*;

Kel'siev's *Ispoved'*; Herzen's *Byloe i dumy*; and some of Ogarev's writings, especially the materials published in *Literaturnoe nasledstvo*, vol. LXI, pp. 459-522. Of the secondary sources, the most recent is a well-documented work edited by Militsa V. Nechkina, *Revoliutsionnaia situatsiia v Rossii v 1859-1861 gg.* (Moscow, 1960). Other noteworthy studies include the following: Ekaterina N. Kusheva, "K istorii vzaimootnoshenii A. I. Gertsena i N. P. Ogareva s Zemlei i Volei 60-kh godov," *Literaturnoe nasledstvo*, vols. XLI-XLII, pp. 82-86; and V. D. Koroliuk and I. S. Miller, eds., *Vosstanie 1863 g. i russko-pol'skie revoliutsionnye sviazi 60-kh godov. Sbornik statei i materialov* (Moscow, 1960).

[18] Subbotin, "Raskol kak orudie," pp. 722-23.

[19] Nikolai I. Subbotin, *K istorii raskola-staroobriadstva vtoroi poloviny XIX stoletiia. Perepiska prof. N. I. Subbotina preimushchestvenno neizdannaia, kak material dlia istorii raskola i otnoshenii k nemu pravitel'stva (1865-1904)*, (Moscow, 1914), pp. 435-36, 843; Kel'siev, *Ispoved'*, pp. 318, 321-24; Aleksandr S. Prugavin, *Staroobriadchestvo vo vtoroi polovine XIX veka: Ocherki iz noveishei istorii raskola* (Moscow, 1904), p. 109.

[20] "V. I. Kel'siev to N. F. Petrovskii," London, July 5, 1862, in Lemke, *Ocherki*, pp. 32-33.

[21] Kel'siev, *Ispoved'*, pp. 329-32; Subbotin, *K istorii raskola*, pp. 203-04. For biographical information on Paul the Prussian see Arkhimandrit Pavel, *Nikol'skago edinovercheskago monastyria inoka Pavla izvestnago pod imenem Prusskago vospominaniia i besedy v glagolemom staroobriadchestve* (Moscow, 1868).

[22] Herzen, *Sobranie sochinenii*, vol. XXVII, p. 501; "Iz perepiski Ogareva s Pavlom Prusskin (pseud. I. Lednevym)," *Literaturnoe nasledstvo*, vol. LXIII, pp. 130-39; Kelsiev, *Ispoved'* p. 333.

[23] Kel'siev, *Ispoved'*, p. 340.

[24] Lemke, *Ocherki*, pp. 20-39; Herzen, *Polnoe sobranie sochinenii*, vol. XVIII, pp. 93-94. It was on Sunday, June 6, 1862 that Vetoshnikov accepted the correspondence from Herzen. The identity of the agent has only recently been established as Grigorii Grigorievich Perets. (N. G. Rozenblum, "G. G. Perets—Agent III Otdeleniia," *Literaturnoe nasledstvo*, vol. LXVII, pp. 685-97.)

[25] Herzen, *Polnoe sobranie sochinenii*, vol. XIV, p. 399; Kel'siev, *Ispoved'*, p. 344.

# NOTES TO CHAPTER IV

[1] "V. I. Kel'siev to London," July 2, 1863, *Literaturnoe nasledstvo*, vol. LXII, p. 183; Vasilii I. Kel'siev, "Ispoved'," *Literaturnoe nasledstvo*, vols. XLI-XLII (1941), pp. 316-17, 342; Mikhail K. Lemke, *Ocherki osvoboditel'nogo dvizheniia "shestidesiatykh godov"* (St. Petersburg, 1908), p. 45.

[2] Professor Shchapov of Kazan University was one of the most prominent exponents of the *oblastnost'* theory. This theory was also propagated by the Ukrainian and Polish nationalists. A good discussion of this subject is in Franco Venturi's *Roots of Revolution* (New York, 1960), pp. 122, 199, 238, 294-95, 316-18.

Kel'siev, *Ispoved'*, pp. 265, 347; Venturi, *Roots of Revolution*, p. 56.

³ Aleksandr I. Gertsen, "Pis'mo iz provintsii. Ot redaktsii," *Kolokol*, No. 3 (March 1, 1860), 531.

Herzen's fear of a violent revolution is revealed in many of his writings, including his memoirs. Perhaps his most concise statement concerning his opposition to violent methods is found in his writings published posthumously under the title "Pis'ma 'K staromu tovarishchu'," *Literaturnoe nasledstvo*, vol. LXI, p. 159.

Bakunin's attachment to the tsar may be gleaned from a pamphlet he published in London in 1862, 'Narodnoe delo: Romanov, Pugachev ili Pestel'?" in Mikhail A. Bakunin, *Pis'ma k A. I. Gertsenu i N. P. Ogarevu* (Geneva, 1896), pp. 396-418.

⁴ *Ocherki istorii SSSR. Period feodalizma XVII v.* (Moscow, 1955), p. 365; Mikhail N. Pokrovskii, *Russkaia istoriia s drevneishikh vremen* (Petrograd, 1922-23), vol. II, pp. 134-39.

⁵ Ivan D. Iakushkin, *Zapiski, stat'i, pis'ma dekabrista I. D. Iakushkina* (Moscow, 1951), pp. 35, 37.

Professor Platon V. Pavlov was exiled in March, 1862, because of a speech he made in commemoration of the millenial anniversary. His article containing a plea for the calling of the Zemsky Sobor, published in 1861, is one of the earliest printed espousals of this revolutionary goal. (Lemke, *Ocherki*, p. 9.)

⁶ Nikolai P. Ogarev, "Tsel' russkogo dvizheniia," *Literaturnoe nasledstvo*, vol. LXI, p. 501.

⁷ Bakunin, "Narodnoe delo," pp. 396-418; Aleksandr I. Gertsen, "MDCCCLXIII," *Kolokol*, No. 4 (January 1, 1863), 1269-70; and his "Pis'mo k Garibal'di," *Kolokol*, No. 7 (January 15, 1864), 1453-56.

⁸ Mikhail A. Bakunin, "Russkim, pol'skim i vsem slavianskim druz'iam," *Kolokol*, No. 5 (February 15, 1862), 1022; Herzen, "Pis'mo k Garibal'di," *Kolokol*, 1454.

⁹ *Obshchee Veche*, No. 1 (July 15, 1862); No. 2 (August 22, 1862); No. 10 (February 1, 1863); No. 19 (July 10, 1863); and No. 22 (November 1, 1863).

¹⁰ Aleksandr I. Gertsen, *Polnoe sobranie sochinenii i pisem pod redaktsiei M. K. Lemke* (St. Petersburg, 1919-25), vol. XV, pp. 210-11; "V. I. Kel'siev to I. I. Shibaev," July 5, 1862, in Lemke, *Ocherki*, pp. 33-34; Kel'siev, *Ispoved'*, pp. 342-44; *Obshchee Veche*, No. 1 (July 15, 1862), and No. 8 (January 1, 1863).

¹¹ Vasilii I. Kel'siev, *Sbornik pravitel'stvennykh svedenii o raskol'nikakh* (London, 1860-62), vol. I, p. 135.

¹² Nikolai I. Subbotin, *Istoriia belokrinitskoi ierarkhii* (Moscow, 1874); Ministerstvo vnutrennikh del, *Sobranie postanovlenii po chasti raskola* (1860), vol. II, pp. 436-43.

¹³ G. [Subbotin], "Raskol kak orudie vrazhdebnykh Rossii partii," *Russkii vestnik*, LXIX (May 1867), 326-27; *Obshchee Veche*, No. 21 (September 1, 1863).

Another opponent of the tsarist government, Prince Peter V. Dolgorukov (1816-68), was also trying to exert influence over Filaret Zakharovich at that time. Dolgorukov, living as an emigrant in Western Europe, published various political pamphlets (*Listok*, *Pravdivyi*, and *Budushchnost'*), in which he denounced the Russian government. Like some of the members of the Kolokol Group, he seems to have believed that the Raskol was the most potent anti-tsarist element in Russia. Dolgorukov sent copies of his pamphlets to Belo-Krynitsa and invited Filaret Zakharovich to contribute articles to his publications. His relations with Belo-Krynitsa are described in Subbotin's "Raskol kak orudie." For Filaret Zakharovich's letters to the Kolokol Group see *Literaturnoe nasledstvo*, vol. LXII, pp. 217-18.

14 Subbotin, "Raskol kak orudie," pp. 328-29.

15 Konstantin N. Nikolaev, "Ocherk istorii popovshchiny s 1846 goda," *Chteniia v imperatorskom obshchestve istorii i drevnostei rossiiskikh pri Moskovskom universitete*, vol. V (1865), pp. 197-335, hereafter cited as *Chteniia*; Ilarion G. Ksenos, *Okruzhnoe poslanie* (Moscow, 1910).

16 Nikolaev, "Ocherki istorii popovshchiny," *Chteniia*, vol. V, pp. 197-335; *Obshchee Veche*, No. 21 (September 1, 1863).

17 Kel'siev, *Ispoved'*, 355. Details concerning the Polish emigrants in Turkey may be found in the following sources: Kel'siev, *Ispoved'*, pp. 345-74; Kel'siev, "Pol'skie agenty v Tsaregrade," *Russkii vestnik*, LXXXI (June, 1869, 520-44, LXXXIII (September, 1869), 290-302, LXXXIV (November, 1869), 152-94, and LXXXV (January, 1870), 260-73; Subbotin, "Raskol kak orudie," *Russkii vestnik*, LXVI (November, 1866), 7-78; Mikhail I. Chaikovskii, "Zapiski Mikhaila Chaikovskago," *Russkaia starina*, LXXXIV (November, 1895), 161-84 and continuing serially until volume CXX (December, 1904), 558-94; Aleksei V. Nikitin, "Osip S. Ganchar, ataman Nekrasovtsev, 1796-1879," *Russkaia starina*, XXXVIII (April, 1883), 175-92.

18 Kel'siev, *Ispoved'*, p. 353; "Bakunin to Herzen and Ogarev," November 10, 1862, in Bakunin, *Pis'ma*, pp. 90-91.

19 Kel'siev, *Ispoved'*, pp. 358-61, 368; "V. I. Kel'siev to Herzen and Ogarev," June 11, 1863, in *Literaturnoe nasledstvo*, vol. LXII, p. 185.

The idea of a Caucasian federation was not a new one. The Polish emigrants in Paris had already translated the Swiss constitution into Turkish, and they had even devised a flag for such a federation. (Kel'siev, "Pol'skie agenty v Tsaregrade," *Russkii vestnik*, LXXXIII (September, 1869), 290-99; and his *Ispoved'*, pp. 358-61.)

20 "V. I. Kel'siev to Herzen and Ogarev," July 2, 1863, in *Literaturnoe nasledstvo*, vol. LXII, p. 185; "V. I. Kel'siev to Bishop Cyril," October 21, 1863, in *Russkii vestnik*, LXVIII (March, 1867), 407-08.

Cyril had become a bishop shortly before he left Russia (at the age of thirty-three), and thus he did not have a bishopric to return to. When he did return, he was not punished for the delay in his departure from Palestine. (D. P., pseud., "Partiia Gertsena i staroobriadtsy," *Russkii vestnik*, LXVIII [March, 1867]), 403-05.

21 "V. I. Kelsiev to Herzen and Ogarev," June 11, 1863, in *Literaturnoe nasledstvo*, vol. LXII, pp. 172-73; Aleksandr I. Gertsen, *Sobranie sochinenii* (Moscow, 1954-64), vol. XI, pp. 337-38; Nataliia A. Tuchkova-Ogareva, *Vospominaniia* (Moscow, 1959), pp. 198-99; "Ogarev to O. S. Goncharov," July or August, 1863, in *Literaturnoe nasledstvo*, vol. LXII, pp. 74-75.

The two Old Believer bishops were Arkady and Olimpy. They were exiled to Russia during the Russian occupation of Dobrudja in 1854. Goncharov spent many years trying to win their release. He wrote numerous letters on their behalf; he held audiences with representatives of the Turkish, Russian, and French governments; and, with the help of Bishop Arkady of Slava, he drew up a petition to the Pope (an unusual step for an Old Believer to take!). It is not known whether this petition was actually transmitted to the Pope.

(Nikolai I. Subbotin, *Perepiska raskol'nicheskikh deiatelei* [Moscow, 1889], vol. II, pp. 91-92.)

In July, 1862, with the aid of the Polish emigrants, Goncharov obtained an audience with the French Foreign Minister regarding the two exiled bishops. Goncharov's interpreter, a Pole named Kossilovsky, told Kelsiev that in the course of this interview the Foreign Minister asked Goncharov if the Dobrudja cossacks knew anything about Emperor Napoleon III. Without hesitating, Goncharov replied that although the Dobrudja Old Believers were uneducated and knew very little about political matters, they all kept the portrait of the French Emperor beside their icons. When Kelsiev asked Goncharov if this was a true account of his interview, Goncharov replied:

> "Well, what else was there to do? I have to please the people. I was interested in freeing the bishops, and I had to please the people. To some, my dear Vasily Ivanovich, one can give a head of sugar, with others one can get away with an invitation to a simple dinner, but in this case—this was a very important minister!" (Kelsiev, "Pol'skie agenty v Tsaregrade," LXXXIV [November, 1869], 189-90.)

All of this tends to show that Goncharov's interest in freeing the two bishops had a great deal to do with his trip to London.

The espionage activities of Goncharov and Bishop Arkady of Slava were in part directed against the London revolutionaries. On May 16, 1864, for example, a Russian consular agent in Izmail (Romanenko) reported to his superiors that he had received a letter written by Ivan Kelsiev. The letter had been given to the agent in Izmail by Arkady. Romanenko also acknowledged receipt of a letter from Goncharov, who had just arrived in Izmail from Tulcea. This letter had been written by Herzen and Ogarev and addressed to Goncharov. (Herzen, *Polnoe sobranie sochinenii*, vol. XVII, p. 282.)

[22] The French-language newspaper, *Courier d'Orient*, is not available to me. It is known, however, that Kelsiev was acquainted with its publisher, a Corsican named Petri. (Kelsiev, *Ispoved'*, p. 371; and his "Pol'skie agenty v Tsaregrade," LXXXIII [September, 1869], 290-91.)

[23] "O. S. Goncharov to Herzen and Ogarev," February 2, 1864, in *Literaturnoe nasledstvo*, vol. LXII, pp. 75-76; "Bishop Arkady to Fathers Onufry and Pafnuty," May 9, 1866, in Subbotin, *Perepiska raskol'nicheskikh deiatelei*, vol. II, pp. 205-08; "I. I. Kelsiev to E. V. Salias," July or August, 1863, in *Literaturnoe nasledstvo*, vols. XLI-XLII, pp. 106-10; and "I. I. Kelsiev to Herzen," September, 1863, in *ibid.*, vol. LXII, pp. 233-34.

[24] On Goncharov's negotiations with the Russian government see Ministerstvo vnutrennikh del, *Sobranie postanovlenii po chasti raskola* (1875), pp. 578-79, 582.

When the Nekrasovtsy first settled in Dobrudja, there was no formal system of land tenure in the province. The man who worked the land owned it, and only if he ceased using it could his land be claimed by another. In the nineteenth century the government began to survey the land and Sultan Mahmut II (1808-39) began the selling of *yarlyks* or titles to the land. The corruption which existed at the Porte allowed persons to purchase the *yarlyks* to land which was settled by others. The Nekrasovtsy were the victims of their own ignorance of the new system and of the shrewdness of others. The threat to their ownership of the land was the chief source of discontent among them in the 1860's.

# NOTES TO CHAPTER V

[1] Aleksandr I. Gertsen, "Ispolin prosypaetsia!" *Kolokol*, No. 4 (November 1, 1861), 918; Nikolai P. Ogarev, "Universitety zakryvaiut!" *Kolokol*, No. 5 (January 15, 1862), 1002.

The "Going to the People" or *Khozhdenie v narod* movement of the 1870's evolved from the populist revolutionary groups which coalesced around Mark A. Natanson and Nicholas V. Chaikovsky. The mass ingression of their followers "to the people" took place in 1873-74. The general aim of these youthful revolutionaries was to teach the peasant masses the ways of revolution. A fervent political religiosity characterized the movement. By the end of 1874 some four thousand revolutionaries had been arrested and the movement collapsed. (There is an informative chapter on the subject in Franco Venturi's *Roots of Revolution* [New York, 1960], Chaper 18.)

[2] "V. I. Kelsiev to Herzen and Ogarev," June 11, 1863, in *Literaturnoe nasledstvo*, vol. LXII, p. 176; Aleksandr I. Gertsen, *Polnoe sobranie sochinenii i pisem pod redaktsiei M. K. Lemke* (St. Petersburg, 1919-25), vol. XVI, p. 105. The proclamation was printed in No. 12 of *Obshchee Veche* (March 8, 1863).

The following incident reflects some of the difficulties involved in Kelsiev's task of "going to the people" in Dobrudja. One day, an Old Believer cossack named Raznotsvetov somehow obtained a package of Kelsiev's proclamations and began to nail them up on the door of the local taverns. As he gained an audience, his enthusiasm grew. He mounted a horse, brought out a sword, and, proclaiming himself a member of the Land and Liberty society, began to urge his drinking companions to follow him to Moscow, where they would establish the Zemsky Sobor. ("V. I. Kelsiev to Herzen and Ogarev," July 2, 1863, in *Literaturnoe nasledstvo*, vol. LXII, p. 176.)

[3] "V. I. Kelsiev to E. V. Salias," autumn, 1863, in *Literaturnoe nasledstvo*, vols. XLI-XLII, pp. 106-10.

[4] "Delo P. A. Shipova i V. I. Kel'sieva," in Vasilii P. Alekseev, ed. and comp., *Politicheskie protsessy 60-kh gg.* (Moscow, 1923), vol. I, pp. 111-13.

[5] *Ibid.*, vol. I, pp. 119-20; "I. I. Kelsiev to E. V. Salias," July or August, 1863, in *Literaturnoe nasledstvo*, vols. XLI-XLII, pp. 109-10; "I. I. Kelsiev to Ogarev," November or December, 1863, in *Literaturnoe nasledstvo*, vol. LXII, p. 240.

[6] "V. I. Kelsiev to Herzen and Ogarev," September, 1863, in *Literaturnoe nasledstvo*, vol. LXII, p. 234.

[7] Vasilii I. Kel'siev, "Pol'skie agenty v Tsaregrade," *Russkii vestnik*, LXXXV (January, 1870), 261-71; "I. I. Kelsiev to Ogarev," November or December, 1863, in *Literaturnoe nasledstvo*, vol. LXII, p. 237.

[8] *Ibid.*, pp. 237-38, 240; Vasilii I. Kel'siev, "Ispoved'," *Literaturnoe nasledstvo*, XLI-XLII (1941), 379; "V. I. Kelsiev to Ogarev," March, 1864, in *Literaturnoe nasledstvo*, vol. LXII, p. 250.

[9] "V. I. Kelsiev to Herzen and Ogarev," February 23, 1864, in *Literaturnoe nasledstvo*, vol. LXII, p. 190.

[10] *Ibid.*, pp. 190, 192-93. In the original the italicized words appear in English.

[11] "I. I. Kelsiev to Ogarev," March, 1864, in *Literaturnoe nasledstvo*, vol. LXII, p. 252; "V. I. Kelsiev to Herzen and Ogarev," February 23, 1864, in *Literaturnoe nasledstvo*, vol. LXII, p. 194.

¹² *Ibid.*, p. 194; "I. I. Kelsiev to Ogarev," November or December, 1863, in *Literaturnoe nasledstvo*, vol. LXII, pp. 246-47; Herzen, *Polnoe sobranie sochinenii*, vol. XVI, pp. 44, 566.

¹³ "I. I. Kelsiev to Ogarev," November, 1963, in *Literaturnoe nasledstvo*, vol. LXII, p. 240, 242.

¹⁴ "V. I. Kelsiev to Herzen and Ogarev," July 16, 1864, in *Literaturnoe nasledstvo*, vol. LXII, 199; Vasilii I. Kel'siev, *Perezhitoe i peredumannoe* (St. Petersburg, 1868), pp. 316-17; Kelsiev, *Ispoved'*, p. 389.

¹⁵ Nikolai P. Ogarev, *Izbrannye sotsial'no-politicheskie i filosofskie proizvedeniia* (Moscow, 1956), vol. II, p. 126; "I. I. Kelsiev to Ogarev," September, 1863, in *Literaturnoe nasledstvo*, vol. LXII, p. 236; "V. I. Kelsiev to Herzen and Ogarev," February 23, 1864, in *Literaturnoe nasledstvo*, vol. LXII, pp. 193-94.

¹⁶ "V. I. Kelsiev to Herzen and Ogarev," June, 1864, in *Literaturnoe nasledstvo*, vol. LXII, pp. 195-97.

¹⁷ "V. I. Kelsiev to Herzen and Ogarev," November 11, 1865, in *Literaturnoe nasledstvo*, vol. LXII, p. 210; "V. I. Kelsiev to Herzen and Ogarev," July 23, 1864, in *Literaturnoe nasledstvo*, vol. LXII, p. 200; Lvov N. Tolstoy, *My Confession: My Religion: The Gospel in Brief* (New York, 1929), pp. 58-59.

¹⁸ Kel'siev, *Ispoved'*, p. 383.

Krasnopevtsev had apparently a pathological urge to commit suicide and made several attempts to fulfill this desire. In Tulcea he constantly talked about the impending event, and the other members of the phalanx became so accustomed to this that they ceased regarding him seriously. One day, when Krasnopevtsev was repeating his well-known plan for his future, Kelsiev humourously informed him that there was a clothesline tied in his garden which would serve the ex-captain's purposes admirably. Krasnopevtsev did not find Kelsiev's remark amusing, but thanked him and said that he would prefer using his own belt. The following day (February 8, 1865) Krasnopevtsev was found hanging from the vane of a windmill. He did use his own belt. This tragedy was a sobering experience for Kelsiev who blamed himself for what had happened. (Kelsiev, *Ispoved'*, p. 386.)

¹⁹ The followers of Lenin published a special newspaper, *Razsvet* [*sic*] or *The Dawn*, directed at the Raskolniks and were politically active within the Raskol right up to the end of the Revolution of 1917. The prime source material on this subject is found in the works of Vladimir Bonch-Bruevich, the editor of the *Razsvet*. See especially his *Izbrannye sochineniia* (Moscow, 1959), pp. 16, 382.

# NOTES TO CHAPTER VI

¹ Vasilii I. Kel'siev, "Ispoved'," *Literaturnoe nasledstvo*, XLI-XLII (1941), 396-97.

² "V. I. Kelsiev to Herzen and Ogarev," October 26, 1865, in *Literaturnoe nasledstvo*, vol. LXII, pp. 204-06.

³ Kelsiev, *Ispoved'*, p. 399; V. P. Ivanov-Zheludkov (pseud., Kelsiev), "Psikhologicheskaia zametka," *Otechestvennye zapiski*, CLXX (January,

1867), 116-19.

⁴ Kelsiev, *Ispoved'*, pp. 399, 402.

⁵ *Ibid.*, p. 405.

⁶ *Ibid.*, pp. 410, 412, 415.

⁷ "Herzen to Ogarev," November 7, 1867, in *Literaturnoe nasledstvo*, vols. XLI-XLII, p. 577.

⁸ Kelsiev, *Ispoved'*, pp. 265-68.

⁹ Aleksandr I. Gertsen, *Polnoe sobranie sochinenii i pisem pod redaktsiei M. K. Lemke* (St. Petersburg, 1919-25), vol. XIX, p. 393; Nicolas Berdiaev, *The Origin of Russian Communism* (London, 1948), p. 35. An informative discussion of Pecherin is Alexander Lipski's "Pecherin's Quest for Meaningfulness," *Slavic Review*, XXIII (June, 1964), 239-57.

¹⁰ Kelsiev, *Ispoved'*, pp. 356-57, 375-76.

¹¹ *Ibid.*, pp. 319, 388; Ministerstvo vnutrennikh del, *Sobranie postanovlenii po chasti raskola* (1875), pp. 646-49.

¹² Aleksandr I. Gertsen, *Sobranie sochinenii* (Moscow, 1954-64), vol. XVIII, pp. 423-25; Aleksei A. Shilov, *Shestidesiatye gody* (Moscow, 1940), p. 207.

¹³ Fedor M. Dostoevskii, *Pis'ma* (Moscow ,1930), vol. II, p. 47; and his *Sobranie sochinenii* (Moscow, 1956-58), vol. VII, pp. 32-33, 41.

¹⁴ Herzen, *Sobranie sochinenii*, vol. XI, p. 335; "V. I. Kelsiev to Herzen and Ogarev," February 23, 1864, in *Literaturnoe nasledstvo*, vol. LXII, p. 194.

Soon after he had begun to work for *The Bell*, Kelsiev was approached by Nicholas Truebner, a printer whose printing facilities were in the service of the Kolokol Group, concerning the possibility of translating the Bible from Church Slavonic into modern Russian. Truebner was interested in obtaining such a translation in order to maintain a monopoly over the printing of Russian books in Britain, for a prominent book collector, Lucien Bonaparte, a nephew of the famous Napoleon, sought to obtain a Russian text of the Bible from another printer. In addition to the prospect of becoming acquainted with the famous book collector Kelsiev also saw in this project the possibility of creating some disturbance within the Russian ecclesiastical order. With remarkable speed, he translated the Pentateuch directly from Hebrew, and Truebner hastily printed it in 1860 under the translator's pseudonym Vadim. When Herzen read the Russian text of the translation, he became apprehensive for the reputation of the "Free Russian Press," as the publishing facilities of the Kolokol Group were called, for Kelsiev had translated the Biblical text literally, disregarding idioms and grammatical rules. Lucien Bonaparte, thus, had acquired an extremely rare book, for only a few copies of it were sold. Herzen claimed that Kelsiev's translation of the Bible frightened the Holy Synod into publishing the Bible in modern Russian. (Herzen, *Sobranie sochinenii*, vol. XI, p. 334.) In reality, however, the Holy Synod had undertaken the translation of the Bible from Church Slavonic into modern Russian in 1856, and a complete text was published in 1876. (Sergei S. Tatishchev, *Imperator Aleksandr II, Ego zhizn' i tsarstvovanie* (St. Petersburg, 1903), vol. II, p. 224.)

¹⁵ Vasilii I. Kel'siev, "Pis'mo k Dimitriiu Vasil'evichu Averkeevu," *Russkaia starina*, XXXV (September, 1882), 635; Kelsiev, *Ispoved'*, p. 259.

¹⁶ *Ibid.*, pp. 294, 310, 312, 319, 329-30.

¹⁷ Herzen, *Polnoe sobranie sochinenii*, vol. XX, p. 382 and vol. XXI,

p. 35; Kelsiev, *Ispoved'*, p. 261; D. (pseud. for A. N. Pypin), "Perezhitoe i peredumannoe. Vospominaniia Vasiliia Kel'sieva," *Vestnik Evropy* (July, 1868), 445-53.

[18] Gabriel R. Derzhavin, "Plaint," in Bernard G. Guerney, ed., *A Treasury of Russian Literature* (New York: The Vanguard Press, 1943), p. 46.

[19] Ministerstvo vnutrennikh del, *Sobranie postanovlenii po chasti raskola* (1875), pp. 646-49.

[20] Aleksandr V. Nikitenko, *Moia povest' o samom sebe i o tom, "chemu svidetel' v zhizni byl"* (St. Petersburg, 1904-05), vol. II, p. 385; Aleksei A. Shilov, *Shestidesiatye gody* (Moscow, 1940), vol. II, p. 210.

[21] Nikitenko, *Moia povest'*, vol. II, p. 436.

[22] Kelsiev, *Ispoved'*, p. 261.

[23] *Ibid.*, p. 352.

# BIBLIOGRAPHY

"Akty otnosiashchiesia k istorii Solovetskago bunta," *Chteniia v Imperatorskom obshchestve istorii i drevnostei rossiiskikh pri Moskovskom universitete.* Moscow: October-December, 1883.

ALEKSEEV, VASILII P., comp., and BORIS P. KOZ'MIN, ed., *Politicheskie protsessy 60-kh gg.* Moscow: Gosudarstvennoe izdatel'stvo, 1923.

ANDREEV, VASILII V., *Raskol i ego znachenie v narodnoi russkoi istorii. Istoricheskii ocherk.* St. Petersburg: V tipografii M. Khana, 1870.

AVVAKUM, PROTOPOP, *Sochineniia,* in *Pamiatniki istorii staroobriadchestva XVII v. Russkaia istoricheskaia biblioteka.* Leningrad: Izdatel'stvo Akademii nauk SSSR, 1927.

AVVAKUM, PROTOPOP, *Zhitie protopopa Avvakuma im samim napisannoe i drugie ego sochineniia.* Moscow: Tipografiia imeni A. A. Zhdanova, 1960.

BAKUNIN, MIKHAIL A., *Pis'ma k A. I. Gertsenu i N. P. Ogarevu s prilozheniem ego pamfletov, biograficheskim vvedeniem i ob'iasnitel'nymi primechaniiami M. P. Dragomanova.* Geneva: Ukrainskaia tipografiia, 1896.

BAKUNIN, MIKHAIL A., "Russkim, pol'skim i vsem slavianskim druz'iam," *Kolokol,* No. 5 (February 15, 1862), 1021-28.

BELOKUROV, SERGEI, *Arsenii Sukhanov.* Moscow: Universitetskaia tipografiia, 1891-94. 2 vols.

BERDIAEV, NICOLAS, *The Origin of Russian Communism.* London: Geoffrey Bles, 1948.

BILLINGTON, JAMES H., "Neglected Figures and Features in the Rise of the Raskol," in Andrew Blane, ed., *The Religious World of Russian Culture; Russia and Orthodoxy.* Vol. II. Essays in Honor of Georges Florovsky. The Hague: Mouton and Company, 1975.

BONCH-BRUEVICH, VLADIMIR D., *Izbrannye sochineniia. Tom I: O religii, religioznom sektantstve i tserkvi.* Moscow: Izdatel'stvo Akademii nauk SSSR. 1959.

BONCH-BRUEVICH, VLADIMIR D., ed., *Razsvet. Sotsial-demokraticheskii listok dlia sektantov.* Geneva: January, 1903-September, 1904. A newspaper.

CHAIKOVSKII, MIKHAIL I., "Zapiski Mikhaila Chaikovskago," *Russkaia starina,* LXXXIV-CXX (November, 1895-December, 1904).

CONYBEARE, FREDERICK C., *Russian Dissenters.* New York: Russell and Russell, Incorporated, 1962.

CRUMMEY, ROBERT O., *The Old Believers and the World of Antichrist: the Vyg Community and the Russian State 1694-1855.* Madison, Wisconsin: The University of Wisconsin Press, 1970.

D. P. (pseud.), "Partiia Gertsena i staroobriadtsy," *Russkii vestnik,* LXVIII (March, 1867), 400-10.

DEMKOVA, NATAL'IA SERGEEVNA, *Zhitie protopopa Avvakuma (tvorcheskaia istoriia proizvedeniia).* Leningrad: Izdatel'stvo Leningradskogo universiteta, 1974.

DOBROLIUBOV, NIKOLAI A., *Polnoe sobranie sochinenii.* Moscow: Gosudarstvennoe izdatel'stvo "Khudozhestvennaia literatura," 1939, 6 vols.

EL'SBERG, IAKOV E., *Gertsen, Zhizn' i tvorchestvo.* Moscow: Gosudarstvennoe izdatel'stvo khudozhestvennoi literatury, 1956.

FEDOTOV, GEORGE P., ed., *A Treasury of Russian Spirituality.* Belmont, Massachusetts: Nordland Publishing Co., 1975. (Volume IV in the *Collected Works of George P. Fedotov.*)

FEDOTOV, GEORGE P. *The Russian Religious Mind (II): The Middle Ages—The 13th to the 15th Centuries.* Belmont, Massachusetts: Nordland Publishing Co., 1975. (Volume IV in the Collected *Works of George P. Fedotov.*)

FLOROVSKY, GEORGES, *Aspects of Church History.* Volume IV in the *Collected Works,* Belmont, Massachusetts: Nordland Publishing Co., 1975.

FLOROVSKY, *Christianity and Culture.* Volume II in the *Collected Works.* Belmont, Massachusetts: Nordland Publishing Co., 1975.

GERTSEN [HERZEN], ALEKSANDR I.:

*Byloe i dumy.* Minsk: Gosudarstvennoe uchebno-pedagogicheskoe izdatel'stvo, 1957. 2 vols.

"12 aprelia 1861 (Apraksinskiia ubiistva)," *Kolokol,* No. 4 (June 15, 1861), 848-49.

"Ispolin prosypaetsia!" *Kolokol,* No. 4 (November 1, 1861), 917-18.

*Izbrannye filosofskie proizvedeniia.* Moscow: Gosudarstvennoe izdatel'stvo politicheskoi literatury, 1946. 2 vols.

"MDCCCLXIII," *Kolokol*, No. 4 (January 1, 1863), 1269-70.
*O razvitii revoliutsionnykh idei v Rossii.* Moscow: Gosudarstvennoe izdatel'stvo khudozhestvennoi literatury, 1958.

"Pis'ma A. I. Gertsena i N. P. Ogareva k V. I. Kel'sievu, 1866-1867," *Russkaia starina,* LXI (January, 1889), 182-90.

"Pis'mo iz provintsii. Ot redaktsii," *Kolokol*, No. 3 (March 1, 1860), 531-33.

"Pis'mo k Garibal'di," *Kolokol*, No. 7 (January 15, 1864), 1453-56.

*Polnoe sobranie sochinenii i pisem pod redaktsiei M. K. Lemke.* St. Petersburg: Narodnyi komissariat po prosveshcheniiu, 1919-25. 22 vols.

*Sobranie sochinenii.* Moscow: Izdatel'stvo Akademii nauk SSSR, 1954-64. 30 vols.

GONCHAROV, OSIP S., "Iz perepiski O. S. Goncharova s Gertsenom i Ogarevym," *Literaturnoe nasledstvo,* LXII (1955), 70-78.

HAXTHAUSEN, AUGUST VON, *The Russian Empire. Its People, Institutions and Resources.* London: Chapman and Hall, 1856. 2 vols.

IAKOVLEV, MIKHAIL V., *Mirovozzrenie N. P. Ogareva.* Moscow: Izdatel'stvo Akademii nauk SSSR, 1957.

IOVCHUK, MIKHAIL T., *Filosofskie i sotsiologicheskie vzgliady N. P. Ogareva.* Moscow: Izdatel'stvo Moskovskogo universiteta, 1957.

IUZOV I. (pseud. of IOSIF I. KABLITZ), "Politicheskie vozzreniia staroveriia," *Russkaia mysl',* bk. V (May, 1882), 181-218.

*Izvlechenie iz rasporiazhenii po delam o raskol'nikakh pri imperatorakh Nikolae i Aleksandre II.* Leipzig: Mezhdunarodnaia biblioteka, 1882.

KAPTEREV, NIKOLAI F.:

*Kharakter otnoshenii Rossii k pravoslavnomu Vostoku v XVI i XVII stoletiiakh.* Sergiev Posad: Izdanie M. S. Elova, 1914.

*Patriarkh Nikon i ego protivniki v dele ispravleniia tserkovnykh obriadov.* Moscow: V universitetskoi tipografii, 1887.

*Patriarkh Nikon i tsar' Aleksei Mikhailovich.* Sergiev Posad: Tipografiia Sviato-Troitskoi Sergievskoi Lavry, 1909. 2 vols.

KARTASHEV, ANTON VLADIMIROVICH, *Ocherki po istorii russkoi tserkvi.* Vol. II. Paris: YMCA-Press, 1959.

KEL'SIEV, IVAN I., "Pis'mo I. I. Kel'sieva E. V. Salias," *Literaturnoe nasledstvo,* XLI-XLII (1941), 106-10.

KEL'SIEV, IVAN I., "I. I. Kel'siev—Gertsenu i Ogarevu. Prilozhenie:

Pis'ma k V. T. Kel'sievoi," *Literaturnoe nasledstvo*, LXII (1955), 219-58.

KEL'SIEV, VASILII I.:

*Galichina i Moldaviia*. Putevye pis'ma. St. Petersburg: Pechatnia V. Golovina, 1868.

"Ispoved'," *Literaturnoe nasledstvo*, XLI-XLII (1941), 253-470.

"Iz byta pol'skikh emigrantov," *Vsemirnyi trud*, n. v. (January, 1869), 81-104.

*Moskva i Tver'*. Paris: YMCA-Press, 1932.

*Perezhitoe i peredumannoe. Vospominaniia*. St. Petersburg: V. Golovin, 1868.

"Pis'mo k Dimitriiu Vasil'evichu Averkeevu," *Russkaia starina*, XXV (September, 1882), 634-37.

"Pis'mo k Episkopu Kirillu," *Russkii vestnik*, LXVIII (March, 1867), 405-09.

"Pol'skie agenty v Tsaregrade," *Russkii vestnik*, LXXXI (June, 1869), 520-44; LXXXIII (September, 1869), 290-302; LXXXIV (November, 1869), 152-94; LXXXV (January, 1870), 260-73.

"Pri Petre. Istoricheskaia povest' vremen preobrazovaniia Rossii," *Niva*, Nos. 38-52 (1871).

(Pseud. V. P. Ivanov-Zheludkov), "Psikhologicheskaia zametka," *Otechestvennye zapiski*, CLXX (January, 1867), 109-24.

(Ed.), *Sbornik pravitel'stvennykh svedenii o raskol'nikakh*. London: Truebner and Company, 1860-62. 4 vols.

"V. I. Kel'siev—Gertsenu i Ogarevu. Prilozhenie: Pis'ma Filareta Zakharovicha," *Literaturnoe nasledstvo*, LXII (1955), 157-258.

KLEVENSKII, MITROFAN M., "Gertsen—izdatel' i ego sotrudniki," *Literaturnoe nasledstvo*, XLI-XLII (1941), 572-620.

KLIUCHEVSKII, VASILII O., "Zapadnoe vliianie v Rossii XVII v.," *Voprosy filosofii i psikhologii*, VIII (January, 1897), 137-55; (May, 1897), 335-58; (September, 1897), 760-800.

*Kolokol. Gazeta A. I. Gertsena i N. P. Ogareva*. Moscow: Izdatel'stvo Akademii nauk SSSR, 1962. 10 vols.

KOROLIUK, V. D. and I. S. MILLER, eds., *Vosstanie 1863 g. i russko-pol'skie revoliutsionnye sviazi 60-kh godov. Sbornik statei i materialov*. Moscow: Izdatel'stvo Akademii nauk SSSR, 1960.

KOSTOMAROV, NIKOLAI I., "Istoriia raskola u raskol'nikov," *Vestnik Evropy*, VI (April 1871), 469-536.

222 VASILY I. KELSIEV

KSENOS, ILARION G. (Ilarion E. Kobanov), *Okruzhnoe poslanie sostavlennoe I. G. Ksenosom i izdannoe staroobriadcheskimi episkopami 24 fevralia 1862 goda. S prilozheniem ustava i omyshleniia, sostavlennykh tem zhe avtorom.* Moscow: "Russkaia pechatnia," 1910.

LEMKE, MIKHAIL K., *Ocherki osvoboditel'nogo dvizheniia "shestidesiatykh godov" po neizdannym dokumentam s portretami.* St. Petersburg: Izdatel'stvo O. N. Popovoi, 1908.

LEMKE, MIKHAIL K., *Politicheskie protsessy v Rossii 1860-kh gg. Po arkhivnym dokumentam.* Moscow: Gosudarstvennoe izdatel'stvo, 1923.

*Literaturnoe nasledstvo.* Moscow: Izdatel'stvo Akademii nauk SSSR. Vols. XLI-XLII, LXI, LXII, LXIII, LXVII.

MALIA, MARTIN E., *Alexander Herzen and the Birth of Russian Socialism, 1812-1855.* Cambridge, Massachusetts: Harvard University Press, 1961.

MALONEY, GEORGE A., S. J., *Russian Hesychasm: The Spirituality of N. I. Sorskii.* The Hague: Mouton and Co., 1973.

MILIUKOV, PAUL, *Outlines of Russian Culture.* New York: A. S. Barnes and Company, Incorporated, 1960. 3 vols.

Ministerstvo vnutrennikh del, *Sobranie postanovlenii po chasti raskola.* St. Petersburg: 1875.

Ministerstvo vnutrennikh del, *Sobranie postanovlenii po chasti raskola sostoiavshikhsia po vedomstvu Sviatogo Sinoda.* St. Petersburg: Tipografiia MVD, 1860. 2 vols.

NIKITIN, ALEKSEI V., "Osip Semenovich Ganchar. Ataman Nekrasovtsev, 1796-1879 gg.," *Russkaia starina,* XXXVIII (April, 1883), 175-92.

NIKITENKO, ALEKSANDR V., *Moia povest' o samom sebe i o tom, "chemu svidetel' v zhizni byl."* *Zapiski i dnevnik, 1804-1877.* St. Petersburg: Tipo-litografiia "Gerol'd," 1904-05.

NIKOLAEV, KONSTANTIN N., ed., "Ocherki istorii popovshchiny s 1846 goda," *Chteniia v Imperatorskom obshchestve istorii i drevnostei rossiiskikh pri Moskovskom universitete,* LIV (July, 1865), part V, 197-335. Documents.

*Obshchee Veche (pribavlenie k Kolokolu),* 1862-1864, in *Kolokol,* vol. X *(Prilozheniia).*

OGAREV, NIKOLAI P.:
*Izbrannye sotsial'no-politicheskie i filosofskie proizvedeniia.* Moscow: Gosudarstvennoe izdatel'stvo politicheskoi literatury, 1952, 1956. 2 vols.

"Iz perepiski Ogareva s Pavlom Prusskim," *Literaturnoe nasledstvo,* LXIII (1956), 130-39.

"Novye materialy o revoliutsionnoi situatsii v Rossii (1850-1861) gg.," *Literaturnoe nasledstvo,* LXI (1953), 459-522.

"Universitety zakryvaiut!" *Kolokol,* No. 5 (January 15, 1862), 1002.

PALMER, WILLIAM, ed., *The Patriarch and the Tsar.* London: Truebner and Company, 1871-76. 6 vols.

PASCAL, PIERRE, *Avvakum et les débuts du Raskol. La Crise religieuse au XVIII siècle en Russie.* Paris: Mouton and Co., 1963.

PAVEL, ARKHIMANDRIT, *Nikol'skago edinovercheskago monastyria inoka Pavla izvestnago pod imenem Prusskago vospominaniia i besedy v glagolemom staroobriadchestve.* Moscow: V universitetskoi tipografii, 1868.

PAVEL, PRUSSKII, "O moem znakomstve s Kel'sievym," *Bratskoe slovo,* II (1889), 690.

*Polnoe sobranie zakonov Rossiiskoi imperii.* First collection (1649 to December 12, 1825), 45 vols.; Second collection (December 12, 1825 to February 28, 1881), 55 vols.; Third collection (March 1, 1881 to December 31, 1913), 33 vols. St. Petersburg: Gosudarstvennaia tipografiia, 1830, 1884, 1916.

PRUGAVIN, ALEKSANDR S., *Staroobriadchestvo vo vtoroi polovine XIX veka. Ocherki is noveishei istorii raskola.* Moscow: Tipografiia tovarishchestva I. D. Sytina, 1904.

[SHCHAPOV, AFANASII P.], "O prichinakh proiskhozhdeniia i rasprostraneniia raskola, izvestnago pod imenem staroobriadstva, vo vtoroi polovine XVII i v pervoi polovine XVIII stoletiia," *Pravoslavnyi sobesednik,* IV (1857), 629-89, 857-91.

SHCHAPOV, AFANASII P., *Sochineniia.* St. Petersburg: Izdanie M. V. Pirozhkova, 1906-08. 3 vols.

SHELGUNOV, NIKOLAI V., *Vospominaniia.* Moscow: Gosudarstvennoe izdatel'stvo, 1923.

SHILOV, ALEKSEI A., *Shestidesiatye gody. Materialy po istorii literatury i obshchestvennomu dvizheniiu.* Moscow: Izdatel'stvo Akademii nauk SSSR, 1940.

SHUSHERIN, IVAN K., *Izvestie o rozhdenii i vospitanii i o zhitii sviateishago Nikona, patriarkha moskovskago i vseia Rossii.* Moscow: Izdatel'stvo voskresenskago, Novyi Ierusalim imenuemago monastyria, 1871.

SMIRNOV, NIKOLAI ALEKSANDROVICH, *Tserkov' v istorii Rossii (IX v.–1917 g.); Kriticheskie ocherki.* Moscow: Akademiia nauk SSSR, Institut istorii, 1967.

SUBBOTIN, NIKOLAI I.:
*Istoriia Belokrinitskoi ierarkhii*. Moscow: Tipografiiia T. Ris, 1874.

*K istorii raskola-staroobriadchestva vtoroi poloviny XIX stoletiia. Perepiska prof. N. I. Subbotina preimushchestvenno neizdannaia, kak material dlia istorii raskola i otnoshenii k nemu pravitel'stva (1865-1904).* Moscow: Izdatel'stvo Imperatorskogo obshchestva, istorii i drevnostei rossiiskikh, 1914.

(Ed.) *Perepiska raskol'nicheskikh deiatelei (materialy dlia istorii Belokrinitskago sviashchenstva).* Moscow: Tipografiia E. Lissnera i I. Romana, 1887, 1889, 1899. 3 vols.

(Pseud. G.) "Raskol kak orudie vrazhdebnykh Rossii partii," *Russkii vestnik*, LXV (September, 1866), 105-46; (November, 1866), 5-78; LXVIII (April, 1867), 690-724; LXIX (May, 1867), 312-56.

SYRTSOV, IOANN I., *Samoszhigatel'stvo sibirskikh staroobriadtsev v XVII i XVIII stoletii.* Tobol'sk: Gubernskaia tipografiia, 1888.

TOLSTOY, ALEXANDRA, *Tolstoy: A Life of My Father.* Belmont, Massachusetts: Nordland Publishing Co., 1975.

TUCHKOVA-OGAREVA, NATALIIA A., *Vospominaniia.* Moscow: Gosudarstvennoe izdatel'stvo khudozhestvennoi literatury, 1959.

*Vekhi. Sbornik statei o russkoi intelligentsii.* Contributors: N. A. Berdiaev, S. N. Bulgakov, S. L. Frank, M. O. Gershenzon, A. S. Izgoev, B. A. Kistiakovskii, P. B. Struve. Moscow: I. N. Kushnerev, 1909.

VENTURI, FRANCO, *Roots of Revolution. A History of the Populist and Socialist Movements in Nineteenth Century Russia.* New York: Alfred A. Knopf, 1960.

WOODCOCK, GEORGE and IVAN AVAKUMOVIC, *The Dukhobors.* Toronto: McClelland and Stewart, Ltd., 1977.

ZEN'KOVSKII, SERGEI A., *Russkoe staroobriadchestvo: Dukhovnye dvizheniia semnadtsatogo veka.* Munich: Wilhelm Fink Verlag, 1970.

# INDEX